National Security: Military Aspects

National Security
Military Aspects

Vice Admiral K.K. Nayyar

Air Marshal B.D. Jayal

Lt. Gen. V.K. Singh

Vice Admiral R.B. Suri

Maj. Gen. Afsir Karim

Foreword by
Brajesh Mishra, National Security Advisor

Rupa . Co

in association with

OBSERVER RESEARCH FOUNDATION

Published 2003 by
Rupa . Co
7/16, Ansari Road, Daryaganj,
New Delhi 110 002

Sales Centres:

Allahabad Bangalore Chandigarh Chennai
Dehradun Hyderabad Jaipur Kathmandu
Kolkata Ludhiana Mumbai Pune

ISBN 81-7167-935-8

Typeset by
Nikita Overseas Pvt Ltd
1410 Chiranjv Tower
43 Nehru Place
New Delhi 110 019

Printed in India by
Rekha Printers Pvt Ltd,
A-102/1 Okhla Industrial Area,
Phase-II, New Delhi-110 020

Contents

Foreword

Developments in the recent past have not only re-defined the notion of national security but have also unveiled hitherto unacknowledged areas of vulnerability of countries. The threats to India's national security and to its core strategic interests have correspondingly followed a sharply upward curve.

The Observer Research Foundation's study *National Security: Military Aspects* is, therefore, both timely and relevant. The events of September 11 have shaped a transformation in the world's view on terrorism and highlighted the growing role of technology in defining national security. The revolution in military technology has completely transformed the conduct of offensive and defensive military operations. We saw, both in Afghanistan and during the Gulf war, the countries can now conduct a war far away from their borders and with minimal involvement of their own ground forces. Our military strategists have to factor in these developments in their long term defence planning.

Our armed forces have a glorious and proud record of serving the nation in a most professional and apolitical manner. It is, therefore, imperative that we continue to provide them with appropriate hardware and software to ensure their access to cutting edge technologies. The integration of the Service Headquarters' with the Ministry of Defence was an important recent reform of the defence planning process.

While the linkages between internal and external security are evident, the growing inter-linkages between terrorism, narcotics and insurgency have added multiple dimensions to our security matrix. The dynamics of new alliances among nations and 'coalitions' with a completely new basis for cooperation, also have significant implications for national security.

Dramatic changes are taking place in our neighbourhood as a result of the 'war against terrorism'. From Afghanistan in Nepal and the Central Asian Republics to Sri Lanka, there has been a sea-change in the attitude to hosting foreign military forces and to developing close contacts with the armed forces of foreign countries. This has obvious long-term implications for the region as a whole, and for India in particular.

Our long term National Defence Policy has to draw all these different strands into a coherent agenda to defend our core national interests. Our approach has to take a broad and holistic view to incorporate dimensions of economic security and social stability in addition to the traditional elements of military preparedness and physical protection of the country and its citizens. While military aspects form an essential dimension of national security, demography, environment, energy and technology are crucial to a comprehensive national security approach.

The realities of the emerging security environment require us to address all these aspects on a priority basis. Defence and national security matters must be given the priority they deserve. The challenge facing us is to institutionalize long-term perspective planning and a holistic approach to national security, so that the territorial integrity and sovereignty of India is preserved, even as we pursue the social and economic development of our people. Ultimately we have to rely on our own capability.

BRAJESH MISHRA
National Security Advisor

23 October 2002

ONE

World View

National security concerns everyone. There were times when the defence of the country and its people was the sole responsibility of a ruler or the government and the military. Today threats can touch common man from diverse directions. Terrorism has already consumed thousands of ordinary people in time of peace and there are forces at work to undermine the country's integrity and cohesiveness in a subtle and invidious manner.

The concept of security itself is undergoing a change. No longer do threats originate only from outside the country's border but also from within the country. Internal change in the society, technological changes, population growth, poverty, economic instability, unemployment, widespread urbanisation, disease, environmental degradation, energy and resource depletion, etc., can destabilise a country and be a source of threat to national security. Fractured political environment, bad governance and corruption can complicate the situation. A nation's currency is as vulnerable as its seaborne trade. Proxy wars, low-intensity conflicts, infiltration across the border, small-arms proliferation, drug trafficking, terrorism and militancy have become household words. This is not all. Extraneous influence is applied to force changes and dictate terms. Aid will be promised if labour laws are changed, subsidies reduced, privatisation encouraged and economy opened to foreign interests. But the same aid will be withheld if the military budget is perceived to be high. Access to technology will be denied on the grounds of dual use. In the Cold War era, nations had come to accept the ground realities and rules. However, all that has changed and uncertainty prevails as the new world order emerges. One thing, however, is certain that the new world would be more conflict prone. Before we proceed further let us examine what are the driving forces that will shape the future.

Nine-eleven, as it has come to be known, was the day when terrorism struck America on its soil on 11 September 2001, destroying the twin World Trade Centre towers and a wing of Pentagon, claiming nearly 4,000 innocent lives. Four commercial airliners hijacked by terrorists of Al-Queda were flown into the buildings—a scenario out of a Hollywood movie—sending shockwaves around the globe. Osama bin Laden sheltered by Taliban in Afghanistan has been accused by the US for masterminding this diabolic attack. In a way, this event has vindicated the Indian stand that terrorism recognises no boundaries, no rules, no conventions and is aimed not at a nation or state but at entire humanity, against the way of life of freedom loving people. The worldwide revulsion at the attacks in the US has awakened the international community into taking concerted action not only against this scourge, but also against those who harbour the terrorists. European Union (EU) and North Atlantic Treaty Organisation NATO declared solidarity with the US by invoking Article five of the Treaty. Russia too had shown willingness to join the coalition. Virtually the entire world condemned these attacks. Response of the Islamic countries has been a mixed one. India has given unconditional support to this war against terrorism, which has to be fought along many fronts with political, diplomatic, financial and military means. This event would also have far-reaching effect on transforming policies of many countries, both within and towards each other. Terrorism will now be a major factor in the gambit of security worldwide.

India has been a victim of terrorism sponsored from across the border for a long time. The world community is gradually becoming aware of the role of Pakistan in sponsoring terrorism in J&K. It is also well-known that Pakistan nurtured the Taliban and helped Al-Queda in exporting terrorism worldwide. There are deep links between these organisations and Jehadis in J&K of Lashkar-e-Toiba and Jaish-e-Mohammed, which claimed responsibility for the car bomb attack on State Legislative Assembly in Srinagar on 1 October 2001 as well as the attack on the Indian Parliament on 13 December 2001. It is paradoxical that the war on terrorism launched by the US-led coalition has Pakistan as its lynch pin a country that itself has been exporting terrorism for the past decade to various parts of the world including J & K. While there is no doubt that the events of 11 September 2001 will significantly affect the way we look at the world, there are other changes which are taking place which will also shape the world view in the long term.

Momentous changes took place in the world order in the last decade of the 20th century. The end of the Cold War set into motion a new world, whose contours are still difficult to perceive. The US–Soviet confrontation ended with the collapse of the latter, though the much promised 'peace dividend' is nowhere in sight. Admittedly, likelihood of a major conflict in the European theatre receded. However, long-suppressed conflicts surfaced in many parts of the globe. They mainly emerged from multi-ethnic reasons and fundamentalism. This era of transition is prone to widespread conflicts and upheavals and is characterised by uncertainty. New spheres of influence and shifting alliances will result in a dynamic balance of power arrangement in a new world order marked with conflicts. In this emerging order the US will try to sustain if not enhance its prime position over other nations.

Demographic changes will affect most of world. The population of the world will grow to 7.2 billion in 2015, up from 6.1 billion in 2000. The increasing population will place heavy demands mostly on developing countries. In advanced economies, population trends are declining and could result in shortfall in the work force and aging populations. In some developing countries, these very trends will increase the working population and provide potential for economic growth. India's population will grow to 1.2 billion by 2015 and Pakistan could swell to 200 million. Some estimates put this as high as 230 million.

Apart from placing heavy strain on resources, the increase in population can be destabilizing particularly in case unemployment coupled with communal tension rises. As far as migration is concerned, two major trends are discernible. These are urbanization and cross-border migration. The movement of population from rural countryside to cities and towns will increase. This will be a major challenge faced by governments for providing jobs, shelter and infrastructure. The movement of people from across our borders will also pose a challenge since it could lead to ethnic imbalance and spark ethnic conflict. There are greater chances of migration occurring from neighbouring countries due to difference in per capita incomes, which may further widen in the future. Illegal migration of economically deprived people could become a more contentious issue. Thus demographic changes will exert influence in shaping events with implication on national and international security.

National resources and environment will also contribute to the shape of the new world order. Overall food production will be sufficient to meet the intake of increasing world population though chronic poverty and lack of infrastructure in some countries could lead to hunger and famine. Despite a 50% increase in demand of energy worldwide, resources would be adequate to meet these demands. Latest estimates indicate that 80% of world available oil and 95% of its gas resources remain underground. Persian Gulf will continue to remain the largest source of oil, though Central Asian Region will also become an important source. The consumption will tilt towards Asia with China, Japan and India becoming the largest consumers of oil energy. In this scenario, it is anticipated that the western world will still continue to draw on the Persian Gulf supplementing their energy needs through the Caspian Sea in the Central Asian Region for quite some time.

While oil would continue to be the main source of energy and might not pose serious problem of supply, it is water whose scarcity will be a major challenge. By 2015, nearly half of the world's population living in Africa, Middle East, South Asia and northern China will face water shortage. Water tables in important grain producing countries like China and India are falling at the rate of 5 feet per year. Though historically water shortage has not led to conflict, sharing of river water would present greater challenge. This is because nearly half of the worlds land surface consists of river basins shared by more than one country, and more than 30 nations receive more than 1/3rd of their water from outside their borders. Water shortage will add to other tensions such as boundary disputes, maritime zone issues and could exacerbate tensions.

Existing environmental issues will continue to defy solution and in many instances grow more acute in the next fifteen years. Large tracts of tropical forests and arable land will be denuded and depleted. Given the resistance by developed nations, green house gas emissions will increase. Losses of biological species living in wetlands and coral reefs will also continue. Existing protocols to contain environmental damage would not be effective, though awareness about their dangers to environment will grow among people at large. Environmental problems will become more acute in developing countries due to population growth, industrialization and rapid urbanization. Global warming will present a major challenge and will make climatic changes more difficult to predict. Melt backs of polar ice, rise of sea level and increasing frequency of storms, floods, heavy rain, etc. will occur. US's attitude to Kyoto protocol is a pointer in case.

The world is changing on another plane too. A revolution is taking place in the field of technology. The world is shrinking into a global village with the advancement in communications and information technology (IT). Most experts agree that quantum leaps will occur in IT and that it will form the basis of conducting world commerce. The integration will boost development in advanced countries. Older technologies will also continue to spread into new areas. One of the side effects of all this could be that terrorist organizations and organized crime could draw on IT to strengthen their activities. Through IT, interaction among terrorists, drug dealers, proliferators of small arms and organized criminals could grow in the form of networks, each drawing on the strength of the other. The sophisticated devices of communication, deception, intelligence gathering are even now being widely used by these nonstate actors. Similarly weaker nations will be able to achieve asymmetrical capabilities with the help of missiles and similar weapons. It is also envisaged that information warfare will rapidly assume an important role.

The end of Cold War also shifted rivalry among nations from ideology to commerce and trade. Global economy and globalization will therefore affect the shape of the emerging world order. As the globe shrinks, flow of information, ideas, values, capital, goods and services as well as people among nations will become easier and the existing barriers are likely to become porous. It is envisaged that globalization will help in hastening economic development. However, this process could be painful to developing nations, as it is not easy to withstand competition from developed countries. End of Cold War has reinstated confidence of many states in open market economy and the virtues of this system are being touted as a panacea by the western world to developing economies. Globalization demands restructuring a country's internal system and opening it up to integrate with the rest of the world. The extent to which each country would accept to do so will depend on how it perceives its interests. Countries that do not become part of the global system will feel left behind and could face economic difficulties. Their reactions in that event are not certain but they could lead to conflicts. Furthermore, their ability to respond to financial crisis will also be effected as time goes by and globalization spreads. The transition will be especially difficult for those developing countries where economic growth is low and disparity in distribution of wealth high, coupled with a non- transparent system of governance. There will however be pressures on the governments to promote economic dynamism and growth in an effort to improve the standard of living of the people. There will be a demand for greater improvement in managing economies, rising trade and commerce and emergence of new markets. Importance of private enterprises and information technology will spur the changes as information becomes freely available. However, as stated earlier countries, which are not able to take advantage of globalization would be more prone to weak economic growth and internal instability. Those countries, which have internal conflicts, will also suffer. The successful integration with the world would require peaceful and stable conditions internally and externally, as the country faces up to the challenges of globalization. Emerging Asian markets of China and India would be major actors in this scenario. While there are beneficial aspects of globalization, there are adverse outcomes too, which will effect economies of different countries. Turbulence in one economy could affect others due to increased integration.

The role of the state is being challenged, as its control diminishes over flow of information technology, arms, migrants, etc. across its borders. How well a country is governed will decide how it will face up to forces generated from outside. States with good and stable system of governance will gain from the changing world while those with ineffective system will lose out and become breeding grounds for fundamentalism, terrorism, grounds of conflict and instability. Generally democracies will fare better in the longer run.

Religion too will play an important role in shaping the future world. The great religion of Islam with a billion adherents is in the midst of civil war among the modernists and the fundamentalists. Such struggles from within are long lasting and have a far-reaching effect on global security. The situation in Middle East and South Asia is particularly volatile. Similarly, religious fundamentalism is growing in the Central Asian Region. Both these areas are also rich in oil. Ethnic problems with religious connotation have also errupted in Indonesia, Malaysia and Phillipines. Since some of these countries feel deprived, the religious fervor is canalized towards militancy and terrorism. Manifestation of such fundamentalist nature is vividly seen in South Asia where "Jehad" is being exported to countries perceived to be offending. The hub of global terrorism is shifting from Mid East to South Asia in the wilderness of Afghanistan and Pakistan. The nexus between organized crime and terrorist organizations will become stronger in years ahead. The income from narcotics trafficking, alien smuggling coupled with toxic materials, illicit fire arms, other contraband and racketeering will provide sufficient funds to continue with terrorist activities employing sophisticated technology. The risk could increase if these groups are able to lay their hands on weapons of mass destruction. Transnational terrorism will be exported from weakly-governed states with internal conflicts, religious tensions, weak economies and porous borders. Certainly such terrorist's attacks will gain in lethality. The problem in such states would be that fundamentalism breeds on economic and political failure and offers itself as an alternative to governance. Thus, countries with weak economies, religious fervor, ineffective system of governance, political corruption and endemic failure of institutions will slide into anarchy, civil war, chaos and misery under the tutelage of fundamentalism. The prime example is Afghanistan, a country that was being propelled into medieval dark ages, without a tear being shed by the international community. It was the 11 September attack that compelled the United States to launch its war against terror which had emanated from Afghanistan and which brought about the rout of Taliban and a new beginning of life for the war-torn Afghanistan. Had this event not taken place, there were chances that Afghanistan would have continued to wither away. Global terrorism would have continued to grow insidiously gnawing away at the vitals of human race.

This thesis has been borne out by the diabolical terrorist strike of 11 September 2001 which claimed the lives of nearly 4,000 innocent people. The origin of this attack was most probably Afghanistan and was suspected to be carried out by Osama bin Laden and his Al-Queda terrorist organization possibly in conjunction with other terrorist outfits. What was surprising was that the terrorists took advantage of openness of civil society and worked for many months without being found out.

India has been highlighting the threat of terrorism for over a decade but the West, including US, did not pay heed to these warnings. Links have now surfaced between terrorists in Kashmir belonging to Lakshar-e-Taiba and Jaish-e- Mohammad and the Al-Queda. Attention of the world community has now focused on global terrorism as the greatest threat to freedom loving countries and fight against this evil has begun. It would be a long, hard struggle, fought with overt and covert means employing full capabilities of the world community on all fronts, military, political, diplomatic and financial. The terrorists would portray this fight as crusade against Islam in order to drive wedge between the forces aligned against them. It would suffice to say that the world would not be same after these attacks. At the same time a realization is dawning on the developed countries that it is necessary to address the root cause of terrorism. In most cases, it is the disadvantaged people who take this route of violence and political causes for their dissatisfaction need to be resolved before a solution can be found against terrorism. It is possible that this factor may induce the developed countries to become more reasonable towards the underdeveloped world and share some of their resources, thus paving way for a more just world order.

ASIAN SECURITY PERSPECTIVE

Asia accounted for nearly half of the world GDP in the 18th century. Though over the last two centuries of colonial era this wealth was eroded by half, recent trends indicate that the recovery has begun and the 21st century will see a resurgent Asia. In this multi-polar world, contours of which are still to take concrete shape, US has a clear primacy interest in both economic and technological terms. Europe is reaching the stage of consolidation with an independent view advocated specially by countries like France and Germany. The induction of Euro is a step towards building of a unified European community. In Asia, China, Japan, the ASEAN, India, Saudi Arabia, Iran and Iraq are keen to play a larger/regional role. In Asia and also in the world, among the imponderables, greatest uncertainty is the shape that China will assume in the future. The implications of the rising economic and military power of China would be far reaching. Added to this are the several hot spots in Asia ranging from the Koreas, to Taiwan, the South China Sea, turmoil in Indonesia, South Asian rivalries, Afghanistan and challenges to newly formed states in Central Asia. The precarious nature of regimes in Saudi Arabia and the mid-east imbroglio will continue to cause tensions. There are even chances that in this cauldron of rivalries and flash points, conflicts will most probably occur in the next 15 years. An upheaval in countries producing oil could adversely affect the energy supply with consequential effects on the security scenario.

Among the greatest uncertainties in Asia, as stated earlier, is the future evolution of China, which is already the largest military power in Asia. Its economy is growing at a fast pace. It is generating enough resources to feed an ambitious military modernization programme. Its access to high tech weaponry from Russia has changed the shape and size of the armed forces. The future thrust of the PLA has also changed from static warfare to power projection far away from the homeland. She has launched a most ambitious futuristic weapons development programme including high-energy microwave beam weapons, ship-based laser cannons and space-based weaponry to destroy communication and reconnaissance satellites. China is the greatest source of proliferation of weapons of mass destruction and missile technology. History has shown that China is not averse to using force in order to achieve its aims. China's attitude towards it neighbours is a constant source of concern. This is more so, since it borders two large energy sources, South China Seas and Central Asia, both of which could become areas of future conflicts.

Most analysts agree that China wants to assert itself as an Asian and world power and has the capability to challenge the US in this region. In this pursuit, China would also want peace and stability in the intervening period so that she is able to achieve her long-term goals. The main area of interest to China watchers would be the effect on the monolithic political structure of China as the economic growth plateaus and how it will be able to accommodate economic plurality. As it looks today, despite the relative ease with which the Chinese are restructuring their economic and financial sectors, their political system and centralized outlook is not best suited for globalization and the winds of change and freedom of thought which is a precursor to the governance of a modern state. Despite great resilience and wisdom, either the economic growth will slow down as a result of the shackles of the political structure or prosperity gained through open economy will empower people to exert force to change the system itself.

A lot will depend on the future relationship between China and the US. In the long term, the US sees China as a competitor but it is doubtful whether China will technologically be able to challenge the US by 2015. In the short term there are many disconcerting notes in their relationship. But these have to be seen in the context of China's US$100 billion trade with the US, which rules out open adverse relations. The only challenge to the US in Asia comes from China. In fact China is seeking to emerge as a super power in her own right and is trying to occupy the space vacated by Russia. Chinese assertion to become co-equal to the US is based on its high economic growth of the last two decades, nuclear capability and military modernization programme. During the Clinton years, America had been moving towards making China a "Strategic Partner" but the Republican administration has since retreated slightly from this position. The Secretary of State, Colin L Powell, in the senate hearing had said: "A strategic partner China is not. But neither is China our inevitable and implacable foe. China is a competitor and potential regional rival, but also a trading partner willing to cooperate in areas where these strategic interests overlap". The Bush administration on assuming power tried to downgrade the relations but it does not want open hostility and has since then retracted its position somewhat. A lot depends on the Strategic Defence Review, which is being currently undertaken by the administration. If China is seen to be challenging the US in the future, a much tougher policy could be adopted. The

US has a sizable presence of troops in Asia numbering nearly 1,00,000 and has established alliances in the Pacific and Persian Gulf region, which are of vital interest to her. A senior PLA person is quoted surmising the US policy as an effort towards integrating China in the world community led by the US!! To what extent will China allow itself to be led remains to be seen.

The US surveillance plane incident in April 2001 provided interesting insight to the relationship between the US and China. The EP-3E had to land on Hainan Island, following a collision with a Chinese fighter plane, while on surveillance mission off the coast of China. The stand off between China and the US showed differing cultures of the two countries. The US found nothing wrong in monitoring the Chinese space from international waters, displaying its technological superiority as the sole superpower of the world. China, on the other hand, deemed it as an attack on her sovereignty reminding her of how in the 1800s, intervention in China by foreign powers had decapacitated the country. To the US, no apology was required to be given; to China the act symbolized "hegemony". It also brought sharply into focus issues of Taiwan and the deployment of Theatre and/or National Missile Defence system. While China considers the unification with Taiwan as the most serious issue to be pursued if necessary by force, America has however always resisted the use of force in this matter, and made it very clear that any force used by China will be answered by force by the US. Recently the Republican administration cleared an arms package for Taiwan. The overall package was sufficient to irk China but perhaps not start an arms race. The US, it is reported, agreed to supply four Kidd Class destroyers, 12 P-3C Orion aircraft, eight diesel submarines, Palladin self-propelled artillery system, MH-53E minesweeping helicopters, Amphibious Assault Vessels and MK 48 torpedoes, Avenger Surface-to-Air Missile systems, submarine launched and surface launched torpedoes among other items. However, Taiwanese request for Aegis naval air defence systems was not accepted. The Aegis is incidentally a part of the recently mooted TMD/NMD system. Should, however, the US go ahead with TMD to secure interests in Asia Pacific region, there are signs that China will see it as an abrogation of the 1972 ABM treaty and enter into a missile upgradation programme. The Chinese feel that TMD/NMD will neutralize their nuclear deterrent and upset the power balance in East Asia opening them to nuclear blackmail. However, since China is not in a position presently to challenge the US, it would be satisfied if it could deter US aid to Taiwan and would, therefore, act in a minimal way so that its overall relationship with the US was not hampered. China also feels a bit let down by Russia having meekly accepted American position on the ABM treaty. Yet China wants to retain a special relationship with the US and it has down played the incident of bugging of President Jiang Zemin's plane.

US has major security interests in Asia. Foremost among them is an assured and uninterrupted supply of oil from the Persian Gulf. During the Cold War era, US policy was primarily directed against Soviet influence in the area as also rivalry in the Indian Ocean. After the end of Cold War and the Gulf operations, the present policy is directed against threats from "rogue states" such as Iran and Iraq. The US policy against these nations has had a mixed result since not every country in the region perceives them as threats. There has also been a perceptible softening of hardliners in Iran. Despite this, the US has advocated National/Theatre Missile Defence System and a Cooperative Defence Initiative (CDI) for the region. This proposal was enunciated in April 2000 and its primary objective was to enhance US forces in the region to provide security to the Strait of Hormuz as well as to the entire Gulf and oil producing countries. The huge reserves of oil and natural gas have made the Gulf a vitally important region to the western world. By current estimate, the Gulf contains about 60% of the world's petroleum reserves 28 tankers ply through the Strait of Hormuz daily. After the Gulf War, the US has maintained presence in the area and now about 5,000 US troops are stationed there. The 5th Fleet monitors the SLOCs through the Strait of Hormuz.

The US proposal of Cooperative Defence Initiative (CDI) for the Gulf countries was aimed at protecting allies from missile attack. The plan was based on an Early Warning System through satellites, which will provide instantaneous information and warning about any missile launch to the regional ally and also track the missile in flight. In addition, there is active defence provided by Patriot SAM system and passive defence by Electronic Counter Measure System. The US will provide basic information and intelligence about a missile attack and the countries themselves, some of whom have already procured the Patriot anti-missile systems, will operate the rest of the system. The CDI will of course make the allies more dependent on military equipment sales from the US and has therefore received mixed response. Some countries feel that the threats have been exaggerated, others say this was to promote arms sale by the US. Despite this, the security of the Gulf will continue to remain the priority objective of the US policy in the region. Apart from Iran and Iraq, Islamic fundamentalism continues to pose threat and more terrorist attacks by the likes of Taliban and Osama bin Laden could take place to US interests. Moreover, it appears that the US has learned form its past mistakes and is not likely to leave this area in a hurry till the last vestiges of terrorism are eradicated. It is, therefore, likely that US military presence will continue in this region and may be enhanced in the future.

The Caspian Sea oil and natural gas reserves are of great importance to the western world. After nine- eleven the US has realized that depending on others to secure its energy interests does not work and that it must control these with its own presence. This is another reason why the US will remain in the Afghanistan/Pakistan area, for the south-eastern route through pipe line of oil and gas from Caspian Sea can be erected through Turkmenistan, Afghanistan and Pakistan. The development of Pakistani port of Gawadar and Ormara are also important pieces of this picture as is the need to have a friendly regime in this area.

Japan too is re-evaluating its policies after the end of the Cold War. How will it perceive the growing power of China on her security will be a moot question. So would be the continuance of the security umbrella with the US. Her willingness to adopt a more positive role in national security and in restructuring her economy will decide the future course of her action. Japan has the potential to become militarily strong and possibly stabilize the power equation in Asia. An important issue is her dependence on oil from Persian Gulf and the long sea lanes of communications. Any disruption in the oil flow will seriously affect Japan. In addition, the Japanese stand on the mutual security pact with the US will also affect the power balance in this area. On the one hand, there are indication that the Japanese may be brought around to increase their involvement in security and accept association with the TMD programme, on the other hand, there are voices seeking greater defence capability independent of the growing dependence on the US. The entire concept of security is being seriously debated. For the first time Japan decided to send its warships to the Gulf region in support of the US-led coalition. At the same time it must be noted that the Japanese economy has recently exhibited some problems in the financial sector. There have also been cases of endemic political corruption. All these will affect the future course of events. The core balance of power in the Asia-Pacific region will revolve around Sino-US relations, Japanese and the Taiwanese involvement and how the ASEAN visualize the growing power of China. The growing presence of the US in Central Asian Republics and Afghanistan; the ratcheting up of relations with Pakistan and India; stationing of US troops in Philippines; the arms sale, to Taiwan all may cause concern to China. While China tries to engage Russia as a "Strategic Partner" against US hegemony, the US seeks to contain Chinese influence through alliances with Australia, ASEAN and possibly advocating more independent posture by countries in the region by building up their defence capabilities. The recent visit of our Prime Minister to Japan has helped clear misunderstandings that had cropped up post Pokharan and there is a better appreciation of the Indian security concerns. There is also a better awareness of the business opportunities and opening up of the Indian economy. The security of the sea lanes from the threat of piracy, flow of arms to terrorist organisations, drug trafficking and illegal immigrants is also an area of common concern.

Russia is in the throes of transformation and its outcome is still uncertain. After the break up of former Soviet Union, Russia is reduced to the level of a great Eurasian regional power. However, there is all likelihood that she will regain her erstwhile stature, though this would take quite some time. Russia was and is a country of extremes extreme climate, hardy people and a violent undercurrent. Her experiment with market oriented economy and a change from the closed centralized system of governance has been marked with severe upheavals. She is passing through a major financial crisis and revitalization of economy is her first priority. But Russia has other problems too. She is facing a decline in her population and great disparity in distribution of wealth, which is causing hardship to large sections of its society. Crime and corruption is deep rooted and widespread here. Russia also faces severe ethnic problems and India has been a source of inspiration to her in this regard. The Military industrial complex, which was the showcase of the power of the former Soviet Union, lies in disarray, as the country cannot afford to operate even half of its capacity. Admittedly the threats of the Cold War era have abated but export of military hardware was a source of much needed foreign exchange and a major decline in the future will affect her economy adversely.

For the present Russia continues to be a major supplier of military hardware to China and India. In fact, her need of foreign exchange appears to be so great that it has embarked on a major drive of modernization of the PLA with sophisticated technology and modern weapons.

Russia and China signed a friendship treaty in Moscow on 9 July 2001 replacing the outdated 1950 treaty. Though this treaty has stopped short of being a Defence Pact against the US and was not directed at a third country, it has forged a strategic alliance against the American move of building National Missile Defence. Both Russia and China have affirmed their faith in the ABM treaty of 1972 stating it to be a "Cornerstone of Strategic Stability" and the "Foundation for reduction of strategic offensive weapons". The joint statement also stressed against arms race in space. The main objective of this treaty was, however, to improve bilateral relations by augmenting trade and resolving border disputes in a peaceful manner. Despite this, Russia has accepted the American abrogation of the ABM treaty stating that missile defence propounded by the US would not affect its security.

Apart from the historical linkages, ties between Russia and India have a further common interest of fighting Islamic fundamentalism. Jihad in Kashmir and Chechnya are both flamed by a common source. Similar problems are showing up in Central Asian Republics and south western province of China. Talibanisation of Afghanistan has made the situation more complex and a serious support to the initiatives of Shanghai Five will be in our interest, more so since instability in the energy resource rich Central Asian Region could cause serious repercussions worldwide. The Central Asian Region is experiencing power play between the western powers, Russia and China in their bids to consolidate their positions in the energy rich region. After the break up of the former Soviet Union, Russian influence in the area has reduced. Nevertheless, it seems for the present that Russian supremacy will not be challenged in the short term. If on the other hand, Russia does not resurge as expected, it could face serious repercussions and China could replace it as an overwhelming player, especially as this region would become an important source of energy for meeting its growing requirement in the future.

India and Russia reached a comprehensive agreement on 7 November, 2001 on the nature of international terrorism, on ways and means to combat it and on the approach that needs to be adopted to satisfactorily resolve the ongoing conflict in Afghanistan. The declaration highlighted, "Whatever be the motive of their perpetration political, ideological, racial, ethnic, religious or any other terrorist acts are unjustifiable". The declaration also added, "In multi-ethnic and democratic countries such as India and the Russian federation, violent actions being perpetuated under the slogan of self-determination in reality represents acts of terrorism which in most cases have strong international links". Both sides also noted the mixes between terrorism and illegal trafficking in narcotics, trade and arms and organized crime. There are mounting concerns about security in Central Asia and South Asia over rising crossborder and state sponsored terrorism; religious extremism and fundamentalism radiating out of Afghanistan and Pakistan. Terrorism is becoming a prominent feature in the non-military threats in Russia, India and Central Asia. This scourge has assumed a new dimension enforced with the help of modern technology. As stated earlier, Information Technology has enabled militant organizations of different hues to network themselves. India is facing the threat of instability through crossborder terrorism sponsored by Pakistan in J&K, Russia in Chechnya and Central Asia in Uzbekistan, Kyrgyzstan and Tajikistan. The fundamentalist regimes in Afghanistan and Pakistan were backing such nefarious activities in the name of "Jihad". Continuing violence in Afghanistan threatened to spill over to India and the Central Asian Regimes. Afghanistan, which was a traditional ally of India over the years, had become a source of fanaticism and extremism. The Taliban did not respect any international norms. Recent destruction of the Bamiyan Buddha's showed their savagery and medieval mindset. The grand strategy was to destabilize multi-ethnic countries in the name of Islam. According to the US State Department in its report on terrorism, Pakistan and Afghanistan had become breeding grounds for international terrorism. The US has branded Harkat-Ul-Ansar (HUA) along with 29 other militant outfits as terrorist groups. It later banned the Lakshar and Jaish, the groups were responsible for terrorist activities in J&K. The HUA is active in Kashmir, Bosnia, Tajikistan, Myanmar, Chechnya and Kosovo. Afghanistan had also become the hub for training foreigners from different countries Pakistan, India, Saudi Arabia, Libya even UK and China to carry out Jehad as well as to take part in military operations on the side of Taliban. Madrasas were growing where young people were indoctrinated in Islamic fundamentalism encouraged to take up Jehad.

Another related and greater problem of this area is drug trafficking of heroin from Afghanistan. A lucrative drug trade in which Afghanistan, Pakistan and Russian mafia are involved, posses a major threat to the stability of Central Asian Regimes. It also provides a source of abundant funds for jihadi movements. Recent seizures indicate that drug trafficking has increased nearly four times in the last five years. Kyrgyzstan now exports more narcotics than Myanmar and Thailand. According to experts, Afghanistan is exporting nearly 75% of the world's opium. Drugs are moving into Russia and Europe along two main channels. First from the "Golden Triangle" of South East Asia via Far East and second from the "Golden Crescent" of Afghanistan and Pakistan via Central Asia. Annual turnover of the illegal drug trade is around $ 50 billion.

Central Asian Region also remains highly susceptible to smuggling of fissile material for weapons of mass destruction (WMD). Though Kazakhstan has renounced itself from being a nuclear power, there are vast uranium deposits in Uzbekistan and Tajikistan. Since illegal drug trafficking thrives in the area, the same routes could easily be used for illegal transportation of WMD material. During the initial phase following the break up of the former Soviet Union, it was feared that unaccounted fissile material could have passed into wrong hands. Such a scenario has caused major concern in the US following nine-eleven. Stability in Central Asian Region is extremely essential and it should not fall prey to undue influence from extra-regional powers. Afghanistan is considered important by Central Asian Republics as it could provide them with an easy route for their oil and natural gas to reach the Persian Gulf for worldwide transportation.

The Taliban despite facing sanctions by the UN continued to wage war against Northern Alliance in Afghanistan and expanded its control, with the assistance provided by Pakistan, where both the Inter Services Intelligence Agency (ISI) and Ultra Islamic Groups give it unqualified support. Events in Afghanistan have a crucial bearing on the security of the Persian Gulf, Iran, Central Asian Region, Pakistan and India. This was conclusively shown by the massive terror strikes on the US in New York and Washington on 11 September 2001, which has changed the entire scenario in this region. While Osama bin Laden and his Al-Queda outfit was the prime suspect, it was the Taliban that gave shelter to them to perpetuate these atrocities. Taliban was the brainchild of Pakistan, born and bred in the madrasas and mosques along its border with Afghanistan and nurtured so that Pakistan could control Afghanistan and gain the strategic depth it so desperately wanted vis-a-vis India. The situation has dramatically changed after 11 September 2001. In the war against the perpetuators of the 11 September carnage, decisive victory has been achieved in Afghanistan by the US-led coalition forces. The Taliban has been destroyed and melted away far more quickly than what was envisaged by most. Whether the Al-Queda network has been routed, only time will tell.

INDIA AND ITS NEIGHBOURHOOD

Thirty years ago India helped Bangladesh in its liberation. It was hoped at that time that both the countries would enhance their friendly relations. But this has not happened to the extent it was hoped for. With the resolution of the sharing of waters from the Farakka barrage, there are no major problems with Bangladesh but some vexed ones linger on. Many areas of India, adjoining Bangladesh, have undergone demographic changes with migration across the border. There could be as many as 15 million Bangladeshi nationals living and working in India but there is no system of identifying them. This problem may become more acute in the future. There is also the problem of sanctuary being available in Bangladesh to insurgents belonging to United Liberation Front of Asom (ULFA) and Nationalist Socialist Council of Nagaland (NSCN). These groups not only get rest, recreation and training but are also supplied with weapons from other sources. Along the border, there are two further issues, which have to be resolved. Firstly, there are enclaves in each other's territory. These must be exchanged. Secondly, there are border areas, which have still not been demarcated resulting in villages and border stretches being in "adverse possession" of either India or Bangladesh. Pyrdiwali was one such village. The April 2001 incident, in which Bangladesh Rifles killed 16

BSF Jawans, occurred because of many such problems having remained unresolved over a long period of time. The gruesome manner of these killings, perpetuated by hardliners in Bangladesh Rifles was aimed at invoking strong reaction from India on the eve of polls. Our border management needs to be made more effective and so also communications between the border forces of India and Bangladesh. As in Nepal, misunderstandings and misperceptions must be cleared quickly to avoid such incidents casting shadows on good relations with our neighbours. There are sufficiently strong "vested interests" on both sides, which exploit such incidents for partisan purposes. Nevertheless, effective patrolling and guarding of our borders have become necessary as problems of this nature would become more acute in the future. Similarly, crossborder crime in the field of smuggling needs to be tackled firmly. Friendly relations with Bangladesh are crucial to India's security. While it would be essential to respond in a carefully calibrated manner, major issues with Bangladesh, result from "human" problems and will increase as population increases and resources deplete in the future. Firm and sensitive handling will be necessary in enhancing relations between India and Bangladesh. In the recent elections, the Bangladesh Nationalist Party has come back to power. This will increase challenges for India. It has been reported that killing of Hindus have increased recently and they are being specifically targeted. The terrorists organizations located in Pakistan have also increased their network in Bangladesh with active support of local ultra-fundamentalist parties.

Apart from being in India's immediate neighbourhood, the geo-strategic importance of Nepal lies in its geographical location between India and China. This is more so because of unresolved border problems between India and China. In addition, because of the open border between Nepal and India, the former has become a haven for illegal trade, smuggling and drug trafficking. In the recent years, growing influence of ISI and terrorists route through Nepal into India, especially the North East have added to our security concerns. Hijacking of

IC-814 to Kandahar via Lahore, in flight from Kathmandu to Delhi, showed how easy it was for terrorists to carry out such nefarious activities.

The asymmetrical size, differing security perceptions and landlocked nature of Nepal have affected relationship with India. The treaty of the Mahakali Integrated Development Project signed on 9th January 1996 was a high mark and considerably improved the relations, which had dipped in the late 80s due to perceived lack of cooperation by India in providing adequate trade routes and outlets. Anti-Indian feelings however still lie not very deep in certain quarters and can be exploited for political purposes as was seen by anti-Hrithik Roshan riots that erupted in December 2000 attributing anti-Nepalese remarks to him. Despite his denials, damage was done to the image of India. The security relationships between India and Nepal are based on the Treaty of Peace and Friendship of 1950. This treaty needs to be modified and updated keeping in view the new realities. It would be in Indian interest to meet the requirements of weapons, equipment and arms requested by the Nepalese Army and build on the close cooperation between the countries. Recent trends in the relations have been towards greater cooperation in trade, transit and investments. The treaty of trade providing preferential treatment to Nepalese goods was extended by five years from 4 December 1996. Like Bangladesh, in Nepal too, anti-Indian rhetoric can be raised to meet short-term political goals, but India being larger needs to show greater magnanimity and responsibility in building a relationship founded on mutual interests and respect with her neighbours. There will also be need to show greater restraint and sensitivity to their concerns. Nepal is a "Hindu Kingdom" and traditionally much closer to India than to China. Placed as it is, Nepal could swing either one way or the other. It would be in India's interest to forge greater confidence and content into India-Nepal relations. The transition from monarchy to democracy in Nepal's multi-ethnic society has not been easy and has made governance more difficult; their sense of nationalism and individually needs to be respected as well as their desire for economic independence. As India grows in economic and military power, its relations with its neighbours would need to be handled with greater sensitivity since actions on our part could be perceived more often as "hegemony" and provoke strong anti-Indian reactions. Our security on the northern front is intertwined with Nepal and a friendly nation can be of great benefit; an antigenastic one could aggravate existing problems into serious concerns.

The massacre of the Royal family on 1 June 2001 by the Crown Prince has once again focused attention on the troubled kingdom. The monarchy played a stablising role in the nascent democracy. King Birendra was a mature person who was aware of the ground realties and skillfully tried to steer the country through the maze of inept governance by the political parties, a rising Maoist insurgency and growing aspiration of people, which remained unfulfilled causing frustration among the common man. Maoist insurgency was started in 1996, by a group of people who boycotted the elections over alleged corruption in the parliamentary system, gaining ground. A "peoples war" has been launched against the established system. The failure of the representative government coupled with political instability where nine governments have changed in the last ten years, added strength to this insurgency in which over 1,600 people have been killed. paramilitary forces seem to be unable to handle the situation. Despite this, the army strangely seems to be inactive against the insurgents. When under pressure, the insurgents shift their training camps to the Indian territory. This would need to be curbed by more effective border management on our part.

Many questions haunt the situation. How would the new ruler King Gynendra be disposed towards India? He is believed to have strong monarchal tendencies and India is seen to be pro democracy. Would the new Monarch be proactive in internal politics at the cost of nascent democratic institutions? How will this affect the political system? What will be his attitude towards Pakistan and China? Could all this lead to greater instability in the country and the region? Would the army be looking to playing a greater role for itself? Events in Nepal need to be carefully watched. In the aftermath of the massacre, one would have expected anti-Indian sentiment to rise or India to be blamed for the royal genocide. This did not occur. India shared Nepal's grief and supported her in a smooth takeover by the new monarch. The next victim of the events in April was Prime Minister Koirala. In July 2001, he resigned in the face of growing activities of the Maoist rebels and charges of corruption. His exit indicated that Nepal is likely to face a long period of instability. Its political institutions have still not strengthened. The Maoist rebellion is growing and the change of monarchy at this juncture has added uncertainty to an already complex situation. Civil war loomed in Nepal as the Maoist insurgents declared the formation of a "revolutionary government" with its capital in Rolpa in western Nepal on 24 November 2001.Closing the door on discussions with the government to negotiate a political settlement, the Maoists seized two districts killing 28 policemen and soldiers. This is the first time since 1996 that army men have been attacked. The rebels run a parallel government in 40 of the country's 75 districts. Return to the gun by the Maoists followed the breakdown of talks with the Dueba government. The Maoists had insisted on abolishing the monarchy, a stand opposed by all the political parties. Moaists killed nearly 120 government troops and police personnel again on 19th February 2002. state of emergency is likely to continue. During the recent visit of the Prime Minister of Nepal to India, issues such as trade and security on the borders figured prominently in the discussions.

India and Myanmar have been linked by cultural and commercial ties which have their roots in ancient history spanning several centuries. These ties were further reinforced with the spread of Buddhism that originated in India. Common struggle against colonial rule further cemented these historical bonds. India and Myanmar share long land and maritime borders, tranquility over which is essential for development of both the countries. This can be achieved by providing impetus to development of border areas. In this regard, the Tamu-Kalewa highway project is an important link from the border to central Myanmar, and the commercial center of Mandalay. Building up of such infrastructural projects will form a basis for taking further steps in economic and commercial cooperation. One of the problems in this regard is the threat from international terrorism linked to drug trafficking, religious fanatism and spread of illegal arms. This can be combated through cooperative efforts in a spirit of friendship, respect for each other's sovereignty and tranquility on the borders. Both countries are active members of the Bay of Bengal Community in BIMST-EC, which would evolve in time. Visit of General Manng Aye, Vice Chairman of the State Peace and Development Council, Myanmar to India in November 2000 was an important landmark in the bilateral relations between the two countries. Both sides accepted that development of border areas is an important step in the future. Towards this end, projects are to be identified in the field of crossborder transport and communication links so as to promote better exchange of people and business. The basic problem of availability of sanctuaries to ULFA and NSCN insurgents in Myanmar also needs to be discussed and resolved. Chinese influence has been spreading in the neighbourhood of India in Pakistan, Nepal, Bangladesh and Myanmar. In this regard, the listening post established in the Coco Island by China provide a platform for intelligence gathering in the Bay of Bengal. China is also involved in the development of naval bases in Myanmar at Munaung, Hainaggyi, Katan Island and Zadaikyi Island. Major waterways connecting the southern province of Yunan to the port of Yangon are being developed and could obviate crossing Malacca Strait and provide a direct access to the Indian Ocean for the Chinese. In itself, these developments do not cause concern, but when seen in conjunction with the Chinese help in building Gawadar in Pakistan, and naval bases in Sri Lanka and Bangladesh, the picture changes dramatically and needs to be watched for assessing Chinese long-term game plan and increase of influence in the Indian Ocean.

Sri Lanka is still struggling to overcome ethnic clashes with the LTTE in the Tamil dominated north and east of the country. India is directly or indirectly involved in Sri Lanka's ethnic strife since 1983. India's intervention in 1987, its changing role from peace keeping to house keeping, followed by operations against LTTE and its eventual withdrawal of troops in 1990 was an exercise in regional power game. Since then India has reverted to its earlier policy of considering the ethnic problem as an "internal issue" of Sri Lanka. India's policy towards Sri Lanka is dictated to a large extent by internal domestic politics of Tamil Nadu. Every major initiative by India has been influenced by this factor. Over a period of time however, disenchantment with the obdurate and violent attitude of LTTE among the Indian Tamils changed to revulsion in 1991 when the LTTE was implicated in the assassination of Rajiv Gandhi. Had the Sri Lanka government been successful in hammering out some settlement to devolve power to Tamil areas, affinity between Indian Tamils and LTTE would have been snuffed. But the Sinhala majority was unable to do so and this has kept the LTTE in the game.

In May 2000, when the LTTE was about to gain control of the Jaffna Peninsula, Sri Lanka requested India to evacuate 20,000 stranded soldiers. India turned down the request under pressure from Tamil compulsions. This was despite the fear that Sri Lanka would approach other powers to assist her and Sri Lanka did turn to Pakistan and Israel for help. The outside help did not materialize. However, as it happened Sri Lankan Army was able to handle the situation on its own. The "hands off" approach followed by India is turning her into a passive onlooker, a situation, which is not in her overall security interests. The recent Norwegian peace initiative between LTTE and Sri Lanka government is a case in point in which India played only a distant informative role. Sri Lanka sits on top of the major trade routes in the Indian Ocean. It also has large and deepwater ports. Any extra-regional power, which is inimical to India's interest, can split India's western and eastern seaboard if it gets a foothold in Sri Lanka. This will cause serious hazard to India's security. Recent changes in the government in Sri Lanka where the opposition has come to power may bring new peace initiatives with the LTTE. A ceasefire has been brokered between the government troops and the LTTE through Norwegian assistance. Though the final solution may be long way off, this is a good step in that direction. The government of Sri Lanka is in the process of holding peace talks with the LTTE in a fresh bid to break the deadlock in this long ethnic strife.

The military coup in Pakistan in October 1999 was a great blow to democracy. The administration did not live up to the many promises made and the country was facing severe difficulties over economic and political issues. Nawaz Sharif, was luckier than Zulfiqar Ali Bhutto and found exile in Saudi Arabia. Here too controversy dogged the regime. The local elections did not generate much enthusiasm among the public and the so-called assurance by the government, that it would provide "clean" political persons did not materialize. On the economic front, the economy is not faring well and the country was on the verge of defaulting on its external loan when the IMF came to its rescue with a US $ 596 million credit. Pakistan's internal polity is also in a state of flux with right wing Islamic parties asserting themselves and seeking a greater role for themselves. For India it meant that the support for "Jihadi" movements in Jammu and Kashmir has now the full fledged support of the administration, not only in moral but in a material sense too. Pakistan's single-minded fascination with Kashmir and its obsession for being counted as equal to India is its undoing. Three wars and more than fifty years later Pakistan still continues to talk of a two nation theory as an unfinished agenda of the Partition. Their policy of confrontation hardens with each failure over passage of time. Every gesture by India towards normalization of ties is interpreted as a sign of weakness. Kargil was set into motion when Vajpayee was on his bus journey to Lahore. Nawaz Sharif had to pay the price for Pakistan's misadventure in Kargil.

Though India is seen as serious threat and virtually all policies are India-centric, Maleeha Lodhi wrote not long ago " The greater threat is from within — a debt-ridden economy in tatters, a society that is fracturing, a federation under unprecedented strain, and a pervasive lawlessness that is symptomatic of a virtual institutional breakdown, rule without law, democracy without consent and power without authority are among the contradictions of the country's present predicament. Pakistan may not yet be an endangered state but is certainly a wounded one, drifting leaderles." This was stated in August 1998 and things have only worsened since then.

The jehad in J&K is being equipped with small arms from the arms bazaars of the NWFP, which have their origin the arms provided to mujahadeens by the US to fight against the Russians in Afghanistan in the 80s. After the Soviet invasion of Afghanistan, the US provided arms assistance worth US$ 3 billion. In 1983, 10,000 tons of weapons were transferred to Afghanistan via Pakistan, which rose to 65,000 tons in 1987. Because of the covert nature of these operations, no one knows the exact quantities and there is ample opportunity for these weapons to find their way into the arms bazaars and into the hands of militants. Most of the Kashmiri militants are armed with these weapons today in J&K. The same arms proliferation is posing a problem for internal stability of Pakistan as sectarian killings become more violent. Pakistani Government tried to stop the illegal flow of small arms but it is yet to be seen how this measure would succeed especially in the tribal areas which serve as the source of such illegal arms. Dara Adam Khel, located in the tribal area 40 km south of Peshawar, is the largest center of manufacturing and supply of illegal arms in Pakistan. The business flourishes here due to the high demand for weapons in the domestic market. All earlier attempts to stop the small arms proliferation here has failed.

The army in Pakistan has always attributed to itself the role of the final arbitrator of the country's destiny. There is now an institutional framework of the National Security Council where the army is represented by sufficient members and could prevail upon the government to toe its line. General Karamat was sacked for suggesting this concept though he earned the displeasure of the army for not going through with it. But the army also felt the heat of the situation.

Firstly, the defence expenditure is frozen to last year's level as dictated by the IMF. This would affect the modernization programmes. Secondly, General Zia had courted the mullahs to increase the constituency of the army. This measure is now backfiring as fundamentalism takes roots in the army. The Islamic right wing influence is spreading in the army and would cause serious problems for Pakistan. When seen in the light of deteriorating economy, rising prices, increasing disparities between the rich and the poor, abundantly available small arms which are proliferating at an alarming rate, a booming drug trafficking network in which the army is involved coupled with a breakdown of law and order and de-federation, a dismal and desperate picture emerges. While lack of good governance and decades of mismanagement is now catching up, the image of Pakistan in the world has slipped considerably. A perceptible shift in the US policy has isolated Pakistan in the international arena. It is only the long, standing military relationship with the US and its need for waging war on terrorism that helped Pakistan in not being declared a rogue state. The advantage that Pakistan held for furthering US interests in this region has evaporated with the end of Cold War. With the rise of rabid Islamic fundamentalism and with harboring terrorist organizations, which export cross border terrorism, it can no longer convince the western world that it has a clout to tone down such frenzy. Its well-connived moderate image is tarnished and has lost credibility for exerting influence on the fundamentalists. The Taliban effect is also backfiring and holding the country in a vice-like grip. No wonder there is deep concern in the West about its nuclear calculation, since the trigger is held in the hands of a leadership, which tends to take extreme steps. The safety of a nuclear arsenal cannot be guaranteed in view of the close ties of the ISI with terrorist organizations nurtured by the Taliban. Pakistan is facing serious challenges from religious fundamentalism, tribal and ethnic passions, and Talibanisation and sectarian violence. There is also a feeling of Punjabi hegemony being forced on the people of Sind, NWFP and Baluchistan. All this spells a rather uncertain future where instability could prevail with conditions worsening over a period of time. Should, however, Pakistan realize her predicament and take measures to pull out of these conditions, things could change for the better. This however would require a change in mindset that proxy war and jihad in J&K do not pay and that it needs to resolve its problems with India in a peaceful manner. Pakistan has fallen in its own trap, which aims at gaining parity with India. India is over five times its size and growing stronger everyday. It is an unequal race that Pakistan refuses to accept. And the only way it will do so is when the pain of lost opportunities becomes unbearable. It will only realize this when the situation becomes untenable. India has once again offered its hand in friendship to open a dialogue under the Shimla Agreement and the Lahore Declaration. India has done so despite the fact that nothing has changed from its principal stand that it would not open a dialogue with Pakistan unless the crossborder terrorism stopped. Time will tell whether Pakistan is able to turn the events in the subcontinent to the mutual benefit of both countries or whether another opportunity would go a begging. General Musharaf has to show that he is capable of taking wise decisions; that he is different from other Generals and that the only way Pakistan can survive is by accepting peace with India and the ground realities of a changed world. (It would be seen later that he was unable to shed his uniform and become a statesman). At the same time it is essential to keep up ones guard since problems between India and Pakistan are complex and deep rooted and would take a long time to normalize. One way of achieving peace in the subcontinent is for India to be militarily and economically strong. A strong and firm India will be respected; a weak India will invite aggression. This lesson of history must not be lost to sight.

Pakistan's obsession with Afghanistan for providing it the so-called "strategic depth" has had far-reaching implications. From the beginning of Soviet invasion in 1979, Pakistan has tried to support one regime or the other, playing a game dabbling inside Afghanistan, siding one warlord then another, in order to keep the situation to its advantage. This has distorted its national thinking as much as its mindset with Kashmir. Sectarianism, militarisation of religion and the reverse, Islamisation of the military, spawning of mullahs and Jehadis and spread of madrasas are all result of this distorted thinking. This venom has slowly spread inside Pakistan and affected administrative and intelligence framework. This resulted in a nexus between the military and fundamentalists within the country and further vitiated a domestic political situation. It must also be noted that Pakistan used Taliban to further its ends in Central Asia. The spread of Islamic fundamentalism and jehadi movement in Uzbekistan, Tajikistan, Krygyztan, Chechnya and Kashmir were spearheaded by Pakistan with the help of its ally the Taliban. It is this very disease, which is now engulfing Pakistan. It is this realization that made President Musharraf speak out against religious fundamentalism and announce recent measures to curb their activities. Whether nine-eleven could force Pakistan to make a paradigm shift is yet to be seen.

ENERGY SECURITY

Energy security is crucial to India's economic growth and well-being and is therefore being examined as an important factor in national security. Earlier, India's requirement of energy was being met by its own huge coal deposits and hydroelectric potential. These resources enabled the country to develop reasonable self-sufficiency. In the 80s and 90s, economic development gained momentum requiring increased input of energy. This was made possible by increasing dependence on oil and gas as sources of energy. Currently oil forms 39% of the total primary energy consumption in the country.

The total oil consumption of India rose from 30.9 million tonnes in 1980-81 to 55.0 million tonnes in 1990-91 and 89.36 million tonnes in 1998-99. According to experts, if the economic growth rate is to be aimed at 7-8% per annum, according to experts, the consumption or crude oil could rise to 200 million tonnes by 2010. As against this, domestic production lags well behind due to many reasons. In 1998, it was 36.4 million tonnes, necessitating imports to the tune of 56.3

million tonnes, costing an amount of Rs 23,828.60 crores. In 2010, the import content could rise to 80% of the requirement. Most of this would come through the seas, making security of sea lanes of communications vital to Indian national interests.

In the future scenario, main demand for oil in Asia will be centered on China, Japan and India. The resources will come from the periphery consisting of the Persian Gulf, Central Asia, North Indian Ocean, South and East China Seas. Since most of the oil is transported overseas, the security of the sea lanes of communication will emerge as a crucial issue for other nations too. Nearly 40% of the worlds crude oil moves through the Strait of Hormuz. The Malacca Strait, South China Sea and the Horn of Africa represent the other choke points. Any disturbance in these areas would impede the flow of tankers carrying oil and directly affect the economy of the consumer countries. Security of sea lanes of communication would require steps to be undertaken towards a concept of regional cooperation. The catastrophic effect on the economies of oil importing states can be easily judged when seen in the context of their dependence on supply of oil and gas as the medium of transportation.

The MOD annual report states that increase "India's security and prosperity is heavily dependent on energy security. An increasing demand for energy in the future requires a special attention to the geopolitics of energy ranging from the nuclear to fossil-based. Energy security can no longer be only a set of political and economic hazards of which India should be the passive victim. Energy security should also mean a set of policies aimed at bringing the regional states together for their mutual benefit. In that sense it is as much, energy for security, as security for energy. The time has come for India to develop an integrated perspective on the issue."

INDIA'S RELATIONS

India's relations with the international community are now on much firmer grounds. India is no more seen as an appendage to the Soviet

Bloc; the jaundiced view of the western world, a reminder of the Cold War era, is no longer prevalent. The after shocks of 1998 Pokhran explosion are also waning and the Indian security compulsions are being better understood and appreciated by the world community. Indian diaspora is also playing a more active role in enhancing awareness about India in the US.

The relations with the US have been qualitatively enhanced over the past few years. India's ready acceptance of US NMD programme has generated a lot of good will. The parity with Pakistan in the Clinton era is no longer prevalent and India is seen by the US as a strategic partner. While non-proliferation remains an important goal of US policy there is a desire to re-energize Indo-US relations and expand its scope. The objective is to re-engage on defence issues and improve military-military contacts, explore potential areas of cooperation while narrowing down differences. During the recent visit of General Shelton, Chairman Joint Chiefs of staff of the US, proposals to revive Defence Planning Group at high level and Executive Steering Group at service level were discussed. Areas of further cooperation have been identified as counter terrorism, security of sea lanes of communications, search and rescue operations, humanitarian assistance, training and capacity building and coordination and cooperation in UN peace keeping activities. The successful visits of the Home and Defence Ministers recently to the US have paved the way for strengthening of ties between the two nations. The complete unanimity of views on fighting terrorism and enhanced cooperation in defence portray the type of relationship that could be formed in the future. India has kept away from the US as a source of military hardware due to various reasons. This is likely to change as the new relationship develops. There is a possibility of building substantive cooperation between the two most long-standing democracies in the world.

Similarly UK and the European community have accepted the ground reality of the subcontinent. India's look East policy has also succeeded in augmenting her potential acceptance by ASEAN and

ARF. New areas of defence cooperation are being explored with Russia, France and Israel. Australia and Japan are also less hostile to India's attaining nuclear weapon capability. A new chapter in India's relationship with Iran has been opened and areas of cooperation are being examined with Central Asian Republics. However, problems remain closer at home, especially with Pakistan and China. The most serious threat in the short term originates due to the proxy war and terrorism unleashed by Pakistan in Jammu and Kashmir and insidious, subversive and communal propaganda perpetuated by the ISI in different states of India as part of the unfinished agenda of Partition.

With China, the relations are more complex. The misgivings created by the 1962 war continue to bedevil our generation. Annexation of Tibet, a 2000 km long border with areas of dispute, nuclear asymmetry and low volume of trade are the main areas of concern. Though the LAC with China is generally quiet, it could erupt anytime if China wanted to adopt a confrontationist posture. However, China is seen as a competitor and a threat in the long term when it completes its military modernization programmes. A strong China would seek to readjust frontiers to its advantage, even risking conflicts with its neighbours. A weak China on the other hand will indulge in WMD proliferation. But few things are certainly clear. If China continues to proceed along its economic plane of growth, more funds would be available for modernization of its armed forces. There are reports that the central government accomplished its target of revenue collections in the first five months of the current year and is flush with funds. It is also reported that the PLA is insisting on a 17% increase in fefence budget next year. 40 of the 160 members of the central commission are from PLA and it has a strong clout in the national decision-making apparatus. By 2015, China is likely to have several hundred missiles ranging from ICBMs with nuclear warhead to intermediate range missiles with nuclear and conventional warheads. In the short term, China is likely to play its cards through Pakistan. The nexus between China and Pakistan in nuclear and military fields is a stated fact of history, accepted even by the United States, who had turned its face away and perhaps in some form even encouraged it, before Pakistan achieved its unstated nuclear capability in 1987. Every missile project in Pakistan since then has been initiated through active Chinese or North Korean assistance and is India specific. Having said this, it must also be stated that China has shown restraint and a new desire to improve relations with India. Both the countries have decided to concentrate on areas of agreement and not to allow the boundary question to influence the relations. In the recent visit of the Chinese Premier, Rong ji, emphasis was placed on exploring business opportunities and enhancing economic ties and trade, especially in the IT sector. While this can be of mutual benefit, it is essential that we observe due precautions so that cases like the Bangalore-based Huwai technologies do not occur where this Indian based company, manned by over 100 Chinese, managed to provide telecom services to Taliban via Pakistan. The recent visit of the Foreign Minister to China was marked by the inauguration of direct air links between New Delhi and Beijing. During the discussions, it was decided to put a time frame to the resolution of the border dispute and focus on enhancing trade between the two countries.

It may be worthwhile at this stage to take a look at a likely scenario in South Asia in the future say 10-15 years hence. A paper "Global Trends 2015", a dialogue about the future with non-government experts was written for the National Intelligence Council in USA and summed up the position in South Asia in 2015 as follows:

- India will strengthen its role as a regional power, but many uncertainties about affects of global trends on its society cast doubts on how far India will go. India faces growing extremes concerning wealth and poverty, a mixed picture on natural resources and problems with internal governance. India's democracy will remain strong, albeit more fractionalized.
- Pakistan will be more fractious, isolated and dependent on international financial assistance. It will not recover easily from

decades of political and economic mismanagement, divisive politics, lawlessness, corruption and ethnic friction. Nascent democratic reforms will produce little change in the face of opposition of an entrenched political elite and radical Islamic parties. Further domestic decline would benefit Islamic political activists who may significantly increase their role in national politics and alter the make up and cohesion of the Military — once Pakistan's most capable institution. In a climate of continuing domestic turmoil, the central government control probably will be reduced to the Punjabi heartland and the economic hub of Karachi.

- Other South Asian states like Bangladesh, Sri Lanka and Nepal will be drawn closer to and become more dependent on India.
- The threat of a major confrontation between India and Pakistan will overshadow all other regional issues. Continued turmoil in Afghanistan and Pakistan will spill over to Kashmir and other areas prompting Indian leaders to take more aggressive, pre-emptive and retaliatory actions.

One does not have to accept the above prognosis in its entirety. However, it appears to be reasonably accurate unless Pakistan has a change of heart and moves away from the path of confrontation with India. Unfortunately there is not much evidence that it has learnt from its past mistakes. On the other hand, international isolation, economic bankruptcy and domestic turmoil may force it to make a temporary truce with India. Pakistan has a fixation with Jammu and Kashmir and believes that the proxy war generated by it will succeed in tiring India's security forces to an extent that India will offer the valley to Pakistan. Such strategic miscalculations have brought Pakistan to a sorry state today. In 1947, had the Indian army not been stopped, the Jammu and Kashmir problem would not have existed now. In 1965, mass infiltration by Pakistan ended in failure. In 1971, Pakistan was cut to size. All this has still not prevented it from using force to try and snatch the valley. Pakistan again tried to alter the LoC in Kargil and once again had to withdraw, when

India repelled its forces. Under such circumstances India's conventional military capability must be strengthened to the level where Pakistan is deterred from taking a path of aggression. No let-up in vigilance on our borders must be allowed to take place. India's security concerns are much larger than Pakistan's and if the latter construes it as an arms race, it is her decision and her problem. The proxy war generated by Pakistan must be stopped and this can only been done by achieving a decisive edge in conventional military capability and a demonstrated national will to use it. The realization that such a war can prove disastrous to Pakistan in the long term (in short term the costs for Pakistan are marginal) might force it to review its strategic policy in J&K.

The Agra summit of 14-16 July 2001 could not reach a conclusion in the form of a joint declaration or a statement. This was mainly due to a wide difference in approach of the two countries that couldn't be reconciled within the short time available. While India stressed that a broad-based approach be followed in which Jammu and Kashmir issue could also be discussed (India had already backed down from her earlier stand that Kashmir is an internal problem and that there is nothing to be discussed with Pakistan except vacation of POK) along with other issues, Pakistan's stand was based on the centrality of Kashmir. The uni-focal fixation of Pakistan with Kashmir held the summit to hostage. India considered Agra as an ongoing step in the process of normalizing relations, which started with the Shimla Agreement and continued with the Lahore Declaration. Pakistan on the other hand dismissed these agreements as they failed to address the core issue of Kashmir. Throughout the various phases of the summit, President Musharraf continued to harp on Kashmir. He repeatedly kept on insisting that everything revolves around Kashmir. If Kashmir is resolved, it will be the greatest confidence building measure and the other issues can be easily tackled. He wanted a time-bound framework under which Kashmiris would be given the freedom of self- determination and the Hurriyat, which according to Pakistan is the voice of the Kashmiris. President Musharraf would also be involved in the talks even went to the extent of saying that if he could not convince India of this, he might as well buy the Neherwali Haveli and live in it. To India's suggestion that cross border terrorism is not conducive to creation of an amiable atmosphere in which the issue of Jammu and Kashmir can be discussed, he likened the violence in Kashmir to Palestine and termed it as an indigenous freedom struggle and denied that Pakistan is encouraging it. Later, he compared the jehadis to Mukti Baheni!!! According to him, there is no crossborder terrorism since he does not accept the word "border" in Jammu and Kashmi, terming it as LoC!!!

India's stand is based on a commitment towards achieving peace and friendship with Pakistan. It wants trust and confidence to be built up and aims to develop mutual relations of benefit and cooperation in which all issues including J&K could be addressed. Operating in segments will not resolve problems. The PM cautioned General Musharraf "Let no one think that India does not have the resolve, strength or stamina to continue resisting terrorism and violence". If the J&K issue is to be resolved, it must include the issue of crossborder terrorism in its ambit. The PM also brought to the notice of General Musharraf the issue of Indian POWs held in Pakistan jails and that the guilty persons of Bombay blasts in Mumbai in 1993 and hijacking of the IA flight IC 814 from Kathmandu to Kandahar are living in Pakistan and should be handed over to India to be brought to justice. As a confidence building measure, the Indian Coast Guard was ordered to release all Pakistani fishermen who had inadvertently strayed into our waters. This gesture needs to be reciprocated by Pakistan. The PM also expressed grave concern that known terrorists are allowed to stay in Sikh gurudwaras in Pakistan. The enhancement of trade between the two countries would be of mutual benefit and had been advocated by business communities in both the countries. A group of experts could be formed to recommend measures in this area. India had also announced certain confidence building measures before the visit such as enhancing people-to- people contact, removal of visa restrictions and establishing more check points along the border to facilitate travel by the people.

Unfortunately, no headway was made on any of these issues, as the Summit did not succeed in narrowing the basic conceptual differences on the issue of Kashmir. Agra has once again proved that the road to peace and friendship is a long haul with many twists and turns. While Agra should not be termed as a failure, the first step on this long road has been taken. More could follow as the Prime Minister had accepted General Musharraf's invitation to visit Pakistan. The disappointment at Agra will however fuel terrorism in the valley and this is exactly what happened. In a span of two days after the Summit, militant violence claimed innocent lives of nearly 50 people, mostly Hindus.

Pakistan does not want to slow down the proxy war machine. It costs her nothing and ties down huge resources in India. It also continues to keep the focus of the international community on Kashmir and causes alienation among the people in the valley and the centre in Delhi since presence and operations of security forces at times hurts the sensitivities of people. There are plenty of misguided youths who can be trained as mercenaries and weapons and labour are cheap. Jehadis collect contributions from people and drug money bankrolls the operations. The Indians don't cross the LoC even to destroy training camps. Since no pain is inflicted, why then should Pakistan give up the proxy war? But Pakistan does not yet realize that this very proxy war machine pollutes its domestic environment. Pakistan trained jehadis are a global nuisance. The world is fed up with Islamic fundamentalists fanning global terrorism. Here lies the war machines real price tag. Pakistan can possibly shrug off India's stand on crossborder terrorism, as it did at Agra, but can it portray to the world community that it is an excellent option for making investments, so vital for its economic growth. Investors are not worried about what happens in J&K, but they are certainly anxious to know what will happen to their money before they invest. Though some sort of fringe realization is coming in Pakistan about the perils of the the proxy war, they hope that it might tire India in giving up the valley before it submerges Pakistan itself. Even a marginal success of proxy war snares Pakistan into believing that its policy is achieving its end and conceals the rot within. India's principled stand at Agra of linking crossborder terrorism and the proxy war with talks on Kashmir issue and its strong resolve to fight jehadi terrorism in Jammu and Kashmir, coupled with the desperate economic outlook in Pakistan and pressure from the international community, may force it to review its policy towards India. The option for India is clear. It must only talk to Pakistan from a position of strength. Reagan's dictum when dealing with the Soviets is apt for India, "Negotiate by all means but always from a position of strength"

Pakistan's hand in perpetuating terrorism and the Taliban movement was so all pervading that its total extent may never be known. But the war in Afghanistan has brought out that some of the ministers in Taliban government were actually Pakistanis; that the entire telecom network of Afghanistan was an extension of Pakistan; that thousands of Pakistani tribals crossed over to Afghanistan to fight along with the Taliban; that thousands of Pakistani nationals actually formed part of the hardcore Taliban forces; that hundreds of Pakistani nationals were killed in the campaign; that with the acquiescence of the US special air lifts were carried out to evacuate Pakistani armed forces personnel and Pakistani nationals from the siege of Kunduz; that Pakistan tried to mislead the US campaign in the initial phases so that Taliban could consolidate its defences; that thousands of Taliban fighters changed side and melted away into the wilderness of the tribal plains in Pakistan adjoining eastern Afghanistan; that two Pakistani nuclear scientists were in contact with Al-Queda; that the financial trail to Mohammad Atta led from Pakistan; that possibility exists of Mullah Omar and Osama bin Laden having found shelter in Pakistan. In joint operations by US and Pakistan troops, large number of Taliban and Al-Queda terrorists were captured from inside Pakistan, among them was the Chief Coordinator of Al Queda, a Palestanian named Zubhaydha. He is the highest ranking Al-Queda leader captured so far by the US in the war against terrorism.

The war on terrorism started in Afghanistan by the US-led coalition in October 2001 has reached its final phase with the collapse of the

Taliban. Military operations are continuing against the remnants of Taliban, localised to districts surrounding their last stronghold, Kandahar. A political solution for establishing a multi-ethnic broadbased government in Afghanistan has been achieved by the formation of the Karzai government. While war on Taliban protected Osama bin Laden and his Al-Queda network is prosecuted, it will take a long time to root out the terrorist networks spread all over the world and the causes that have sprouted such virulent fundamentalist hatred. An area, which is causing great concern, is the availability of 'suitcase' type of nuclear device to terrorists organization like the Al-Queda. Two Pakistani nuclear scientists are being investigated by the US for links with Osama bin Laden. This scenario which was imagined to come alive in a Hollywood blockbuster some time ago, is very much possible after nine-eleven. The US President in his State of the Union address drew attention to such a threat and warned the countries which made materials of mass destruction that they could become targets of US-led war on terrorism. In this fluid situation many questions remain and their answers could have a reaching affect on the geopolitical situation, not only in our region, but the entire world. An attempt will be made to list such imponderable factors:

- Will the focus on the war against terrorism, led by the US, remain strong after Osama bin Laden and his organisation is destroyed in Afghanistan, which is the immediate objective of the campaign?
- Will this campaign target other nation states? Who will decide such targets? What will be the effect of such operations on the unity of the coalition?
- So far civilian casualties have been minimized. However, continuous military operations and aerial bombings could lead to more deaths of civilians in Afghanistan and elsewhere. What would be the effect of such killings on the Muslim states, especially when emotions run high?

- The war against terrorism could get out of control if it is seen to be against Islam. How can a clash of civilizations be avoided since that could lead to unimaginable convulsions in many multi-ethnic societies?
- India has the second largest population of Muslims. What will be the effect on their psyche?
- There is a deep struggle among the moderates and fundamentalists in Islam. This will have a far- reaching effect on their attitude towards the rest of the world. Its outcome has not yet been fully evolved and could lead to upheavals within the nations themselves.
- Causes of terrorism are complex but most of them are because of a feeling of deep resentment among people, which is fuelled by hardliners and fundamentalists taking recourse to religion. Some of these emanate because of the unjustness in world order. Will the world community try to remove such discrimination between developed and developing/underdeveloped nations, thus paving way for a more just world order?
- Will the US learn from its past experience that means are as important as the ends when its interests are at stake? Will it stop pursuing its aims in an aggressive and unilateral manner as it did during the Cold War in total disregard to other nations? This is more so since the world has changed after the demise of the former Soviet Union and the "evil empire" no longer exists? Will the US realize that its actions cause deep animosity among ordinary people in many states including the Islamic states. There are many instances of the past, where it helped repressive regimes to further its own ends causing irreparable damage to world order. Even today many regimes (undemocratic) are being shored up by the US.
- Will the US remain deeply engaged in areas like Afghanistan/ Pakistan/Indian Ocean for long periods to further its own interests and stability in the region? Will it turn out to be like the post 91 Gulf scenarios? The continued presence of US forces in the Gulf areas and Saudi Arabia is also a cause of resentment among the people.
- Will US realize that Pakistan is a swamp where terrorism breeds?

Will it apply pressure on Pakistan to become moderate? Will the jehadi mindset in Pakistan be eradicated? Will the infiltration and cross border terrorism in J&K reduce? If Pakistan turns a new leaf and becomes more moderate by giving up jehad in Jammu and Kashmir, will US pressurize India to offer concessions to Pakistan on Kashmir?

- One of the causes of the intransigent attitude of Pakistan towards India is the central role played by the Pakistani Army in the formulation of policy in Pakistan. Will the Pakistani Army, which thrives on the anti-India syndrome, change its mindset?
- Is the newly found US-Pak closeness a tactical alliance against the compulsions of the Afghan situation or something more permanent?

Pakistan's credibility and claim over Kashmir is coming under great strain following the mounting evidence that the same terrorists and Jihadis flit from Kashmir to Kandahar to Kunduz in Afghanistan and back. Reports indicate that many of the foreign fighters trapped in Kunduz are Pakistani soldiers and agents. This has finally begun to open the eyes of the Americans to Islamabad's subterfuge. Americans are now beginning to understand that the same jehadis who operate in Kashmir will strike at their interests too. Pakistan's perfidious game in Kashmir is coming out in the open in front of the world community. There is a growing realisation that brazen infiltration of jehadis in Kashmir and Afghanistan has gravely damaged its case in Kashmir. Musharraf's insistence that the struggle in Kashmir is indigenous looks more and more spurious to the world at large. Only the need to keep Pakistan in the coalition has stopped the US from openly naming it as a sponsor of terrorism. Furious efforts were made by Pakistan to send planes to Kunduz to lift its armed forces personnel and nationals to save them from being taken as prisoners by the Northern Alliance. The routing of the Taliban has finally laid to rest the policy of Pakistan of making Afghanistan its courtyard. This was the most serious setback to Musharraf who tried his best to salvage whatever little shreds remained of his policy in Afghanistan. What will be the outcome in the long run is difficult to see at the moment. Will the defeated Taliban flee from Afghanistan and take shelter in the Pashtun areas of Pakistan, where the sentiments offer popular support to their cause? Many of them are being captured inside Pakistan by the US troops. Will they see Pakistan as a friend who has betrayed them? What will be their reaction in that event? Will such a situation lead to civil war in Pakistan? Will areas west of Indus, both Baloochis and Pashtuns, question Islamabad's authority? What will be Islamabad's reactions? Will the Taliban be swung to Kashmir to rage a "freedom struggle" in the year of the state's general elections? What will be the attitude of the US in the war against terrorism once its war in Afghanistan is completed? In this fluid situation one thing is clear. We must find a lasting solution urgently for the Kashmir problem. We must also guard against influences that tend to splinter our society.

This analysis has devoted a lot of space to India's relation with Pakistan and the consequential effect on Indian security. There has been no let-up in the infiltration and terrorist activity from across the border in J&K. This is mainly due to the fact that the recent measures taken by General Musharraf against terrorism have been more out of compulsion to appease the West rather than out of conviction to steer a moderate path. However, it must be admitted that if India proposes to play a larger role, it has to somehow divest itself of the millstone of Pakistan and devote its energies to many other areas requiring attention. The immediate priority in this regard is to urgently find a lasting solution to J&K that will remove the alienation of its people. In the long-term, India will overcome many challenges that might come its way. It is envisaged to become a regional power with a strong democratic polity and a strong economic and military capability. With every succeeding year as India attains this stature, the extent of the problem posed by Pakistan is likely to diminish. India's fight against terrorism is also expected to receive international support as more and more countries join in this war. The road ahead towards economic growth needs stable, secure and peaceful conditions. Threats to national security are becoming more invidious and complex and need to be responded to effectively. India is the largest state in South Asia and it must be sufficiently strong militarily, not only to ward off any threats to her security but to deal with threats to smaller countries of the region.

TWO

Technology and Security

BACKGROUND

Evolution of warfare from manual combat to modern day nuclear stand-off has been a direct consequence of the march of technology. Lethality, mobility, surprise, stealth, speedy intelligence and effective command and control, all essential ingredients of warfare from times immemorial, still retain their essential character. It is technology, however, that has completely transformed their application and resultant impact on warfare.

Historically, technology has been the foundation on which coercion and conquest have been built. Invention of gun-powder was a revolutionary step towards greater lethality. Today the world's nuclear warheads are lethal enough to destroy this planet many times over. Mobility underwent changes as animal power was superseded progressively by internal combustion engines and then jet and rocket engines enabling current levels of performance of warships, aircraft and spaceships. Invention of telegraph led to the enhancement in the speed of communications and later covered a spectrum of powerful electronic devices from intelligence gathering and radar to Information Technologies, the very heart of what is now being termed as Revolution in Military Affairs (RMA).

It is significant that for the first time we are now seeing a shift in emphasis. Today technologies driven by civil uses of communications, transportation, other industries, space and aerospace are as much contributors to military weapon systems as pure defence related technologies. A wider industrial and economic base thus promotes security enhancement and makes military technologies more affordable due to their wider application, economies of scale and amortization of R&D investments.

There is as yet another shift dictated by the compulsions of modern day governance where destabilizing forces are not always clearly identifiable and the battleground not geography specific. Such forces are apt to use the world's media and the Internet as their platforms and responses by governments will be minutely scrutinized for their collateral damage, loss of innocent lives, violation of rights and so on.

Adding to these is the impact of the emphasis that globalization and international trade place on maintaining international peace and stability. Many of these factors individually or in concert are resulting in new roles of peace-keeping and peace-enforcing that are internationally being handed over to armies. These new roles demand techniques, tactics and equipment that are role-specific and for which traditional armies are not adequately equipped either physically or mentally. Technology, once again, is playing a leading role in how these evolving new-world security challenges can best be met.

Any study of the direction that future warfare and role of national security agencies will take must, therefore, begin with a look at the state of technology and its future direction.

CHALLENGES TODAY

The global economy today is becoming highly dependent on access to information that in turn depends on space applications and the electromagnetic spectrum. Free flow of trade and commerce, which is the essence of the global economy, relies heavily on access to world's land, sea and air routes for free flow of goods and space assets for flow of services. Fossil fuels remain the main source of energy that drives world economies. Energy security has therefore come to form an integral part of any nation's security calculus. The ongoing revolution in military technology now termed as Revolution in Military Affairs (RMA) is altering the face of conventional warfare so completely that doctrines, weapon systems and forces that were central to old military doctrines are rapidly becoming obsolete and will need to be superseded. RMA is also adding a new threat of empowering non-state actors, terrorist organizations, international criminal outfits and other irregulars with the power to disrupt, dislocate and even destroy with weapons of mass destruction.

NUCLEAR WEAPONS

Ever since the use of nuclear weapons over Hiroshima and Nagasaki there has been a constant evolution in the lethality, range, accuracy and destruction assurance of the nuclear weapon system. When aircraft were the only means of delivery, there was no guarantee that all the enemy's weapons would be eliminated in a first strike. At the time this was considered as a "delicate balance of terror".[1] It was with the advent of the ballistic missile that the concept of nuclear deterrence took shape. Refinements like basing missiles in silos or carrying them in submarines added to survivability and enhancement of deterrence. Greater yields and multiple warheads led to the stage of "mutually assured destruction" followed by the inevitable acceptance by the US and erstwhile Soviet Union that a nuclear war can not be won and must not therefore be fought. Invariably it was technology, driven by

---

1 *Securing India's Future In The New Millennium' — Countering Missile Threats* — by K. Subrahmanyam. P 248

the desire to maintain operational superiority, that resulted in this nuclear weapon doctrine evolution.

That there has been no conflict involving major powers since the end of Second World War, can be attributed to the fact that nuclear weapons have acted as deterrents. It is ironical that while nuclear powers in general and the US and erstwhile Soviet Union, the two Cold War protagonists in particular, had amassed huge arsenals of nuclear warheads capable of destroying the world many times over, they had also been compelled to put in practice sophisticated command and control systems, hot lines and foreign policy initiatives to ensure that the threshold of employing such weapon systems remained unacceptably high.

While the potential of nuclear weapon technology remains frightening, it can be argued that it has ensured world peace. As long as such weapon systems remain in national armouries it is, however, the specter of failure of intelligence, command and control systems or stable governance leading inadvertently to a nuclear exchange that must still haunt the world.

With NPT having been extended indefinitely, the nuclear five expected their nuclear club to remain exclusive. India's nuclear tests in 1998 have consigned that hope to the dustbin of history. The Indian government's announcement of the tests on 11 May 1998 also referred to Indian weaponeer's ongoing interest in computer simulation and sub-critical experiments.[2]

The May 1998 BARC Newsletter quoted yields of the Pokhran II tests. The yield of thermonuclear device was stated as 45 kilotons and that of the fission device as 15 kilotons. The three smaller devices were described as experimental with yields of approximately 0.2, 0.5 and 0.3 kilotons respectively. Western experts expressed doubts about the claimed yields of the May 11 tests and whether the two May 13 tests even occurred. The Indian science establishment was angry that their

---

2 *India's Nuclear Bomb*, George Perkovich. P 423

most triumphant achievement, the thermonuclear device was being questioned.[3] On 21 May 1998, the Indian government announced that it was voluntarily undertaking a moratorium on further nuclear tests.

George Perkovich in his book 'India's Nuclear Bomb' concludes "Indeed there is no evidence that the "requirement" to develop and test thermonuclear weapons came from anyone but the scientists themselves, continuing the process of scientific "push" begun by Homi Bhaba... Yet nuclear weapons in both senses of the term are supposed to serve strategic purposes. To have a strategic purpose the Indian H-Bomb required a doctrinal context. But no such doctrine had been developed and decided officially in India prior to the production of the H-Bomb."[4]

An additional irony is that the Indian armed forces have not formed part of the nuclear weapons design, development and decision making process. As Brahma Chellaney wonders: "Will civilians by themselves prepare targeting strategies for war scenarios or do what the Prime Minister has identified as an essential minimum-deterrence requirement maintain deployed nuclear weapons? Will the DRDO, which has devised a nuclear doctrine and command-and-control system, fire nuclear weapons when India suffers a first strike? The paradox of a country proclaiming a nuclear deterrent without the necessary military underpinnings can only make it more vulnerable in a regional situation where it confronts a well-armed, ambitious nuclear power and a state whose nuclear-weapons programme has always been run by the military."[5]

Nuclear weapons without the backing of strategic and operational doctrines can be no more than superficial political or diplomatic tools. Operationally, India has not been able to follow its nuclear tests with a coherent national strategic policy and a nuclear doctrine. The danger

---

3 Ibid. P 426, 427

4 *India's Nuclear Bomb*, George Perkovich. P 431

5 *Securing India's Future In The New Millennium — Nuclear Deterrent Posture* by Brahma Chellaney. P 197

inherent in self imposed restrictions on further nuclear testing without clear strategic aims and an employment doctrine is that technology development towards miniaturized and multiple nuclear warheads and refining computer simulation techniques will be thwarted.

The policy of no first use and minimum nuclear deterrence declared by India and its moratorium on further testing need to be viewed from the perspective of not India, but those sought to be deterred. Any doubts cast on Indian nuclear weapon capability, however trivial or motivated, amounts to negation of India's nuclear deterrence.

There is another pitfall that India must guard against. Faced with international and even domestic pressure from some quarters, there has been a tendency to limit development testing of delivery missiles, warheads and the total integrated system to the very minimum. Militaries across the world follow a rigid system of testing weapon systems that are to finally enter their armouries. Essential in this sequence is the final user testing and acceptance by the services concerned whose ultimate task will be to handle such weapon systems in times of need. For systems of deterrence that may not ever be put to operational test and yet if needed must assure success, the approach of frugal testing is technically unsound and operationally flawed.

The price that India has had to pay for this ad hoc approach to a strategic weapon system, indeed the most horrific that mankind has seen, is that while the international scientific community argues about Indian nuclear test claims, the government neither declares its strategic compulsions based on the promised Strategic Defence Review nor does it evolve an integrated operational and planning structure and associated integrated command and control system. India's policy of limited testing of warheads and missiles, keeping the military outside the planning and decision making loop and its self-imposed moratorium on further testing or its intentions to consider signing the CTBT, all contribute to casting doubts on the credibility of its deterrent and would be strategically and operationally flawed While there is confidence that Indian scientists have the capability to conduct computer simulation experiments, from the military point of view these must be validated by explosive tests. With this background it is difficult to convince even nuclear amateurs, leave alone the Cold War nuclear protagonists, of India's nuclear deterrence. Nuclear warheads and associated delivery systems are instruments of national security. Notwithstanding their wider international and political ramifications, their intrinsic value lies in their being perceived as effectively operational and usable at the hands of the military. India's nuclear doctrine based on a comprehensive Strategic Defence Review must be unambiguously laid down. Alongside, it must be backed by an integrated operational and planning structure and an associated integrated command and control system.

BALLISTIC MISSILES

While the Germans first used the V2 missiles, it was the Sputnik launch that spurred the US into missile development programmes, which have culminated in the ballistic missile race and ultimate primacy of the ICBM (Inter-Continental Ballistic Missiles) as a nuclear weapon delivery platform. The principal reason for ICBM superiority over aircraft or cruise missile delivery systems is their very long range determined by ballistic trajectories into space that in turn makes interception and neutralization a major technological challenge. From liquid fuelled missiles, the ICBMs have progressed to solid fuelled ones. From land based ones have evolved the submarine launched ones and multiple warheads have replaced single warheads. The Submarine Launched Ballistic Missile (SLBM) scores over its land based counterpart because of the carrier's stealth and mobility thus preventing neutralization by the adversary and ensuring a retaliatory or "second strike" capability.

Technologies that contribute to an operational ICBM are principally rocket motors (liquid and solid), guidance systems (both in-flight and terminal), telemetry, control and re-entry. In-flight inertial guidance systems can either be replaced by Global Positioning System based systems or use Global Positioning System (GPS) data for in-flight updates. In either case dependence on space-based GPS satellites becomes essential.

With permanent extension of the Non-Proliferation Treaty (NPT), nuclear weapon powers had hoped to limit the spread of nuclear weapons. This, however, did not alleviate their fear that long-range missiles could still be used for delivery of chemical or biological warheads. By putting in place the Missile Technology Control Regime (MTCR) they had hoped to prevent the spread of missile technologies and missile transfers.

While India has developed the requisite technologies for the tactical Prithvi missiles and the intermediate range Agni missiles, it has still to develop the requisite technologies towards solid propulsion systems, cryogenic engines, accurate guidance systems with ability to update in flight and terminal guidance, all of which are a pre-requisite towards developing ICBMs. In-flight and terminal guidance systems also depend on space based GPS and sophisticated reconnaissance systems.

While technologies to develop and operationalise ICBMs with multiple warheads are mature and available with the nuclear five, like the rest of the nuclear and missile regime India will have to develop the necessary technologies and their integration to operationalise ICBMs with multiple warheads.

Finally, while Indian atomic, space and defence scientists can take credit for much of the developments that have brought India to the present state of nuclear and missile development, there is still a long way to go. With its limited missile and aerospace infrastructure, limited R&D funding, absence of any meaningful exports in defence and missiles and limited quantitative requirements, India is still dependent on foreign sources for many specialized components and systems. It is this imperative of developing countries like India that makes them victims of technology denial or denial of dual-use technologies. This is a paradoxical situation. India has the technological base to become self-reliant, yet such a route becomes economically difficult to sustain without economies of scale of production. That is why while India has achieved some selective measure of success in nuclear and missile programmes, it is nevertheless struggling to operationalise modern combat aircraft, tanks, engines and other weapon systems.

Ideally stand alone research, design and development would be the route to go. This however, needs huge investments, corresponding resources and adequate time. In neither case can India afford these specially since the very credibility of its nuclear deterrence posture not regionally but internationally depends on operational availability of such weapon systems?

While conducting its strategic security review, it is vital for Indian policy makers not only to articulate a clear nuclear and missile strategy, but to also show how this can ensure security in the face of the internal and external challenges, some of which have been discussed in the preceding paragraphs.

A repeat of the mistaken policy made in the pursuit of India's nuclear weapons programme, where the programme culminating in tests was driven by the political and scientific institutions, keeping the military institutions in the dark, must not be made. A case in point is the view that "Indian technological capabilities have progressed so rapidly that it is no longer necessary to conduct multiple tests of the same missile system before operationalising it".[6] This perhaps echoes the view expressed by the Indian scientific community, but it runs counter to the mature and well defined procedures for in-service induction of weapon systems.

The very basis of credible nuclear deterrence is that in the eyes of others India's capability is credible. In Indian military minds there are serious doubts. Doubts about the efficacy and reliability of the integrated weapon system based on the very limited testing that has been done and that too without military involvement.

India's missile development programme must continue towards finally achieving operational ICBMs. This will include capabilities for multiple and decoy warheads as also necessitate capabilities for space

---

6 *Securing India's Future In The New Millennium — Nuclear Deterrent Posture* by Brahma Chellaney. P 175

based GPS and reconnaissance systems for terminal accuracies. India has formally declared a policy of "no first use". This coupled with a minimum nuclear deterrence policy requires that India be able to absorb a "first strike" and retain a credible command, control and response capability. Without a SLBM capability, which assures survivability of the second strike forces, the Indian nuclear posture is at best militarily fragile and perhaps serving only a limited political and diplomatic strategic purpose. High priority must, therefore, be accorded to develop an operational SLBM capability to keep this high-risk window to the barest minimum.

ANTI BALLISTIC MISSILES

The Anti Ballistic Missiles (ABM) treaty of 1972 limited the US and USSR to the deployment of to two sites each, banned further research on existing technologies and prescribed mutual consultation if new technologies were to be attempted.[7] In 1983 President Reagan called on the US scientists to develop defensive measures against nuclear weapons to make them impotent and obsolete. This so called "Star War" programme was meant for defence against a saturation attack by Soviet nuclear warheads and was overtly ambitious. While huge investments were made in various technologies, it did achieve the dubious distinction of pushing the Soviet Union into an unaffordable arms race.

Once the Cold War ended, the US under the Clinton administration continued with a more modest theatre ballistic missile defence (TMD) plan. After Iraq's Kuwait adventure, the potential threat now became rogue states that may launch a few warheads.

It is, however, the recent announcement by President Bush that the US plans to erect a national missile defence (NMD) shield and plans to take friends and partners along, that has not only turned

---

7 *Securing India's Future In The New Millennium — Countering Missile Threats* by K.Subrahmanyam. P 249

the nuclear weapon world topsy turvy, but also sent governments and security analysts scrambling back to their security drawing boards. The prompt and positive initial response by India in "that there was a strategic and technological inevitability in supporting such a move", drew both support and criticism from varying sections of the strategic community.

Some of the technologies that are being considered for the NMD are infrared satellites along with ground-based radars for detection of launch and guidance with ground based interceptor missiles achieving the kill. Alternately a powerful 'oxygen-iodine laser' mounted within a mother aircraft which detects missile launch, determines trajectory and then destroys the target with a 3-5 second burst of laser beam is also under consideration. Laser detection and destruction could also be done from a group of orbiting satellites. Whatever the final technical solution, there are two historical fallouts of the US decision. Firstly, space will inevitably see offensive militarization and possible action. Secondly, technology is once again in the center of a complete change in the international security paradigm. As an Indian official explained "this is not about something as trivial as missile defence. This is about a new security paradigm".

It is for the first time in recent history that India, with its moral repugnance to nuclear weapons and its frustrations with the old nuclear order where there was no control on the spread of nuclear missile and technology, may see light at the end of the tunnel. India was a reluctant entrant to the nuclear club. Having declared a nuclear "no first use" and minimum nuclear deterrent policy, it was still faced with huge challenges to blend its nuclear security requirements with those of technology development, affordability and punitive action. It is possible that diplomatic and international relations' windows may now be opening that will enhance India's security without unnecessary flow of resources towards higher and higher nuclear and missile technology expenditures. While the final concepts and technologies are still to evolve even in the US, India can at best use diplomacy and strategic and technological partnerships to ensure that it stays on the right side of development of space as the next frontier. Opting for stand-alone R&D efforts towards operationalising anti- ballistic missile systems will not be an affordable or cost beneficial option.

SPACE

There are upward of 500 military satellites in orbit today primarily performing communications, surveillance, navigation and weather monitoring functions. In essence space technologies have brought in a military revolution in the command, control, communication, computerization, intelligence, information, surveillance and reconnaissance (C4I2SR) functions of warfare. Much of these have now been classified under the generic term Revolution in Military Affairs (RMA)—of which more will be discussed later.

The Gulf War employed a wide variety of new space and intelligence assets to assist mission planning, command and control of the war, provide real-time identification of ground targets for close air support, and ensure that allied forces gained and maintained the initiative. Undoubtedly both space and intelligence platforms are destined to become crucial force multipliers in future conflicts.

Because space is already playing and destined to play a crucial role in the future, it is only a matter of time before conflict moves into space. The USAF Manual AFM 1-1states "Aerospace Control assures the friendly use of aerospace environment while denying its use to the enemy. (It) includes all missions whose objectives are designed to gain and maintain control of the aerospace environment."[8]

The Outer Space Treaty of 1967 prohibits militarization of space. As we have earlier seen, this did not prevent the US from carrying out experiments towards its now defunct "Star Wars" programme. The new NMD announced by the US President is destined to take offensive operations into the frontiers of space.

---

8 *Impact of Emerging Technologies on Air Power* — USI Paper1/98. Air Marshal Bharat Kumar (Retd). P 84

Notwithstanding the treaty, with space playing such a crucial role in the C4I2SR aspects of future military operations, it is inconceivable that efforts at denial of use to enemy will not be resorted to. Such action need not necessarily be offensive in nature. After all GPS satellites already offer differing categories of accuracy to the US military as against other users. Total denial, should operational necessities dictate, is probable.

India is one of the few countries that have the ability to put satellites in geostationary orbit. It will be in a position to offer launch facilities for commercial exploitation, thus enabling resources for further research and development in exploiting space for both commercial and military uses. As with all current and evolving technologies, the challenge to India is not so much technological as one of prioritization and affordability. The primary lesson for countries like India is, therefore, to have essential indigenous space platform capabilities for their future operations while forming partnerships with others to make space launch assets both affordable and not denied during times of crises. A concurrent approach must be to have duplication of essential terrestrial backup facilities for communications and command and control/surveillance within airborne platforms.

India must strive to continue to develop space technologies, offer launch facilities for commercial exploitation and use resources for further R&D to stay abreast in selected space technologies both civil and military. The next century will clearly belong to space technologies and those that lag may do so forever.

A crucial task of the Air Force is surveillance of national air space in peace and war. Space is already teeming with platforms and sensors that contribute significantly to today's operational capability of most nations. With ballistic missile trajectories taking them into space, monitoring and tracking space objects is now an operational imperative. Missile threats demand an organization that is capable of responding instantly in peace and war. Very close monitoring of civil air movements or satellite orbits and analyses of unusual occurrences in peacetime will ensure closer control of air activities across the country's air space. This will also be a vital input to intelligence assessments. A Joint Air Space Management Authority needs to be set up under the Air Force with elements of civil aviation and space organization duly represented. Its task will be monitoring, tracking and analyzing all movements in air and space over the country at all times of day and night.

AIRBORNE WARNING AND CONTROL SYSTEM (AWAC) AND JOINT-STARS E-8

During the entire Gulf war air campaign AWACS aircraft were continuously airborne controlling more than 3,000 coalition sorties each day. As a tribute to their effectiveness, despite having to control aircraft flown by pilots from numerous air forces speaking several languages, not one case of air-to-air fratricide was reported.

Although the JSTARS (USAF-Grumman Joint Surveillance Target Attack Radar System) was still under development during the Gulf war, one aircraft was on station every day tracking every vehicle that moved on the ground. Joint-STARS identified and targeted Scud missiles and launchers, convoys, trucks, tanks, surface-to-air missile sites and artillery pieces for coalition aircraft. These command and control platforms are destined to play a vital role in future land/sea/air battles. As Space platforms mature, many of these functions will inevitably shift into space.

The integrated land/sea/air battle scene of the next war, howsoever limited in India's context, will need highly integrated and sophisticated command and control systems for both effective operations and prevention of fratricide. While induction of AWACS is planned, command and control platforms for conduct of integrated land/sea/air operations need to be developed.

CRUISE MISSILES/UNMANNED AERIAL VEHICLES

US and Russia have operational cruise missiles equipped with both conventional and nuclear warheads. The US forces used cruise missiles, both land and ship launched extensively during the Gulf War in Afghanistan. In the first use of this weapon system to inflict punishment in peacetime against targets in different continents, the US used them against targets in Sudan and Afghanistan in retaliation for terrorist attacks on its embassies in Africa.

Technologies for the use of cruise missiles are well established. Because the airframes are not reusable and do not need sophisticated pilot support systems, the airframes are small and light. This reduces radar and visual signature and enhances payload/range capability. Modest turbo jet engines, sophisticated auto pilots, use of composite materials, on board pre-programmed inertial/GPS systems, terrain following/matching and terminal guidance using digital mapping data are some of the unique features of this weapon system. Essentially, dependence on accurate data on terrain *en route* and the target radar/optical picture is the key to a successful mission. These in turn are dependent on sophisticated reconnaissance and navigational capabilities with support from air and space based platforms. While cruise missiles do not have ranges matching ICBMs, the ability to launch them from ships gives the nations possessing such systems the capability to attack most potential targets from the safety of international waters, as the US attacks on Sudan and Afghanistan have clearly demonstrated.

Below the threshold of surface-to-surface missiles and without resorting to violations of countries' air space and exposing their aircrew, this is a weapon system that in the emerging scenario will be used to punish or coerce in the international arena. It is not without significance that the first use outside of a war scenario has been towards neutralizing supposed terrorist targets within the safety of international hideouts. As the threat of rogue states and international terrorism takes on greater significance in international arena, cruise missiles are destined to play a greater operational role.

Unmanned Aerial Vehicles (UAVs) are already proving to be very useful in varied roles of reconnaissance, surveillance and target identification/designation. The primary advantage is their small size, low observability and no pilot-risk approach. In addition, because there is no need for a pilot and associated support systems, the vehicle becomes highly cost-effective. India has already developed its pilotless target aircraft (PTA) and an unmanned aerial vehicle (UAV) christened Nishant. It also uses UAVs for tactical/photo-reconnaissance, target designation, ELINT and other allied roles. The capability to develop a family of cruise missiles therefore exists and would need to be exploited. The crucial issue will be availability of spacebased GPS and terrain/target mapping data towards mission accomplishment.

The next logical evolution is towards Uninhabited Combat Aerial Vehicles (UCAV) that will perform operational roles as well. Its utility for offensive operational roles in highly defended areas to prevent pilot attrition is unexceptionable. There is, however, a conflicting situation here. Manned aircraft are better suited for offensive operations in a fluid battle scenario because of the inherent flexibility that they provide with the pilot being in the loop. While UCAVs can have control systems that are remotely piloted, semi-autonomous, autonomous or fully adaptive with artificial intelligence, none of these can provide the flexibility that a combat pilot can.

While technologically there are no hurdles for the UCAV concept, the debate of manned versus unmanned combat missions needs to be confined to operational and cost-effectiveness reasons and kept away from purely philosophical and emotional ones. The ongoing RMA process points to UCAVs playing a vital and useful role in certain areas of offensive air operations thus posing a challenge to strategic, operational and tactical targets of the adversary.

Such revolutionary change brings with it doctrinal, operational and organizational challenges. Management of the air space and that of integrated air operations between manned and unmanned combat platforms are some such challenges. Much will depend on how militaries approach this potential and whether they are willing to innovate and adapt old doctrines and organizational structures to exploit such technologies. Manned aircraft will, therefore, continue to form the bulk of combat air arms, duly complemented by UCAVs for specific roles.

INFORMATION TECHNOLOGY

The (US) National Defence University defines Information Warfare (IW) as " an approach to the armed conflict focusing on management and use of information in all its forms and at all levels to achieve a decisive military advantage especially in the joint and combined environment. Information-based warfare is both offensive and defensive in nature — ranging from measures that prohibit the enemy from exploiting information to corresponding measures to assure the integrity, availability, and inter-operability of friendly information assets. While ultimately military in nature, information based warfare is also waged in political, economic and social arenas and is also applicable over the entire national security continuum from peace to war and from 'tooth to tail'. Finally, information-based warfare focuses on the command and control needs of the commander by employing state-of-art information technology such as synthetic environments to dominate the battlefield."[9]

Information revolution is being driven by the ongoing evolution of cyberspace with the help of microprocessors and related technologies. So rapid and far reaching are these changes that it is difficult for security planners to contemplate their precise impact on current and future threats and challenges leave alone attempt solutions. Considering that the speed and power of processors is doubling every eighteen months and prices nearly halving, this is not surprising. The cost factor also determines that unlike old times when defence technologies were within means of only the wealthy nations, today these are available to even private individuals—amongst whom would be hackers and terrorists.

In January 1995, the US Secretary of Defence formed the Information Warfare Executive Board to facilitate "the development and achievement of national information warfare goals" and RAND

---

9 *Impact of Emerging Technologies on Air Power* — USI Paper1/98. Air Marshal Bharat Kumar (Retd). P 66

was tasked to provide an analytic framework for identifying key Information Warfare issues to enable the US to develop a sustainable national consensus on an overall USIW strategy. The following summary from the RAND report[10] puts the problems and challenges in an overall US perspective:

The study highlighted seven defining features of strategic information warfare along with their consequences:

- Low entry cost implies that networks may be subject to attack and disruption not just by states but also by non-state actors.
- Blurred traditional boundaries imply that one may not know who's under attack by whom, or who's in charge of the attack.
- Expanded role for perception management implies that new information-based techniques may substantially increase the power of deception and of image-manipulation activities, dramatically complicating government efforts to build political support for security-related initiatives.
- A new strategic intelligence challenge is posed by poorly understood strategic IW vulnerabilities, thus diminishing the effectiveness of classical intelligence collection and analysis methods. A new field of analysis focused on strategic IW may have to be developed along with new organizational relationships.
- Formidable tactical warning and attack assessment problems imply that the United States may not know when an attack is under way, who is attacking, or how the attack is being conducted.
- Difficulty of building and sustaining coalitions will be faced, as reliance on coalitions is likely to increase the vulnerabilities of the security postures of all the partners to strategic IW attacks, giving proponents a disproportionate strategic advantage.
- Vulnerability of the US homeland is implied as information-based techniques render geographical distances irrelevant and targets in

10 RAND-1996. *Strategic Information Warfare — A New Face Of War.* Roger C. Molander, Andrew S. Riddile, Pete A. Wilson.

> the continental United States become just as vulnerable as in-theater targets. Given the increased reliance of the US economy and society on a high-performance networked information infrastructure, a new set of lucrative strategic targets presents itself to potential IW-armed opponents.

The essential and far-reaching conclusion of the RAND study was that in the US, key national military strategy assumptions are obsolescent and inadequate for confronting the threat posed by strategic IW.

While the above study was confined to the US security environment, the above analysis applies equally to other countries. It emphasizes the magnitude of the problem and challenges facing governments and institutions alike. With technology progressing ever so rapidly and technology base of India expanding even more, security planners would need to understand the impact of the IW process on India's security environment. Appropriate strategies to exploit Information Technology and prevent IW damage must be put in place.

STEALTH

Stealth is about reducing a weapon platform's visual, infrared, radar or acoustic signature, thus reducing detection by the adversary and enhancing surprise. In every one of these areas considerable success has been achieved by application of technology, the extreme examples being the USAF Stealth fighters and bombers. New weapon systems would need to apply stealth techniques to the extent the design and cost factors permit.

ELECTRONIC WARFARE (EW)

In terms of application of information age technology, EW comes close to Information Warfare. Any techniques that degrade functioning of the electronics of weapon systems can be considered forms of EW. Beginning with EW to confuse an adversary's radars and weapon systems, EW is expanding to become all pervasive as weapon systems begin to depend more and more on avionics, computers and communications. In many ways, EW has taken the form of tactical warfare between combat teams consisting of operational and software personnel. This is one reason that advanced countries sometimes need actual operations to debug systems in actual conditions! In the near future EW techniques will use massive electromagnetic pulses, computer logic bombs and computer viruses to degrade weapon system effectiveness. This is an area that will continue to evolve both technologically and in terms of evolving tactics.

NIGHT/ALL WEATHER CAPABILITY

Considerable progress has been made in permitting night/all weather operations by use of modern technologies. In spite of this one of the lessons of the Gulf War was that many systems that incorporated complex or advanced technologies needed specific operating conditions and were, therefore, limited in their operational usability. Militaries will continue to demand flexibility for all weather day and night operations and as operational experience is gained (from experiences like the Gulf War, Kosovo or the recent Afghan campaign) optimum solutions will be evolved for which much of the technology exists.

LAND/SEA/AIR PLATFORMS

Military platforms whether they are land, sea or air based all share characteristics that are essentially defined by the age-old parameters of warfare, namely speed, maneuverability, stealth, high payload to platform ratio, survivability and defensive counter measures. In every one of these spheres material technology and extensive use of computer-aided design and manufacture is playing a major part. As newer technologies are developed in each of these areas their impact will be felt directly on platforms and weapon systems at the hands of the fighting forces. The latter in turn will need to adapt strategies, tactics, training and logistics not only to take full advantage of technological enhancements but also ensure that the adversary does not get the better of them. In no sphere is this more vital than in the area of information/ electronic technologies and warfare, a subject briefly covered earlier.

Technologies, however, come at a price and defence budgets are never unlimited. Armed forces that are smart and innovative in adapting strategies, tactics, training and logistics to take full advantage of technological enhancements while retaining appropriate technologies will retain the winning edge. Those that also use technologies optimally for greater cost effectiveness will be able to afford more and retain numerical superiority.

CONVENTIONAL WEAPONS

In the ultimate analysis the culmination of offensive/defensive operational missions is target destruction. Weapons of today are more precise, have greater lethality, enable greater stand-off launch ranges, have greater punch per unit weight/size and are smarter, some verging on the intelligent. As technology progresses so also will the performance and lethality of weapons. There is, however, a flip side. One lesson of the Gulf War was that effectiveness of many high technology weapon systems was limited due to stringent operating conditions. Two broad conclusions emerge. One that wars when they do take place will be more precise, more destructive and bloody and consequently of shorter duration. And two, that as far as weapons are concerned, high technology and complexity does not necessarily translate to effectiveness and operational usability in a given operational environment. Optimum blend of different technology levels thus remains a powerful tool at the hands of planners and tactical commanders.

NON- LETHAL WEAPONS

The US Department of Defence (DOD) defines non-lethal weapons as "Weapons that are explicitly designed and primarily employed so as to incapacitate personnel or materials, while minimizing fatalities, permanent injury to personnel and undesired damage to property and the environment".[11]

In their thesis "Weapons of Mass Protection"[12] the authors have argued that non-lethal weapons first received serious notice after their use in the Gulf War. Carbon circlets were dropped on Iraqi power stations to deny electricity to the enemy, obscurants were used to deny the enemy targeting information about US troop movements, and electromagnetic weapons — reportedly including non-nuclear electromagnetic pulse — were used successfully to limit casualties.

The authors have categorized non-lethal weapons as:

- Anti-personnel or anti-materiel
- Electromagnetic, kinetic, or chemical
- Non-lethal and anti-lethal

Among technologies identified as non-lethal are acoustic, laser, high-power microwave, non-nuclear electromagnetic pulse, high-power jamming, obscurants, foams, glues and slicks, super-caustics, magneto-hydrodynamics, information warfare, and soldier protection. Among technologies identified as anti-lethal are counter-sniper, counter-mortar, anti-missile, and high-precision weapons, including low collateral damage kinetic munitions with reduced lethality.

The authors conclude that non-lethality requires no massive investment in new technology, but a re-evaluation and re-direction of mature research programs into the weaponization and the fielding of usable systems that conserve life and are environment friendly and fiscally responsible. Non-lethality further posits that the technologies that yield non-lethal systems will comprise a real peace dividend.

---

11 *Impact of Emerging Technologies on Air Power* — USI Paper1/98. Air Marshal Bharat Kumar (Retd). P 54

12 *Weapons Of Mass Protection — Non-Lethality, Information Warfare And Air Power In The Age Of Chaos* — Chris Morris, Janet Morris, Thomas Baines

Non-lethal weapons are technology's answer to the emerging reality where modern peace-keeping, peace-enforcing and counter terrorism in urban areas are becoming routine military missions, where society is intolerant to both military and civilian casualties, where collateral damage is unacceptable and where damage and destruction will be seen on international TV.

It is worthy of recollection that the IAF experimented with glue based runway denial weapons as early as the 1965 Indo-Pak conflict. Non-lethal weapon technology is one area that lends itself for application with low investments providing usable and effective solutions especially in conditions of limited conflicts. R&D towards such application of technologies must be given high priority. Because such technologies are not necessary high profile, R&D agencies must avoid looking down at them. Alternatively user services must take on R&D within their Systems Commands.

BIOLOGICAL WEAPONS

The 1972 Biological Weapons Convention outlaws manufacture, storage or use of toxic weapons. Recently the 56 nation talks on arriving at a protocol for enforcement of the convention were suspended as the US withdrew from the talks. The US felt that the draft under discussion would be ineffective in stopping countries from violations and would expose US commercial secrets of the bio–tech industry to industrial espionage. According to a British science publication *Nature*, genetic engineers already have it within their grasp to devise a lethal bio-weapon. Small changes in the DNA of well-known bacteria and viruses could turn these agents into mass killers. At the hands of terrorists or rogue states their damage potential cannot be under estimated.

Until formal and implementable international agreements on banning biological weapons are reached, the danger to the world from such weapons will remain more so in the hands of non-state actors. Proof of this, if at all needed, has come in the form of letter borne

Anthrax threat that emerged in the US after the 11 September 2001 terrorist attacks on the New York Trade Centre and Pentagon. India must, therefore, have effective disaster management plans to counter such threats.

SECURITY MANAGEMENT IN THE INFORMATION AGE

Clearly current and emerging technological evolutions will continue to have a profound impact on how future security is organized, managed and executed, all this within the confines of resources that a developing country like India can afford. Existing systems of security management that have failed even the relatively modest and benign security environment of the past decade or so are ill equipped for the task ahead.

Technological changes are altering the face of conventional warfare so completely that weapon systems and forces that were central to old military doctrines are rapidly becoming obsolete and will need to be superseded. This requires transformation of the security apparatus, a clear appreciation of the security challenges ahead and a national security strategy to meet such challenges. It needs a transformed higher security management system starting at the apex level right down to the field where authority and accountability go hand in hand. It needs an integrated and seamless system of analysis of threat and responses and redefining of roles and missions of all the three services towards efficient and cost effective security. It needs integration and prioritization of re-equipment plans, standardization of equipment for economies of scale and inter-operability. It needs pooling of hardware for cost effective training, maintenance and logistic support. It needs focused and prioritized effort at defence R&D and production.

The security management model that presently exists in India has its genesis in the armed forces of the pre-independence days with incremental changes brought in by circumstances. It is therefore out of tune even with the current technological and security environment and its needs. The ongoing RMA and rapid technological advances demand not an evolutionary change, but a well-conceived transformation of how security is organized, managed and executed. Technology is also driving costs and making affordability an essential ingredient of national security planning.

Most of all it needs leadership at every level that is both visionary and committed to transformation to meet the challenges that are now being thrown up. A transformation that will need discarding of old ideas, philosophies and prejudices. A leadership that is willing to down-size and share roles laterally. One that is willing to look at innovative solutions to new technological challenges.

Faced with this challenge, the recommendations of the Group of Ministers in February 2001 towards "Reforming the National Security System" are merely the first steps towards a modern defence management system and are by no means the ultimate. And yet the storm created even by these modest changes indicates the attitudinal challenges that face the Indian security establishment of the future.

SCIENTIFIC & TECHNOLOGICAL HUMAN RESOURCE DEVELOPMENT

Of the two capitals essential for technological growth P.V. Indiresan[13] says "human capital is reliable, while financial capital is ephemeral and untrustworthy. Further, as a rule, financial capital chases human capital; that is why so many software firms come to India. Thus, if we have human capital, we need not worry about financial capital. The converse is not true. That makes a skilled workforce a more reliable asset than finance. Development based on human capital is dependable; that based on financial capital is undependable".

Further quoting D.Christiansen[14] he concludes "A country that trains its engineers and technologists well, then rewards them with

---

13 *Securing India's Future In The New Millennium* — 'The Role Of Science And Technology'. P.V.Indiresan. P 41

14 D. Christiansen 'Engineering Excellence: Cultural and Organizational Factors'. IEEE Press, New York 1987

both real and physical income, should have little trouble competing in a world economy that thrives on trading high quality, high-tech products over international boundaries".

That India possesses high quality scientific and technical manpower is borne out by the achievements of its people in the international arena. Consequently one would have expected India to achieve far greater success in the area of technology especially in the defence sector. Yet India continues to import a large proportion of its defence requirements from overseas thus pointing to some drawbacks.

The fundamental weakness that appears to run across the entire Indian human resource landscape is that administration and administrators have come to occupy the top place in the very hierarchical structure of Indian society. Administration, whether in public or private sector is no more a means to an end, but perceived to be the end in itself. As P.V. Indiresan says with regard to scientists and technologists not only are emoluments insufficient "even more important is the relative status of scientists and engineers compared to that of administrative officers. In India, most technologists serve in government establishments and under conditions substantially inferior to that of administrators. In the private sector, too, the situation is similar. As a result of this calculated discrimination, top level scientists and technologists in the country have developed the self-image of servants".[15]

The result is that many scientists and technologists perceive rising up the management ladder as a measure of success rather than aspiring for technological or scientific achievements. Specially so in defence and government laboratories and institutions where accountability matters little and where merit and technical excellence mean less than authority and power. Scholarly and dynamic scientists find this ethos out of tune with that of the task of research and technology development. It is not surprising that many a scientist who has left

---

15 Securing India's Future In The New Millennium — 'The Role Of Science And Technology'. P.V. Indiresan P 45

lucrative assignments at top institutions in the West to come and work closer home at lower emoluments have regretted their decision and a majority have returned.

One example should bring home the point. The LCA (Light Combat Aircraft) programme is by far the biggest challenge to the defence scientific community apart from being the most cost-intensive development project. A post of Director General ADA (Aircraft Development Agency) was conceived to guide and steer this project. The first incumbent resigned even before the project had commenced. An incumbent specially recruited in the US was not permitted to function and left. Thereafter the post has never been filled and the Chief Designer has also been the Project Director, an organizational model not practiced elsewhere in the aerospace world.

As P.V. Indiresan says "In S&T establishments, for example, administration should play a facilitating role rather than one of control. That is, scientists should be in a position to demand service from the administration, rather than be supplicants of administrators. In order to ensure that such privileges are not misused, only competent should be allowed entry into S&T establishments".[16]

There is little doubt that if India is to achieve even a small measure of its potential as a technological power then organizational and institutional reforms are essential towards training and employment of the most valuable potential, the scientist and technologist. Their status in society must reflect the authority and position accorded to them in driving India ahead technologically. In administratively driven India this means a major attitudinal challenge.

DEFENCE RESEARCH AND DEVELOPMENT ORGANIZATION (DRDO)

The Defence Science Organization was set up soon after independence. Over the years it has grown substantially and today Defence Research

16 Securing India's Future In The New Millennium — 'The Role Of Science And Technology'. P.V. Indiresan P 46

and Development Organization (DRDO) is a Department of Defence with a network of fifty-two laboratories/establishments spread across the country.

The mandate of DRDO as reflected in Ministry of Defence (MOD) Annual Report 1997-98 is:

- to enhance self-reliance in defence systems through design and development leading to production of state-of-the-art weapon systems, sensors, platforms and equipment to meet laid down service requirements and
- to undertake development of expertise and emerging technologies which would be required for such future programmes.

The first mandate reflected above would apply to various technologies that go into design and development of weapon systems as the task of design and development of state-of-the-art weapon systems is the legitimate responsibility of the defence production agencies. Judging by some of the recent programmes like the Integrated Missile Programme, MBT and LCA, DRDO has assumed responsibility to even design, develop and produce complete weapon systems. This has had an adverse bearing on the functioning of the production agencies whose design and development departments have become subservient to DRDO. In the longer term this will also have an adverse impact on the quality of in-service product support that will be forthcoming to the user service once the weapon system is inducted. Equally, by getting involved in production, the scientific and research aspects of DRDO have suffered considerable dilution.

With a vast array of resources both human and infrastructural and liberal project funding from the user services, the general expectation was that the services would have benefited considerably from this national asset and made the Indian armed forces truly self-made sufficient in their weapon system requirements after fifty years. For reasons too complex to enumerate, which encompass organizational, personal and inter-departmental issues, this has not happened. Instead programmes like the PTA, Indra Radar, RPV, LCA, MBT and a host of others have become bogged down, denying the armed forces vitally needed operational capability. And even those systems that have found their way into service are dependent on imported systems, sub-systems and components. In the ultimate analysis, of the two primary aims of DRDO earlier mentioned, neither the services nor defence PSUs appear to have seen any significant benefits.

DRDO has spread its activities far and wide. Today it covers a canvas stretching from pure research to pre-production of weapon systems and from space and missile technologies to boots and clothing. While there are some notable successes on the missile front, in nearly every other area, promises made have not been kept. It speaks of the total disregard for the services in the existing management structure that the say of DRDO or the defence PSUs has carried more weight than that of the services.

Often the MOD has superseded services' professional views on future weapon systems over inflated claims made by DRDO. Not only have the armed forces' re-equipment plans suffered serious set-backs, but a sense of mistrust has replaced an integrated national approach to self-sufficiency. Programmes earlier mentioned and a host of others are testimony to this weakness, which primarily stems from a flawed higher defence management structure and where those that determine the services' future re-equipment are not accountable for the final operational consequences.

The concept of pure defence research leading to evolution of technology and materials which then find application in the defence industry towards design and development of weapon systems against service staff requirements has been lost. The tremendous potential within the defence research labs both in terms of infrastructure and human resource has failed to make an appreciable impact either on self-sufficiency or on the fighting potential of the armed forces.

The nation has invested huge sums in infrastructure and human resource development of organizations responsible to promote a defence capability. Notwithstanding this farsighted planning, self-reliance is nowhere in sight and the armed forces are still being forced to import weapon systems. Experience has shown that inter-organizational and inter-personal turf battles have taken precedence over national security compulsions.

The nation and more specifically the armed forces continue to pay a heavy price for which there has been no individual or organizational accountability. Defence services, production agencies and DRDO each have a clearly defined area of responsibility. Accordingly their human resource development and organizational ethos reflect the organization's specific role. When this equilibrium is disturbed, as has clearly happened in India's case, then all suffer.

Today DRDO has failed to deliver on ambitious projects, defence production agencies have been starved of their design and development departments and the services saddled with serious operational gaps. Yet no organization or individual can be held to account.

In the final analysis India's defence capability must encompass self-reliance in areas where technology denial is a threat along with fruitful strategic partnerships to enable not only affordable weapon systems for the armed forces, but sustainable R&D and industrial base through export and economies of scale. These challenges cannot be met with the present archaic and compartmentalized structure of defence industry.

The following institutional and organizational changes are necessary towards a focused, integrated and harmonious approach to defence research and development:

- DRDO should be tasked for research into materials and emerging technologies that will find application in future weapon systems. Design and development of weapon systems must not form part of their charter.
- On a staff project basis DRDO should undertake specific projects of engineering/technology towards promoting self-sufficiency in spares/components/materials of weapon systems that are procured from overseas.

- After an in-depth rationalization exercise, all laboratories/ establishments of DRDO not related to the above roles should be transferred to respective production agencies or Systems Commands of the respective service. Those not relevant can be sold to the private sector or to CSIR or closed down.
- Projects undertaken by DRDO must be in response to specific futuristic staff targets and funded by the service. Project and financial management will be with active participation of the sponsoring service.
- A one time review and rationalization of all existing projects with regard to their viability in DRDO needs to be done with active participation of the user service.

Post-Kargil, the government has embarked on reforming the national security system based on the GOM (Group of Ministers) report of February 2001. This is an opportune time for an in-depth restructuring of the defence research and production roles and responsibilities so that the nation gets the best value for defence investments and those invested with authority in every organization and at every level are also accountable. If this opportunity is lost, then history will repeat itself.

ORDNANCE FACTORIES AND DEFENCE PUBLIC SECTOR UNDERTAKINGS

For decades, under the slogan of self-reliance, Ordnance Factories and defence PSUs have held the armed forces as captive customers. Armed forces' budgets have been compelled to bear the entire burden of overheads, idle labour and outdated technology within these undertakings. On nearly every occasion they have had the first preference to respond to a service staff requirement. Often orders have been placed by the MOD against service advice. Not only have the PSUs then imported systems/sub-systems/components, but also projects have still suffered vast cost and time over runs. Notwithstanding this massive public investment, when the erstwhile Soviet Union collapsed, all the three services suffered acute spares shortages. The MIG 21, which was under production in India for over three decades, suffered the same fate. Today the services are forced to appeal to the private sector to come to their assistance, although apart from public seminars and platitudes, little progress has been made.

Some years ago a massive restructuring and rationalizing of the US defence industry was undertaken with prodding from the US government. At the time the change was being overseen by Jacques Gansler, Under Secretary of Defence for Acquisition and Technology, who as early as 1980, when outside the Government had said "In order to understand the economic operation of the US defence industry, it is first absolutely essential to recognize that there is no free market at work in this area and that there likely cannot be one because of the dominant role played by the Federal Government. The combination of a single buyer, a few large firms in each segment of the industry, and a small number of extremely expensive weapons programmes constitute a unique structure for doing business".[17]

This sums up the challenge to governments and their defence industries across the globe. How to keep this unique structure for doing business, finely balanced between free market on the one hand and absolute state control on the other? No longer can the government, the services and the defence undertakings think strictly in institutional and compartmentalized terms.

Emerging challenges offer opportunities to look at change. Defence industry by virtue of its technological edge and security applications is a crucial strategic industry. National governments in the west have long recognized this linkage and continue to evolve policies that both support the industry and retain its competitiveness.

While governments, defence forces and the defence companies in the West are consolidating and restructuring to meet emerging challenges, there is no such urgency visible in the Indian scene.

---

17 The Defence Industry, Jacques Gansler. MIT Press. 1980

Successive Indian governments have held the view that public ownership automatically safeguards national strategic interests. This flawed logic coupled with political, bureaucratic and scientific control has brought Indian defence industry to the brink.

The Indian government while treating all defence PSUs as security related, has done nothing to prepare these vital industries to face emerging challenges. Policies during the hey-day of non-alignment discouraged arms exports thus insulating the Indian defence industry. Today the industry lacks marketing knowledge and skills. Unless the government evolves a strategic policy for its defence undertakings, aerospace being the most important by virtue of its technological edge, and frees day-to-day management from its control, nothing can change.

In the emerging defence market place, a weapon system is no longer a unique national product. Systems and components are sourced internationally and even customized to suit requirements of different customers. This opens up opportunities for Indian defence PSUs to exploit their core strengths preferably in partnerships with bigger international companies. In a fiercely competitive industry this is the only way to find a place in the international market. Design and development in selected areas, integrating civil and military production, component and system manufacture, integration and testing of avionics and weapon systems, repair and overhaul of civil and military platforms/engines/components, writing and updating software are some areas of Indian strength that come to mind. There are many more and opportunities are endless. Unless defence PSUs diversify into the civilian sector and gain a foothold in the export market, they cannot serve national strategic interests.

By virtue of their technological edge and security applications, defence PSUs can be classified as strategic. The following reforms are necessary:

- Production agencies and Ordnance Factories (OFs) must take on the responsibility and establish capability to design and develop weapon systems meeting service requirements.

- Production agencies must also be responsible for providing in-service design, modification and product support.
- Projects undertaken by production agencies must be in response to specific service Staff Requirements and funded by the service. Project and financial management will be with the active participation of the sponsoring service.
- Self-reliance cannot be a justification to promote OFs/PSU interest over pure military requirements. The former is a long term ideal, the latter a security imperative.
- OFs/PSUs must compete for services' requirements against the private sector
- A one time review and rationalization of all existing projects with regard to their viability both in OFs and production agencies needs to be done with active participation of the user service.
- Contracts must be awarded on fixed cost basis.
- Management must be freed from government interference.
- For survival in the market place strong investment in R&D, exports and economies of scale are pre-requisites. This is possible if linkages are established with similar industries of like-minded countries for a wider technology and market base and economies of scale. Countries with whom India looks for strategic partnerships would be likely candidates for defence industry partnerships.

It needs fresh thinking on the part of the government. The services and defence PSUs to evolve what must be the optimum route to exploit the rapidly changing international armaments scene to India's strategic and commercial advantage. The first step is to free defence PSUs and OFs from the mindset of a PSU and put it into the arena of professional corporate management. Only then will Indian defence industry emerge from the shadows of governmental lethargy and exploit its vast untapped potential.

Areas that can no longer be ignored are, divesting some of the government's holdings, freeing management decision making of bureaucratic and scientific interference, rationalizing and consolidating the existing infrastructure and human resources towards efficient defence and aerospace activities and shedding the rest. These are major issues, but ones on which the very survival of a strategic industry rest. The "unique structure of doing business" earlier referred to will take on different shades depending on many factors. Indian government needs to recognize that India has to define its own unique structure and then introduce institutional reforms. Time is of essence".[18]

PRIVATE SECTOR

For too long Indian government policy guided by the antiquated Industry Policy Resolution, has kept the private sector outside of the defence procurement process. While the supposed reason has been security considerations, the larger issue appears to have been the wider politico-economic debate of retaining the Public Sector in defence and strategic areas. Nowhere has the glaring weakness of this concept been more evident than within the defence apparatus. In an area where technology is the driving force, defence research and development have been reduced to bureaucratic exercises with services as captive customers, having to make do with old technology, poor quality, delayed deliveries and substantially higher costs for the massive overheads.

Recently, the government has allowed the private sector to set up wholly owned units for defence manufacture permitting even foreign investment up to 26%. Much will depend on what restrictions and guidelines are imposed on the private sector. However, one thing is certain. If the government fails to make long-term commitments thus exposing private sector investment decisions to the vagaries of bureaucratic uncertainty and if the services do not tailor their stringent

---

18. *Indian Defence Review. 'Challenges facing Indian Aerospace Industry'* — Air Marshal B.D. Jayal (Retd)

Military Specifications to realistic levels, then we may find the private sector shying away from the defence sector. If we are to encourage private sector participation in defence production, then the government must act as a facilitator, at least to begin the process.

In the developed countries it is the commercial world that has been the technology driver in space, computers, electronics, material sciences, computer aided design and manufacture, genetic engineering and so on. The militaries are merely reaping the benefits of these civil-led R&D efforts towards defence applications. While this will happen as Indian economy expands, to accelerate the process the defence sector will have to promote the private sector.

DEFENCE TECHNOLOGY COMMISSION

Defence research, development and industry form the bedrock of national security power. Its R&D drives technology and promotes self-reliance especially against denial regimes. Its exports support both R&D and the industrial base thus promoting affordable weapon systems for national security. While India possesses all the pre-requisites for a sound industry, its contribution to the building of the nation's defence, air, space and IT power have not been in keeping with this potential. Lack of an integrated and mission oriented approach is the cause.

The only way to harmonize actions towards clear strategic and security goals of self reliance, security, affordability, defence research and development, immunity from technology denial regimes or technology warfare measures and doing all this in a coordinated and prioritized manner, is to set up a national Defence Technology Commission working in close concert with Indian Space Research Organization. The commission should consist of technocrats and professionals tasked to steer the development of space, aeronautics, missiles, information and defence technologies towards clearly defined strategic goals and national requirements. The services as the largest operators must be key players within the commission.

ARMY/NAVY/AIR FORCE TECHNOLOGY & SYSTEMS COMMANDS

The role of these Technology and Systems Commands will be to drive technology upgradation, operational/technical innovations to weapon systems and carry out developments and modifications to enhance the operational capability of the services. Modern weapon systems and corresponding support infrastructure are becoming both powerful and more complex. Whether such systems are being evaluated for procurement from overseas, being developed indigenously or indeed being modified to suit services' operational requirements/tactics, there is need for systematic and a multi disciplinary approach to these tasks to ensure that in the final analysis the services get a weapon system meeting their operational requirements in time and at an affordable price.

By and large modern weapons and systems are bought from overseas. There is not much that is not known about them. There is tremendous potential to modify platforms, marry different weapon systems to evolve combinations and evolve software solutions that will meet the services' tactical needs in an ever-changing battlefield environment and keep the adversary guessing. This is technological innovation for tactical surprise.

Each service also has establishments dealing in IT and operational software. These are by and large distributed weapon-system wise e.g. separate for communications, radars, weapon platforms, etc. Software is emerging as the brains behind weapon systems. It is vital that while hardware can be imported or even indigenously produced, the software must be designed and developed by operational people who will also be able to blend operational tactics into software design. Every service must plan to have a dedicated software development center within their Technology and Systems Command to exploit this vital and rapidly evolving operational asset. By keeping this within the service, the latter will also be able to ensure security of their potential and tactics.

Functional commands designated as Technology and Systems Commands need to be set up in each service to harness software and technology towards enhancing weapon system capability, generating operational software and acting as interface between technology and operations. Responsibilities of Technology and Systems Commands could be:

- To be the driving force in introducing and integrating future technologies into operational weapon systems and tactics of Operational Commands.
- Represent the service in the Defence Technology Commission.
- Evaluation of weapon systems against service Staff Requirements.
- Joint monitoring of indigenous staff projects along with active participation with developing agency during the development and testing phase.
- Acceptance of newly inducted weapon systems and formulating their handling, operating and maintenance manuals.
- Modification of platforms and weapon systems to meet changing operational needs.
- Maintenance of operational software in platforms, weapons, air defence networks, communications, EW etc.
- Generate Information War solutions.
- Maintain a close link with operational commands to synergize operational and weapon systems tactics for optimum operational effect.
- Standardization and inter operability norms with other service Systems Commands.

TECHNOLOGY DENIAL/WARFARE

A report in *The Economist*[19] pinpoints globalization and rapid technological change as two factors posing a threat to national hegemony. In fact it is the galloping advances in Information Technology that are responsible for the current pace of globalization.

19 *The Economist*. Survey Of The World Economy. 28 September 1996.

The latter in turn fuels economies of those that are able to sustain technological superiority thereby enabling greater resource allocations to further fuel technology. The challenge to the national security of those outside this charmed circle, like India, is how to break into this exclusive club. Depending on the model chosen to achieve technological independence, parity or co-operation will depend on the security profile of these countries.

Not unnaturally, technology can be used as a weapon to enhance or degrade security depending on which side of the technology divides one's perspective is from. This could be done in many ways. It can take the form of technology denial as was done by the US government in respect of super computers to India or their preventing Russia from supplying cryogenic engine technology or freezing of technology transfer of LCA flight controls. Or it could be done by targeting indigenous technology where the latter poses a threat by either dumping products at prices which can not be matched indigenously or by weaning away the scientists and engineers by offering them lucrative and technologically rewarding assignments.

In a world of free markets many of these tactics are fair game. The danger is not when this happens overtly, but when this is done in a covert manner. Countries like India who both depend on foreign know-how while also developing their own must not only put in place institutional safeguards, but also aggressively guard against any form of technological attack.

AFFORDABILITY

While there was much relief at the incremental increase in defence budget in the Finance Bill for 2000-2001, this still amounted to less than 3% of the GDP. High technology weapon systems have increased in costs by up to twenty times in the last two decades, far surpassing normal inflation or foreign exchange variations. Corresponding maintenance and manpower costs have also increased disproportionately. Some twenty percent of modernization and maintenance costs of the services are incurred in foreign exchange. Continuing erosion in the rupee value puts further pressure on the service financial planners. Analysts have opined that if the current ad hoc and somewhat disjointed approach to security, force and equipment planning continues then even a 5% GDP defence budget may be inadequate clearly not an affordable option for developing India.

Criteria of affordability must now guide the very basis of national security planning. A top to bottom integrated approach rather than a distributive "do with what you get approach is needed. To enable this a national security policy determined by the National Security Council should guide the MOD's defence strategy. This strategy will need to be translated by an integrated military mechanism into force development objectives for each service and specific military roles and missions jointly and individually.

Blind pursuit of high technology/high cost weapon systems is wasteful. Recent conflicts with extensive use of air power have revealed the limitations of such an approach. Equally, procedural and bureaucratic delays in decision-making are eating heavily into allocated resources, clearly highlighting the urgent need for restructuring and decentralizing the defence financial management system.

It needs recognition that many of the technologies that come under the generic term of RMA are still in the process of evolving and most relating to space-based applications also involve huge R&D investments and will be prohibitively expensive and possibly beyond the reach of even many developed nations. Blind technological pursuits or slogans of self-reliance then become mere mirages. It is here that the Defence Technology Commission would need to set prioritized, achievable and affordable goals including partnerships with civil or outside industries.

NON-STATE ACTORS

Globalization of world trade, commerce and finance coupled with rapid communications and transportation has made it easy for organizations or individuals inimical to the interests of India to operate from havens overseas and indulge in anti-national activities either directly or through proxy. Such transnational criminal organizations will become increasingly adept at exploiting technology to form groupings across international borders and conduct operations seamlessly. Easy money from drug trafficking, smuggling, trafficking in human beings, illegal arms trade, smuggling of toxic materials, hazardous wastes, military technologies and other contraband will be used to subvert corrupt leaderships, compromise governments and even enter the political spectrum to subvert national interests. Much of this is already happening. What must concern security planners is when these organizations begin to have access to nuclear, biological and chemical weapons and technology; they will not hesitate to use these in furtherance of their nefarious goals.

Covert threats such as these did not exist when peacetime intelligence and policing systems were evolved decades ago. Powerful technology in the hands of proxy or fringe groups can create security threats far in excess of earlier peacetime ones. Where does the role of civilian agencies end and that of the services begin? The line is getting ever more blurred. Like in the case of defence, there is need to relook at the entire edifice of peace-time intelligence, policing, paramilitary forces and the military such that planning, equipping, training and command and control for such threats and exigencies leaves no room for error. The need is for the systems to remain pro-active and neutralize events before they result in catastrophe. As in the case of defence management, challenges of technology at the hands of non-state actors makes it compelling for central and state governments in India to modernize and integrate policing, associated intelligence and disaster management operations. This is a challenging task.

REVOLUTION IN MILITARY AFFAIRS (RMA)

A combination of Information Revolution, rapid advances in weapon systems' technology, use of space applications and precision guided munitions all add to the generic RMA process. It is now possible to integrate vast amounts of inputs, from intelligence to real time target information from sources on land, sea, air and space, process it and permit meaningful decision making at the operational commander level to enable effective and timely response. In this environment those armed forces that fail to keep up with technology will lose their deterrence and fighting edge.

Contrary to expectations space applications will continue to contribute towards force enhancement rather than force application within the next decade plus. While the strategic logic of space power would indicate upgrading military capabilities in space, this is an unlikely scenario. Overdependence on space applications is undesirable as it is prohibitively expensive and can be countered by terrestrial means. A major weakness in exploiting even the existing potential of space applications by the US is reportedly organizational and legacy constraints. This in turn inhibits timely, focused and effective operational use of spacebased inputs. An important pointer is how availability of commercial imagery from space has enabled commercial organizations to influence space policy in the US.

A space command responsible for planning, managing and executing all space military applications and coordinating with ISRO is necessary. Those aspects of GPS, high-resolution imagery, communications, command and controls that are force multipliers must be promoted indigenously. Commercial use of launch and other facilities must financially support some military activities. Backup to space applications must always be available.

IW targets will not be confined to the military. Indeed any institution involved in the daily running of the country from government to power distribution and banking, all using computerization will be targets. IW defenses have to be planned by all, not just the military institutions.

The next battle will be seen in every drawing room and street corner and the dynamics of casualties and media handling by the services will sway national mood and politics. IW has the destructive power to manipulate this information database. Security planners can no longer be insensitive to this reality.

"For the United States, the RMA entails, in the words of its erstwhile Under Secretary of Defence, the following: "our military will seek to project power without putting a large number of forces at risk. Massed forces will be replaced by massed firepower precisely placed on targets. Modern, so-called 'reconnaissance/strike' warfare (often referred to as the essence of the 'Revolution in Military Affairs') is based on real-time, all-weather, accurate and secure information systems combined with long range, unmanned, 'brilliant', highly-lethal weapons designed to achieve precision kills. Technology has also enabled us to reduce dramatically our response as geopolitical events warrant. The type of regional conflict that we will see more frequently in the 21st century is likely not to allow six months to build forces and deploy them. There also will no longer be 'free' ports or airfields. Aggression will be instantaneous, with little warning, brutal, and difficult to defend against".[20]

So unpredictable is the future that even as the US Defence Department was finalizing its review of defence, the events of 11 September 2001 occurred. The subsequent US military response has had to face these new challenges and evolve unique solutions.

The Indian security establishment would not only need to clearly articulate its interpretation and application of RMA, but do so in the evolving international terrorism and operational context. This will give military planners clearly defined objectives.

THE FUTURE

Below is an extract of a paper titled Global Trends 2015[21], approved for publication by the US National Foreign Intelligence Board under the authority of the Director of Central Intelligence. The paper prepared

---

20 *Securing India's Future In The New Millennium — Challenges To India's Security In The New Millennium* by Brahma Chellaney. P 566-567

21 *Global Trends 2015: A Dialogue About the Future With Non-government Experts*, NIC 2000-02, December 2000

under the direction of the National Intelligence Council is based on discussions with non-government experts. It aptly sums up the role of S&T in the future security scenario not only of the US, but internationally.

Fifteen years ago, few predicted the profound impact of the revolution in information technology. Looking ahead another 15 years, the world will encounter more quantum leaps in information technology (IT) and in other areas of science and technology. The continuing diffusion of information technology and new applications of biotechnology will be at the crest of the wave. IT will be the major building block for international commerce and for empowering non-state actors. Most experts agree that the IT revolution represents the most significant global transformation since the Industrial Revolution beginning in the mid-eighteenth century.

The integration or fusion of continuing revolutions in information technology, biotechnology, materials science, and nanotechnology will generate the following:

- Dramatic increases in investment in technology, which will further stimulate innovation within the more advanced countries.
- Older technologies will continue lateral "sidewise development" into new markets and applications through 2015, benefiting US allies and adversaries around the world who are interested in acquiring early generation ballistic missile and weapons of mass destruction (WMD) technologies.
- Biotechnology will drive medical breakthroughs that will enable the world's wealthiest people to improve their health and increase their longevity dramatically. At the same time, genetically modified crops will offer the potential to improve nutrition among the world's one billion malnourished people.
- Breakthroughs in materials technology will generate widely available products that are multi-functional, environmentally safe, longer lasting, and easily adapted to particular consumer requirements.
- Disaffected states, terrorists, proliferators, narcotraffickers, and organized criminals will take advantage of the new high-speed

information environment and other advances in technology to integrate their illegal activities and compound their threat to stability and security around the world.

CHANGING NATURE OF WARFARE

Introduction

In broad terms strategy can be defined as the art of harnessing the powers of a nation to accomplish the aims and objectives set forth either in peace or war. It follows therefore that in order to formulate either national or military strategy, national aims and objectives need to be clearly defined.

The closest enunciation of such objectives was laid down in the Draft Indian Nuclear Doctrine that was released for discussion.[22] Para 1.2 of the Preamble states "India's primary objective is to achieve economic, political, social, scientific and technological development within a peaceful and democratic framework. This requires an environment of durable peace and insurance against potential risks to peace and stability. It will be India's endeavor to proceed towards this overall objective in co-operation with the global democratic trends and to play a constructive role in advancing the international system towards a just, peaceful and equitable order".

A purely military strategy for a nation is no longer possible. A clear-cut line of demarcation between military, economic, and political matters no longer exists. Consequently, the development of military strategy takes into consideration political and economic factors, and, conversely, political strategy must be firmly based on military and economic power realities.[23]

---

22 *Indian Nuclear Doctrine* — National Security Advisory Board

23 Strategy, *Microsoft® Encarta® 98 Encyclopedia.* © 1993-1997 Microsoft Corporation. All rights reserved. Arleigh Burke

The broad contours of India's military strategy are defensive, ensuring security of land, sea and air frontiers to enable sustained economic and social development. As long as nuclear weapons remain in the inventory of some nations, a minimum nuclear deterrent must be visible to prevent adventurism under the threat of nuclear weapons.

The evolving globalization of economies, RMA and the high cost of such technologies and weapon systems and the changing nature of threats, all pose challenges of change. Challenges that force choices to be made and priorities to be set towards achieving maximum security for available investments. In the ultimate analysis those nations that evolve an optimum strategy will be the ones able to face the future with greater security and confidence.

Major developments make the entire exercise of cost effective integration of air, land and sea warfare into the future an exciting and challenging one for leadership at all levels. A task demanding vision, astuteness and professionalism. Vision, because new challenges both operational and economic make old concepts and philosophies somewhat redundant. Astuteness, because overlapping of roles and high costs make inter service and institutionalized co-operation imperative. And professionalism because galloping advance in technology is pointing towards intellect and knowledge being key players alongside skill and valor in future application of military power.

The armed forces cannot be expected to plan for, train and fight an integrated battle if the institutions they represent are not operationally integrated. This calls for a review of the higher defence organization with an integrated operational charter.

In their report "The Principles of War in the 21st Century: Strategic Considerations "[24] the authors conclude that modern day principles of war are the culmination of labours to condense the lessons of war

---

24 *The Principles Of War In The 21st Century: Strategic Considerations.* William T. Johnsen, Douglas V. Johnson II, James O. Kievit, Douglas C. Lovelace, Jr and Steven Metz

which in itself are based on historical treatises by military practitioners, philosophers and historians. These have been based on experiences of Napoleonic and Industrial Age warfare and though the concepts at the tactical and operational levels are well understood, their applicability at the strategic level has been less exhaustive.

"Whether or how these principles apply at the strategic level of war under the conditions of rapid technological change that many are calling the 'Information Age' and its military offspring, the Revolution in Military Affairs (RMA), is an open-ended question".[25]

In order to arrive at any strategic formulations for security planning, it is necessary that we look at various factors both internal and external that will determine the nature of war in an age where technology is progressing in leaps and bounds, where proxy wars, ethnic cleansing and terrorist challenges are becoming more common. And where it is not so much threats to national boundaries, but terrorism, fundamentalism, subversion and narco-trafficking that are becoming the major and often subterranean threats. And finally, weapons of mass destruction and terror or tools of the information age at the hands of such individuals and groupings can no more be factors that do not draw the strategic planners' attention.

Science And Technology — A Strategic Dimension

While the impact of science and technology today stands well understood, at the rate technology is advancing few will venture to guess what impact it will have even into the near future. Will the divide between the developed and developing countries reduce or will it increase? Even within developing countries will this create greater divisions and tensions or vice versa. How will alienated ethnic, religious and fundamentalist groups use technology to further their own divisive agendas?

Some trends are however already visible. Increasing reliance on computers and their networks in the daily life, governance, economies

25 Ibid

and infrastructure of countries makes even orderly life and governance susceptible to cyber warfare. Since the latter, unlike present day military technologies, is both affordable and easily accessible with no geographical boundaries it becomes an attractive tool at the hands of disaffected states and terrorist organizations. Biotechnology along with other technologies may offer further openings for such states and organizations to resort to use of biological warfare.

The terrorist attacks on the Pentagon and World Trade Centre have, however, drawn attention to an even more basic fact. Neither superior weapon technologies nor access to massive resources or firepower is needed, if the enemy is not conventional. By resorting to innovation and surprise disproportionate damage has been inflicted to the psyche and economy of the most powerful nation on earth.

Information Technologies — The Challenges

The serious threats are "to the large, complex and fragile interconnected information infrastructures of wired nations". The innate vulnerabilities of these systems are open to attack by hackers, terrorists or antagonistic governments. After examining how military operations, communications, electric power supply, banking and finance, transportation and other vital services could be affected, Strategic Survey 1998/99 notes that existing security concepts provide some protection, but nowhere near enough. It will take focused effort to expand these concepts and create new solutions to thwart the malicious attacks that are certain to be mounted in the future.[26]

Affordable Defence — Challenge For Innovativeness

An essential input to security planning relates to the criteria of affordability. Devoid of this, doctrines and planning lose their meaning. Because of the flawed higher defence organization and lack of integrated military planning, Indian defence budgets have traditionally been distributed between the three services in percentages that have

26 Strategic Survey 1998/99 Strategic Policy Issues

historical rather than security or operational significance. Each service plans for the worst-case scenario and presents its needs and requirements. The budget cannot support these requirements. Since the budgeting and accounting systems are accounting based rather than operational based, no meaningful operational trade offs are possible. Consequently there has been a perceptible decline in the level of modernization and operational readiness of the services as even a small border skirmish recently demonstrated.[27]

In the sphere of self-reliance and production of defence equipment, as militaries across the globe are shrinking, aerospace industries are pooling resources and rationalizing towards cost-effective operations and affordable weapon systems.

In the evolving climate with costs of design and development of weapon systems escalating and with both civil and military technologies converging, India will have to evolve new models of defence research and development leading to production. Neither is the concept of total self-reliance viable any more, nor one of limited production quantities catering only to the internal requirements.

Defence research of the future must be mission oriented towards specific goals where technology denials may work to India's disadvantage. Production agencies must be joint ventures aiming to design and develop world-class equipment for the indigenous and export market in a cost efficient manner with the benefit of economies of scale. And finally, the users themselves must control operational software, the heart of weapon and command and control systems.

Recent Conflicts — Trends

The closing stages of the last millennium and opening of the new witnessed three operations, all of which hold portends for the future. The Gulf War triggered by Iraq's occupation of Kuwait territory saw

---

27 *Indian Defence Review*. Indian Nuclear Doctrine — A Discussion — Air Marshal B.D. Jayal

the allied force under the leadership of the US join hands in fighting a modern integrated land/sea/air war with use of all the conventional technologies including the IT age C4I2SR technologies. It was also a war where one of the principal guiding tactics was to keep the allied casualties low so as not to invite adverse domestic criticism. The conflict gave the powerful nations of the world an opportunity to test and verify their high technology weapon systems and IT age command and control systems.

Undoubtedly lessons were learnt for future design, development and tactics. A GAO (General Accounting Officer) report states that "the effectiveness of many systems that incorporate complex or advanced technologies may be limited in future missions, since many of these systems require specific operating conditions to operate effectively". Also that many of the claims about weapon system performance were overstated, misleading, inconsistent or unverifiable".[28] Two important points emerge. Firstly, conduct of war in the modern day technological environment requires a sophisticated degree of integration of planning, command, control and execution using the most modern air and space technologies. And secondly even the most modern weapon systems suffer from mundane limitations notwithstanding their very high costs.

The Kosovo conflict was a contrast. For the first time NATO ventured beyond its conflict zone to use massive air power as a means of punishment in a limited conflict scenario. NATO's strategic concept now reserves the right to eliminate a self-perceived threat even by using nuclear weapons. It claims a right to "humanitarian intervention" in other countries, asserting that this right transcends the sovereign jurisdiction of the targeted country over its internal affairs.

While this displays the unilateral arrogance of technology and power, and needs to be analyzed in the geo-political context, it is worth recalling that notwithstanding massive use of airpower for over

28 Operation Desert Storm: Operation Desert Storm Air War (Letter Report, 07/02/96, GAO/PEMD-96-10)

one month, the ultimate damage to the Yugoslav forces was extremely limited. Clearly, reluctance to commit ground forces and risk casualties proved to have serious limitations, irrespective of the sophistication of aerospace technology possessed and applied .Two valuable lessons emerged. One that nations with superior technology and firepower must not underestimate the potential of lesser adversaries in a limited war scenario. A Vietnam lesson repeated in modern technology context. And the second even more important conclusion was that while air power will play a vital and determinant role in any future conflict, applied in isolation its potential is at best ambivalent.

In contrast the first war of the 21st century has caught every one by surprise. Barely a month before, the thought that terrorists could strike such a massive blow within the US was not thinkable. The war in Afghanistan by virtue of a combination of air power special operations routed the Taliban quicker than many had anticipated. While the opening stages of the war against terrorism have been traditional air strikes supported by special operations and in that sense conventional, this is not a conventional war. There are no geographical boundaries to defend and no visible enemy to target. And as events unfold more and more of this war will have to be fought covertly away from traditional battlefields and into virtually every area of governance, corporate boardrooms, religious seminaries, banking systems and the like. As events unfold strategic thinkers and military planners will be forced to scramble to rewrite theories and plans.

Strategic Threats — Nuclear/WMD

China and Pakistan, both India's neighbours with whom there are unresolved border disputes, are also declared nuclear powers. While both China and India have declared a policy of 'no first use', Pakistan has not. India has declared a policy of "a minimum nuclear deterrence". While within the delivery systems available to India, the policy of deterrence vis-à-vis Pakistan is viable, India will need to develop and operationalize longer-range missile systems for the deterrence to be credible vis-à-vis China. Within the confines of these parameters it is expected that the countries will put in place adequate command and control systems and mutual safeguards to ensure that a stable deterrent regime is in place. Since international opinion will not tolerate an unstable nuclear regime, it can be assumed that there will be adequate international pressure on all the countries to ensure that this happens.

The threat from Pakistan is, however, somewhat different from what conventional Cold War nuclear wisdom would indicate. Their fragile democracy is frequently replaced my military regimes, who have all along maintained control of the nuclear programme. Of late they have fallen prey to the jihad sentiment of Islamic fundamentalists in their fight to wrest the state of Jammu and Kashmir from India. A quicksand from which the military regime may not find retraction easy. Events following the US offensive operations in Afghanistan have further complicated Pakistan's internal dynamics. The danger of Pakistan nuclear arsenal slipping into the control of fundamentalist elements is always a probability to which the international community has to be alive. This is the strategic threat for which Indian security planners must prepare.

There is as yet another threat looming that of the non-state non-conformist organizations with agendas removed from the international diplomatic domain. Ones like the perpetrators of the World Trade Centre attacks. To them WMDs of even the lowest level of sophistication provide power far beyond their legitimate means. They may use airborne platforms like civil aircraft in the garb of civilian operations, UAVs or indeed platforms on sea or use them in lieu of conventional terrorist weapons. It is this threat outside international diplomatic domain that appears to be most damaging for security planners in India.

In essence India's nuclear doctrine has been declared as one of "credible minimum nuclear deterrence". In this policy of 'retaliation only', the policy states that the survivability of India's arsenal is critical. Further India has declared a policy of "no first use" and said it will "not resort to the use or threat of use of nuclear weapons against States which do not possess nuclear weapons, or are not aligned with nuclear weapon powers".[29] Clearly, the message from India is one of a responsible nuclear weapon state imposing upon itself limitations without international treaty obligations with a view to sending a sobering message.

While four of the nuclear five have not even declared a policy of "no first use", China has done so with some qualifications. Significantly neither has Pakistan accepted the philosophy of "no first use" nor has it shied away from brandishing the nuclear weapon threat as it did during Kargil. In the regional context what this signifies is that while the Cold War legacy of a stable nuclear deterrence can prevail with respect to China and India, Pakistan remains a question mark with all its attendant dangers and ramifications. International effort at drawing Pakistan into this regime must therefore remain the strongest challenge to the international community within the next decade. As long as this does not happen, Indian security planners must take note.

Ballistic Missile Defence

In unveiling his administration's plans for the Nuclear Missile Defence shield (NMD), the US President emphasized the dangers of the Cold War policy of mutual assured destruction on which the 1972 ABM Treaty was based. He justified change, as the Soviet Union was no longer an adversary. Identifying the changing threat he talked of nations for whom terror and blackmail are a way of life and who seek weapons of mass destruction to intimidate their neighbours. He gift-wrapped the dumping of the ABM Treaty by promising that this new framework must encourage still further cuts in nuclear weapons. Crucially, he still supported the NPT, which legitimizes nuclear weapons in the hands of five nuclear powers. What was left unsaid was that as long as there were nuclear weapons with others, only an NMD shield would confer on the US an unfettered and lone superpower status! And it is this ambition to remain as the only super power that will drive the US to forge ahead with this programme duly supported by the scientific-military-industrial complex.

---

29 *Indian Nuclear Doctrine* — National Security Advisory Board

Notwithstanding what the world may say, therefore, and more specifically with the lessons of World Trade Centre and Pentagon attacks, there appears every possibility of the US proceeding with its plan. There is also little doubting that sooner rather than later technological challenges will be overcome and some form of an ABM defence available to the US at least.

According to the website of the Federation of American Scientists, around $ 122 billion had already been spent on development of missile defences till a few years ago and tens of billions of dollars would still need to be spent. If nothing else, this should put paid to those with aspirations to join this exclusive club. More importantly, Indian policy makers must beware of claims being made by some quarters about India's potential to develop ABMs!

CONVENTIONAL WARFARE

Limited Wars

Until Pakistan's Kargil misadventure, India-Pakistan had seen the longest period without an all out war. Since the mid-eighties, as the specter of nuclearisation had gained ground so also had the improbability of an all out war in the conventional sense. It was an accepted belief amongst security planners that whilst India had outstanding territorial disputes with both Pakistan and China with live borders manned by the army, with all three now having declared themselves as nuclear powers, chances of an all out war were now remote. This myth was shattered by Pakistan's Kargil adventure no doubt fuelled by a restive and ambitious military machine egged on by Islamic fundamentalists. In the event, Pakistan could well be the exception to the following conclusion by a paper prepared under the direction of the US National Intelligence Council after discussion with non-government experts.[30]

30 Global Trends 2015: A Dialogue About the Future With Non-Government Experts, NIC 2000-02, December 2000. National Intelligence Council

"The risks of escalation inherent in direct armed conflict will be magnified by the availability of WMD; consequently, proliferation will tend to spur a reversion to prolonged, lower-level conflict by other means: intimidation, subversion, terrorism, proxies, and guerrilla operations. This trend already is evident between Israel and some of its neighbors and between India and Pakistan. In the event of war, urban fighting will be typical and consequently, civilian casualties will be high relative to those among combatants. Technology will count for less, and large, youthful, and motivated populations for more. Exploitation of communal divisions within an adversary's civil populations will be seen as a key to winning such conflicts — increasing their bitterness and thereby prolonging them."

The worst-case scenario in the India-Pakistan context in the next decade can thus be a miscalculation of the Kargil type by Pakistan towards achieving limited objectives, which could find a matching or retributive response. A limited conflict short of an all out war could be the result. Such a conflict will be intense, short and sharp. The responsibility on the shoulders of military commanders at all levels will be such that while fighting an intense limited battle, adequate restraint is exercised to ensure that the nuclear threshold is not approached inadvertently.

In the event of a limited border war with Pakistan or China, technology is unlikely to play an over riding role of the kind witnessed during the Gulf War. Pakistan will make every effort to create communal divisions within India, an aspect fuelled by their ability to use Information Warfare techniques under the garb of religion. There is danger of tensions and fighting within communally sensitive areas in the country thus resulting in civilian casualties and public outcry, affecting law and order and fuelling political divides thus affecting governance at state and central levels.

Limited wars by their very nature have limited objectives. Success or failure is therefore more visible than in an all out war. Add to this the fact that present day revolution in information technology enables the public to monitor the performance of its forces virtually from the ringside and one realizes why loss of scores of aircraft in previous air wars or over a thousand of our army men in Sri Lanka, did not evoke the type of public response that the loss of a mere three aircraft and around five hundred soldiers did in Kargil. As the Indian security establishment plans its the future, this responsibility must weigh heavily on its shoulders.

Threat/Sabotage of Offshore Assets and Island Territories

Offshore assets whether they are related to energy exploration/ exploitation or oil and gas transportation have a direct bearing on national energy security. Equally by their remote location they are more vulnerable to attack and sabotage both in war and peace. An even greater threat exists for the security of India's offshore Island territories of Lakshwadeep, Andaman and Nicobar Islands. A&N Islands by virtue of their distance from the mainland need special attention and an adequate deterrent military posture. Formation of a tri-services joint command for A&N Islands and augmenting of infrastructure for adequate forces have recently been announced. These are positive deterrents and were long overdue, as the threat will remain.

UNCONVENTIONAL WARFARE

Proxy Wars/Terrorism — A New Dimension

A challenge that India has now been facing for over a decade is the phenomenon of a proxy war. A war where individuals and organizations with the support of a government are trained, organized, equipped and supported in their acts of crossborder terrorism. As India grows economically and militarily stronger disaffected states and separatist outfits fuelled either by ethnic, religious, drug or criminal considerations will recognize the futility of challenging the power of the state in open conflict. Current IT revolution has already enabled such organizations to be networked and interact towards global integration and transfer of information/resources, and use of deception and denial techniques. These actors whether they be states, ethnic or fundamentalist organizations, organized criminals or drug traffickers, will all find it easy in an age of the global economy and networked commerce to challenge the government of the day by resorting to either cyber warfare, cyber crime, proxy warfare or in extreme cases to use of weapons of mass destruction in peace time. It is this threat more than any other that must draw the attention of Indian security planners.

Strategic Survey 1998/99 examines the evolving nature of terrorism and concludes that those who are driven by religious fanaticism, or individual hatred of government and society will slowly supersede traditional politically motivated terrorists. It concludes that, within a world being re-fashioned by profound political and technical changes; terrorism will continue to pose a threat. The emerging threats of terrorist use of NBC weapons or "cyber attacks" cannot be dismissed out of hand, but the danger should be seen in proportion. This will not for some time be as great as that presented by guns and bombs. Yet, while conventional terrorism continues to exact a deadly toll and to be economically and physically disruptive, the effects of even these tragic attacks should not be exaggerated.[31] The recent terrorist attacks in the US where hijacked aircraft were used as missiles have certainly added a new dimension to the entire facet of terrorism.

It is ironic that the terrorists who planned out the attacks in New York and Pentagon should have recognized that for the present the technology in their possession was inadequate to shake the world profoundly. They did the next best think of innovating and use of surprise.

There is little doubt that in the rapidly changing technological and global security environment and with considerable pressure on resources for development, the Indian security establishment also needs to take a fresh look at the entire edifice of security planning, organization, structure, roles/missions and execution with a view

---

31 Ibid

towards major transformation. A beginning has been made with the Group Of Ministers (GOM) recommendations on restructuring defence management.[32]

Because of India's location in the middle of two of the world's leading narcotics producing and exporting regions North West Pakistan and Afghanistan on one side and Myanmar on the other, it can not expect to remain unaffected by drug trafficking and associated fallout of organized crime and terrorism. Such groups and organizations with financial resources far beyond their means and with access to weapons, communications and technology will perforce look for soft targets to further their illegal activities. Today individuals or groups can fund and direct terrorist and criminal acts across the globe from the safety of sanctuaries and hideouts. The Purulia arms drop case in India's context and the more recent New York Trade Centre and Pentagon cases in the US are a mere preview of the potential of things that are possible. Clandestine carriage of a weapon of mass destruction and its release over a populated target from an aircraft posing as a civil transport is no more a fictional nightmare. The need to actively monitor and control every object operating in Indian air space is urgent. Equally every space object over Indian space needs to be monitored and to the extent possible its mission and capabilities docketed and known.

Militancy/Separatism

The Annual Report of the MOD (1997-98) identifies militancy and separatist movements in Jammu and Kashmir and thc north-eastern states of India as constituting non-military challenges to India's security. "The phenomena of terrorism, separatism and extremism in all forms are being used as instruments of de-stabilization, primarily against pluralistic and democratic states."[33] India has since independence seen militancy and separatist movements in the north-

32 Reforming the National Security System — Recommendations of the Group of Ministers — February 2001.

33 MOD Annual Report 1997-98

eastern states. Such movements based on perceived religious, ethnic, cultural, caste, linguistic or other social grievances are not new to India and are now spreading across the globe. While Indian security forces have considerable expertise in combating such movements, two points merit consideration. The threat from such fringe outfits will multiply as they obtain greater access to technology of weapons and communications. Perennial deployment of the military for such internal security operations also eats into the ethos of the military to combat external aggression. Since this threat will continue to remain in the Indian context, rather than approaching the problem in an ad hoc manner, some innovative restructuring solutions need to be evolved.

Subversion

A multi cultural, ethnic and religious society like India with its diverse socio-economic strata will always provide a fertile ground for disaffected individuals, groups or organizations to sow discontent. The challenge to governance in a free society like India's is to differentiate between legitimate grievances and subversion. The latter if not identified and crushed results in disaffection amongst the larger populace and erosion of confidence in governance. India is no stranger to this phenomenon having suffered at the hands of Pakistani Intelligence agencies. This is a challenge to Indian governance and intelligence agencies both of whom have to modernize their structure, operations and laws to prevent such a threat.

Narco-Terrorism

According_to the MOD Annual Report "non-military challenges to India's security also include the linked problems of drugs trafficking, terrorism and organized crime. Involvement of insurgent and criminal groups in the drug trade is especially worrisome".[34]

---

34 Ibid

Sabotage

As Indian economy grows, so will its infrastructure of banking, finance, commerce, energy distribution, nuclear power plants, communication networks, railways, ports, civil aviation infrastructure and the like. The flip side is that such infrastructure dependent on modern computers and networking will also be susceptible to disruption through cyber warfare apart from being vulnerable to physical damage by sabotage using conventional or even non-conventional weapons. While the latter can be prevented by physical means, the former is more elusive and can be launched even from offshore locations with the added benefit of anonymity.

Any disruption of significance undermines not only commercial and economic activity, but also dents national image in the eyes of the world economic community. National morale and associated fallouts on national governance are the other casualties.

Information War

In the evolving information age it is relatively easy for states, organizations or even individuals inimical to the interests of India to launch psychological operations or resort to denial and deception techniques. A classic example of this was the disinformation campaign planted recently in Nepal against an Indian actor. Within days the country was brought to a halt and the government found itself in jeopardy.

A more sophisticated approach was followed by Pakistan during the recent Agra Summit, the full impact of which is still being discussed across the country. The potential for such mischief in a culturally, ethnically, religiously and politically diverse country like India is unimaginable.

Similar damage can be done to the operations of the security forces in times of crises or to bring them to disrepute in the eyes of the world or communities when they are engaged in counter insurgency or anti-terrorist campaigns within the country.

The first challenge is to understand the potency of "Psychological Warfare". Sophisticated monitoring, intelligence and pre-emptive responses are the answer to tackle such threats. This needs a whole new approach to laws relating to IT and its policing and implementation. Technologies to integrate many of these functions are within the capabilities of the country and must be evolved on priority. Reactive responses so typical of India's past security history will extract a heavy price in national security terms.

Peace Enforcing/Keeping

While this topic does not lend itself to featuring under the heading of warfare, it does highlight that in an increasingly inter-dependent world the Indian military will increasingly be looked upon to lend a hand in international peace enforcing/keeping operations. Past operations have shown that Indian forces have gained a healthy respect of the international community when they have been entrusted with such a task. As with all other aspects of national security, such roles are also becoming more complex and demanding .The Indian security establishment must plan and train to discharge such functions as a responsible member of the international global order.

Outlook for the Next Decade

The Indian security establishment rarely publishes papers and concepts for the future. It therefore becomes difficult to understand the basis underlying its plans and responses for the future. An equally disturbing trend that has existed for some time but which has come into the open after the Kargil conflict is the total lack of integration amongst the three wings of the armed forces.

It is worth looking at what other international players of interest to the Indian subcontinent are thinking. The Peoples Liberation Army published a paper titled 'The US Military's Soft Ribs and Strategic Weaknesses"[35] in which it advocated launching an 'electronic Pearl Harbour blitzkrieg' using advanced cyber warfare and electromagnetic

35 *The US Military's Soft Ribs and Strategic Weaknesses* — PLA — October 2000

interference technologies to cripple US military capability in Asia. Defence analysts specializing in China have observed that PLAAF and PLAN fully understand the importance of joint command, control, communications, computer and intelligence networks for effective battle space coordination and have developed capabilities accordingly.

A Chinese white paper on national defence issued in November 2000 also called for aggressive expansion of China's hegemony in Asia. In this the PLAAF advocated use of non-lethal means like massive electromagnetic energy pulses, computer logic bombs and network viruses to sabotage computer networks and command and control systems along with psychological operations using the media to undermine economies of potential rivals. In pursuance of this philosophy the Chinese have already increased their naval and air force budgets while curtailing that of thc army.

In the US the Defence Secretary in the Bush administration had ordered a comprehensive review of post Cold War strategy. Within this, eighteen separate reviews covered nearly every aspect of US defence policy. The review was headed by Andrew Marshall, who runs the Pentagon office responsible for predicting future threats and responses and maintains that nature of war is changing and this requires a new look at future roles, weapon systems, force levels and where the military puts its troops. As an example, because of the efficacy of long-range cruise/anti-ship missiles the survivability and viability of large surface vessels and aircraft carriers was being debated. Militaries being conservative, it is not surprising that the review had touched off some of the most heated complaints from the military services. Barely was the review complete when the terrorist struck at New York and the Pentagon. Not unnaturally, this changed context is non-being configured into future thinking.

Another report by the US policy research institute Centre for Strategic and Budgetary Assessments[36] reflects that today the effort in the US is on improving and modernizing today's' version of the

36 *A Strategy For Long Peace* by Stevens Kosiak, Andrew Krepinevich & Michael Vickers, CSBA Report

military. The authors argue that the priority should be to look afresh and transform the military rather than persisting with today's version. This should be done within the framework of projected resource constraints.

SUMMARY

General

There is little doubt that in the rapidly changing technological and global security environment and with considerable pressure on resources for development, the Indian security establishment needs to take a fresh look at the entire edifice of security planning, organization, structure, roles/missions and execution with a view towards major transformation. A beginning has been made with the Group Of Ministers recommendations on restructuring defence management.[37] If the Indian security establishment can take a cue from the above-mentioned CSBA conclusion, then the coming decade should be one of transformation and consolidation.

The biggest challenge to Indian governance and the security establishment is to accept the inevitability of change and to set about managing such change towards costeffective security.

Technology

India's nuclear doctrine based on a comprehensive Strategic Defence Review must be unambiguously laid down. Alongside, it must be backed by an integrated operational and planning structure and associated integrated command and control system.

India's missile development programme must continue towards finally achieving operational ICBMs, capable of delivering multiple and decoy warheads. High priority must be accorded to the development

37 Reforming the National Security System — Recommendations of the Group of Ministers — February 2001

of an operational SLBM capability to ensure an assured second-strike capability.

In the context of ballistic missile defence, while the final concepts and technologies are still to evolve even in the US, India can at best use diplomacy and strategic and technological partnerships to ensure that it stays on the right side of this development as stand-alone R&D efforts towards operationalizing such systems will not be an affordable option.

The next century will clearly belong to space technologies. India must, therefore, strive to continue to develop space technologies, spacebased GPS and reconnaissance systems and offer launch facilities for commercial exploitation such that these resources can augment further R&D to stay abreast in selected space technologies, both civil and military.

The integrated land/sea/air battle scene of the next war, howsoever limited in India's context, will need highly integrated and sophisticated command and control systems which need to be developed. A Joint Air Space Management Authority needs to be set up to monitor, track and analyze all movements in air and space over the country at all times of day and night.

Cruise missiles are destined to play a greater operational role as the threat of rogue states and international terrorism takes on greater significance in international arena. These need to be developed. Availability of spacebased GPS and terrain/target-mapping data towards mission accomplishment will be critical to these systems.

The ongoing RMA and rapid technological advances demand not an evolutionary change, but a well-conceived transformation of how security is organized, managed and executed. The Indian security establishment would not only need to clearly articulate its interpretation and application of RMA, but do so in the evolving international terrorism and operational context.

With technology progressing ever so rapidly and technology base of India expanding even more, security planners would need to understand the impact of the IW process on India's security environment. Appropriate strategies to exploit Information Technology and prevent IW damage must be put in place. High technology and complexity with regard to weapon systems does not necessarily translate to effectiveness and operational usability in a given operational environment. Optimum blend of different technology levels thus remains a powerful tool at the hands of planners and tactical commanders.

Technologies come at a price and defence budgets are never unlimited. Armed forces will need to be smart and innovative in adapting strategies, tactics, training and logistics to take full advantage of technological enhancements while retaining appropriate technologies.

The flip side is that unlike old times when defence technologies were within means of only the wealthy nations, today these are available to even private individuals—amongst them would be hackers and terrorists. This challenge is already a reality.

Non-lethal weapons are technology's partial answer to the emerging scene where peace-keeping, peace- enforcing and counter terrorism in urban areas are becoming routine military missions. R&D towards such application of technologies must be given high priority.

Countries like India who depend on foreign know-how while also developing their own must not only put in place institutional safeguards, but also aggressively guard against any form of technological attack.Until formal and implementable international agreements on banning biological weapons are reached, the danger to the world from such weapons will remain-more so in the hands of non-state actors. This is a task not just for the security forces, but also for the nation as a whole, which must have an effective disaster management plan to counter bio-terrorism.

The government, services and defence PSUs need to evolve an optimum route to exploit the rapidly changing international armaments scene to India's strategic and commercial advantage. To encourage private sector participation in defence production, so vital for a dynamic industry, the government must act as a facilitator, at least to begin the process. Post-Kargil, the government has embarked on reforming the national security system based on the GOM report of February 2001. This is an opportune time for an in depth restructuring of the defence research and production roles and responsibilities.

A National Defence Technology Commission working in close concert with Indian Space Research Organization needs to be set up to harmonize actions towards clear strategic and security goals of self reliance, security, affordability, defence research and development, immunity from technology denial regimes or technology warfare measures in a coordinated and prioritized manner.

Functional commands designated as Technology and Systems Commands need to be set up in each service to harness software and technology towards enhancing weapon system capability, generating operational software and acting as interface between technology and operations.

A Space Command responsible for planning, managing and executing all space military applications and coordinating with ISRO are necessary. Those aspects of GPS, high-resolution imagery, communications, command and controls that are force multipliers must be promoted indigenously. Commercial use of launch and other facilities must financially support some military activities. Backup to space applications must always be available.

Criteria of affordability must now guide the very basis of national security planning. This can be well served by a top to bottom integrated approach rather than a distributive "do with what you get" approach.

Disaffected states, terrorists, proliferators, narco-traffickers, and organized criminals will take advantage of the new high-speed information age. What must concern security planners is when these organizations begin to have access also to nuclear, biological and chemical weapons and technology; they will not hesitate to use these in furtherance of their nefarious goals. This poses a challenge of integration not only of the security apparatus, but many other national and state agencies.

Nature of Warfare

Major developments affecting security across the globe are being forced by technology, geopolitical factors, disaffection and terrorism. These in turn are changing the nature of warfare. The entire exercise of managing security in such a dynamic environment is, therefore, an exciting and challenging one for leadership at all levels, a task demanding vision, astuteness and professionalism. This calls for a review of the higher defence organization with an integrated operational charter.

Whatever may be the other security compulsions, India must have a known and credible nuclear retaliatory capability with a sound command and control system in place. Nuclear deterrence requires potential adversaries to be convinced of the efficacy of second strike and effective command and control assures the international community of India being a responsible nuclear power.

In the regional context while the Cold War legacy of a stable nuclear deterrence can prevail with respect to China and India, Pakistan remains a question mark with all its attendant dangers and ramifications. International effort at drawing Pakistan into this regime must, therefore, remain the strongest challenge to the international community within the next decade. As long as this does not happen, Indian security planners must take note.

With nuclearization of the subcontinent, chances of a full-fledged war have receded. But as Kargil demonstrated, future wars will be limited. Limited wars by their very nature have limited objectives. Success or failure is therefore more visible than in an all out war more so when present day revolution in information technology enables the public to monitor the performance of its forces virtually from the ringside. As the Indian security establishment plans the future, this responsibility must weigh heavily on its shoulders.

While the first war of the 21st century has caught the major powers by surprise, India, which has faced the ugly face of terrorism for over a decade, could well have said "I told you so"! The opening stages of the war against terrorism have been traditional air strikes and in that sense conventional, but this is not a conventional war. There are no geographical boundaries to defend and no visible enemy to target. And as events unfold more and more of this war will have to be fought covertly away from traditional battlefields and into virtually every area of governance, corporate boardrooms, religious seminaries and the like. As events unfold strategic thinkers and military planners, not excluding India, will be forced to scramble to rewrite theories and plans.

The danger of Pakistan's nuclear arsenal slipping into the hands of fundamentalist elements is a probability to which the Indian security establishment not only has to be alive but for which prompt and adequate responses must be planned.

The threat of non-state non-conformist organizations with agendas removed from the international diplomatic domain has recently been demonstrated. To them WMDs of even the lowest level of sophistication provide power far beyond their legitimate means. They may use airborne platforms like civil aircraft in the garb of civilian operations, UAVs or indeed platforms on sea or use them in lieu of conventional terrorist weapons. It is this threat outside international diplomatic domain that appears to be most damaging for security planners in India.

Like in the case of defence management, challenges of technology at the hands of non-state actors makes it compelling for central and state governments in India to modernize and integrate policing, associated intelligence and disaster management operations. This is a challenging task.

Threat exists for the security of India's offshore Island territories of Lakshwadeep, Andaman and Nicobar (A&N) Islands as also of India's offshore assets on which depends India's energy security. A&N Islands by virtue of their distance from the mainland need special attention and an adequate deterrent military posture.

Militancy and separatist movements in Jammu and Kashmir and the north-eastern states of India constitute non-military challenges to

India's security. While Indian security forces have considerable expertise in combating such movements, the threat from such fringe outfits will multiply as they obtain greater access to technology of weapons and communications. Also perennial deployment of the military for such internal security operations eats into the ethos of the military to combat external aggression. Since this threat will continue to remain in the Indian context, rather than approaching the problem in an ad hoc manner, some innovative restructuring solutions need to be evolved.

IW targets will not be confined to the military. Indeed any institution involved in the daily running of the country from government to power distribution and banking, all using computerization will be targets. The next battle will be seen in every drawing room and street corner and the dynamics of casualties and media handling by the services will sway national mood and politics. IW has the destructive power to manipulate this information database. IW defenses have to be planned by all, not just the military institutions.

A multi cultural, ethnic and religious society like India with its diverse socio-economic strata will always provide a fertile ground for disaffected individuals, groups or organizations to sow discontent. The challenge to governance in a free society like India's is to differentiate between legitimate grievances and subversion. The latter if not identified and crushed results in disaffection amongst the larger populace and erosion of confidence in governance. This is the potency of "Psychological Warfare" a concept well employed by Pakistani ISI in India.

While sophisticated monitoring, intelligence and pre-emptive responses are the answer to tackle such threats, the flip side is that such infrastructure is dependent on modern computers and networking. This will also be susceptible to disruption through cyber warfare apart from being vulnerable to physical damage by sabotage using conventional or even non-conventional weapons. While the latter can be prevented by physical means, the former is more elusive and can be launched even from offshore locations with the added benefit of anonymity.

This needs a whole new approach to laws relating to IT and its policing and implementation. Technologies to integrate many of these functions are within the capabilities of the country and must be evolved on priority. Reactive responses so typical of India's past security history will extract a heavy price in national security terms.

Energy security can no longer be only a set of political and economic hazards of which India should be the passive victim. Energy security should also mean a set of policies aimed at bringing the regional states together for their mutual benefit. The time has come for India to develop an integrated perspective on the issue.

Indian forces have won international acclaim for their peace-keeping roles. In an increasingly interdependent world the Indian military will be looked upon to lend a hand in such international roles. The Indian security establishment must plan and train to discharge such functions as a responsible member of the international global order.

THREE

Military Buildup in the Region

INTRODUCTION

When considering the region where military build-up should be of concern or at least of interest to India, the region we need to look at is the arc that stretches from the Gulf of Aden, through West Asia, South Asia, South East Asia and thence through China and Japan. Some of these regions such as West Asia and South East Asia have had historic ties with India and its security. It was this for example, which led the British to treat these areas as part of the outer ring of India's defence. It was this realization of the centrality of India to this region that led Pundit Nehru to state, while speaking to the Constituent Assembly in March 1949, "Look at the map. If you have to consider any question affecting the Middle East, India inevitably comes into the picture. If you have to consider any question concerning South East Asia, you cannot do without India". In addition to these there are some other countries whose military postures and build-up could impinge on India's security concerns, these are, South Africa and Australia. One extra regional power, which plays a major role and has a substantial military presence in the region, is of course the United States of America.

This survey does not intend to go into a detailed enumeration of the military forces of each country in the region, but to cover the general trends in military development in the region and their impact if any on Indian security. The nuclear dimensions of the build-up in the region will be discussed separately.

WEST ASIA

West Asia has been for some years now, particularly after the Gulf War, the world's largest arms market. This particularly applies to the grouping of the Gulf Cooperation Council (GCC) states. The GCC comprises the UAE, Kuwait, Oman, Qatar and Saudi Arabia. They all seem to have become a happy hunting ground for all the western arms manufacturing nations. The other country in the region quietly building up and modernizing its armed forces is Iran.

GULF COUNCIL STATES

The Iraqi invasion of Kuwait and the subsequent Gulf War fuelled insecurities in the Gulf states. Western armed industry, i.e. USA, UK and France have taken advantage of these insecurities to get these states to indulge in a splurge of arms acquisitions. Between 1992 and 1999 the GCC states spent $ 55.7 billion on arms purchases of which Saudi Arabia alone spent $ 28.9 billion. The combined defence budget of the GCC states for 1999-2000 came to approximately $ 28.41 billion of which Saudi Arabia's share was $ 18.4 billion. To put this expenditure in perspective, India's defence budget for the same period was approximately $ 10.5 billion. What this heavy defence expenditure has produced are armed forces who are qualitatively very well equipped, though with a heterogeneous collection of equipment. The total armed forces of the GCC come to approximately 2,50,000. The land forces, given the terrain and presumed threat, have concentrated on mechanized forces. The combined armies would field about 1800 Main Battle Tanks (MBT) with about 500 top of the line M1 Abrams and 150 Le Clerc. The rest are combinations of US M60s and French AMX-30s. The GCC countries have also taken pains to strengthen their air forces and can field some 650 combat aircraft, again a combination of US and French aircraft, including F16s and Mirage 2000s. As regards naval forces, the emphasis appears to have been on coastal defence and keeping the sea-lanes open. The major surface combatants are, 11 frigates, mainly with Saudi Arabia, 6 Corvettes and 30 missile craft. The build up continues, both Oman and the UAE are reported to have signed contracts for F16 aircraft from the USA. The UAE order is for 80 F16 block 60 aircraft the latest in the line.

There is also, of course, a substantial foreign presence in the area with detachments of US Forces both air and ground located in most of the states. British and French air assets are also deployed in Saudi Arabia to police the "no fly zones" over Iraq. The US presence and its effect on security in the region will be considered in detail later in the chapter.

The other interesting aspect of the military buildup in the GCC is the presence of CSS-2 missiles in Saudi Arabia. These Chinese missiles have a range of 2,800 km and were designed to carry a nuclear warhead. It has never been clear why Saudi Arabia obtained these missiles and how it intends to use them. Was this a buildup for the Islamic bomb?

The military build-up in the GCC states can affect Indian security in various ways. If it acts as a force for stability in the Gulf, preventing any Kuwait type misadventure by Iraq or Iran it would be to India's advantage. Given our great dependence on oil from these states to meet our energy requirements and the large Indian work force in these areas, stability is an essential requirement for India's progress. The question that really needs examination is what would be the reaction of these states to an Indo-Pak conflict. Presently, when there is no direct-armed conflict between India and Pakistan, the Gulf states maintain wary neutrality. While they will vote for an anti-India resolution at the OIC their actions do not go beyond that. Even during the Kargil conflict they remained neutral, adding to the voices asking both sides to show restraint. However we need to accept that in case of an all out war their sympathies are likely to be with Pakistan, mainly because of the pull of Islam. This applies especially to Saudi Arabia. The sympathy may change to active steps if it appears that Pakistan faces defeat. Actions could vary, from an oil embargo on India, to providing escorts to Pakistan shipping vessels passing through the Gulf, to providing safe havens to Pakistan naval forces in their ports. Saudi Arabia could also fly its AEW (Air Early Warning) aircraft to provide support to Pakistan and at an extreme level may even transfer some equipment, particularly aircraft, to Pakistan. There is unlikely to be any direct intervention by the armed forces of the Gulf countries.

The reaction would also depend on the extent that India is able to convince these states, particularly Saudi Arabia, that an Indo-Pak war is not a Hindu-Muslim war and that India does not want to either conquer Pakistan or break it up but has been forced to go to war under grave provocation. The duration of the war would also make a difference the shorter the war the lesser the chances of any intervention. The other major factor, which would impinge on the GCC's attitude, would be the US approach and the extent to which they are able to persuade them to remain neutral and stay out of an Indo-Pak conflict.

India can also help its cause by increasing military-to-military contacts with the GCC states. While there have been some joint naval exercises, we need to institutionalize these. We also need to offer vacancies in all our training institutes so as to expose the armed forces of these countries to India and our basically secular polity. The Indian foreign ministers visit to Saudi Arabia in January 2001 appears to have had very positive results; this needs to be followed up.

IRAN

The other country in West Asia whose military build up is of interest is that of Iran. Iran has faced a daunting task of rebuilding its armed forces after a long drawn out war with Iraq. During the reign of the Shah, Iran was firmly in the US camp and as such most of its military equipment was from there. This pipeline was completely cut off after the Shah's overthrow. Iran has shown considerable ingenuity in keeping much of this equipment operational; nevertheless the long drawn out Iran-Iraq war did lead to a degradation of equipment. During this period Iran turned to China and to an extent to the Soviet Union to replenish its arsenal.

The current defence budget of Iran is about $5.7 billion. It has approximately 5,50,000 men under arms; the bulk, about 3,50,000, being in the army. The army is organized into four Corps headquarters, four armoured divisions and six infantry divisions. The mechanised formations have a mix of equipment, the bulk being of Russian origin, T72s and BMPs. Its Air Force has some thirteen combat squadrons with SU24s and Mig-29s being the most modern in their inventory. Major combatants in the navy include five submarines, three of these being of the Kilo class. There are also three frigates and a number of missile craft. In addition to the regular armed forces there is also the Revolutionary Guard Corps of 1,00,000 motivated personnel organised into two armoured, five mechanised, ten infantry and one special force divisions.

What is of interest is not the present state of the Iranian armed force but their projected acquisition plan. In 1998 Iran had indicated to Russia its intention to buy weapons systems worth about $2 billion. The equipment on order included eight S-300 PMO1 air defence systems, 25 Mil-17 helicopters, eight Sukhoi SU-25 aircrafts and other miscellaneous military equipment. Iran also expressed the desire to upgrade its Kilo class submarines and to build maintenance centres for its Russian built aircraft. They also wanted to set up a crew training centre for its T-72 MBT's. However, none of these plans came to fruition due to US pressure on Russia not to supply arms to Iran.

Nevertheless, after the visit to Moscow by the Iranian President, Muhammed Khatami, the Russian President, Vladimir Putin, confirmed that Russia would supply arms to Iran despite the US threat of sanctions. Figures of orders between $4 billion to $7 billion are talked about. If this comes through it should aid Iran considerably in modernizing its forces.

Although at one stage Iran was considered to be close to Pakistan, the recent years have seen a cooling off between the two. This is basically because of the attacks on Shias in Pakistan and more so, due to Iran's belief that it is Pakistan, which had created, aided and abetted the rise of the Taliban in Afghanistan. For all its belief in fundamentals of Islam, Iran does not support the type of Islam which the Taliban tried to enforce in Afghanistan.

India's relations have in the meanwhile seen a steady progress. The Indian Prime Minister visited Iran in April 2001 and had wide ranging discussions with the Iranian government. The joint declaration after the meetings, among other things reaffirmed both countries opposition to terrorism. Iran has been very keen to supply gas to India, preferably by a pipeline passing through Pakistan. This is still under discussion. There was some talk that this could be discussed between India and Pakistan during the recent visit of General Musharraf to India. This does not seem to have happened. India has concerns that Pakistan may cut off supplies through this pipeline in case of Indo-Pak hostilities and has stated that Iran would need to guarantee that supplies would continue. It would be in the interest of Indo-Iranian relations if an agreement on this could be reached at an early date.

As far as Indo-Iranian military relations are concerned, there is ample scope for expanding these particularly in the repair and maintenance of Russian equipment in which India has considerable expertise. India could also offer training in handling such equipment. India should also propose joint naval exercises with Iran.

Iran poses no direct threat to India. The threat, if any, arises if there is a repetition of an Iran-Iraq war or if Iran gets into a military confrontation with any of the Gulf states, with some of whom it has territorial disputes. Iran-Saudi Arabian relations have tended to be cool but there have been recent efforts by both sides to mend these. Cooperation between Iran and Saudi Arabia would contribute greatly to stability in the Gulf region.

SOUTH ASIA

Compared to the other regions of Asia, South Asia as a region spends less on defence than the other regions even though South Asia encompasses two of Asia's bigger military powers — India and Pakistan. The smaller South Asian nations have very modest military establishments, Nepal and Bangladesh, having the lowest per capita expenditure on defence of all Asian nations. Sri Lanka, understandably, ranks a little higher given its ongoing internal strife. However, the only country in the region whose military build-up is of interest to India is that of Pakistan.

PAKISTAN

Ever since it was founded, Pakistan has suffered a sense of insecurity vis-à-vis India. This chapter is no place to discuss the reasons for this but it is this factor which has determined Pakistan's constant effort to match India militarily even at the cost of the strains this has produced on its polity and economy. Lacking natural resources and the industrial base that India has, Pakistan has always looked to external players to bolster its military might and help it to match India's. Pakistan initially, allied with the West during the Cold War, not because of any great ideological reasons but solely to obtain modern weapons from the US and accesses to its training establishments. This accretion of military strength and apparent weakness of India's military as demonstrated by their defeat in the Sino-Indian conflict of 1962, led Pakistan to indulge in the 1965 venture in Kashmir. This did not succeed and in fact had an adverse effect in that US military aid was discontinued. Pakistan promptly forgot its commitment to combat communism and turned to

China and the two, having a common enemy in India, developed close military and political relations. China then became the main source of arms for Pakistan.

The Soviet invasion of Afghanistan, however, gave Pakistan an opportunity to move back to the US camp. Pakistan was now declared a "front line state" and arms aid poured in. Much of these arms had no relation to any threat to Pakistan from Afghanistan or the Soviet presence in that country. Arms like SP artillery, attack helicopters armed with TOW anti-tank missiles, F16 aircraft, maritime reconnaissance aircraft had no relationship with any threat Pakistan faced at that time. Between 1981 and 1986 Pakistan received $3.2 billion in military and security related aid. A further six year package of $4.02 billion (half as military assistance) commenced in 1987 but was cut off in 1990 when the USA finally decided not to turn a blind eye to Pakistan's nuclear weapons programme. This did not, however, stop military sales to the country that, in 1994 was worth $1.03 billion. It was only after the nuclear tests in 1998 that a complete ban on arms transfers to Pakistan was imposed by USA.

However, contrary to the belief of many, the USA has not been the main supplier of armaments to Pakistan; this distinction lies with the Peoples Republic of China. Nearly 80% of Pakistan's MBT's and 60% of its combat aircraft come from China. That country has also been the main source of supply of nuclear weapons technology, designs and components for SSM's. Pakistan has acquired weapons from other sources too France (aircraft and submarines), the UK (frigates) and the Ukraine (tanks). Pakistan is believed to have received financial aid from the Gulf states, particularly Saudi Arabia, for some of its arms purchases. The sanctions imposed by the western powers after nuclear tests, the down turn in the economy and the World Bank and the IMF insistence on cutting back defence expenditure as a condition for financial bail out has however affected further acquisition and build-up. Pakistan has reduced its defence budget by Rs 2 billion in 2001. Any further build-up would therefore be dependent on the lifting of sanctions and funding.

A fledgling military industry makes Pakistan self-sufficient in small arms and their ammunition. It also manufactures anti-tank guided weapons and low altitude, shoulder fired SAM systems based on Chinese designs. Pakistan is also to manufacture the third of the Agosta class submarines it is acquiring from France and is reported to be looking to manufacture Chinese designed frigates and also designing and building its own MBT.

Pakistan maintains a fairly large military establishment of nearly 6,00,000 personnel on its active strength the Army alone accounts for 5,20,000 of these. The Army fields two armoured divisions, 19 infantry divisions and a number of independent brigades. The mechanised formations are well equipped for mobile offensive operations being supported by SP artillery, both medium (155 mm) and heavy (203 mm) as well as attack helicopters. The Pakistan Army has near parity with Indian forces that can be deployed against Pakistan, as even though the Indian Army is numerically stronger, 9,80,000 to Pakistan's 5,20,000, a proportion of the Indian Army will always have to be left on the eastern and northern borders facing China. To an extent this would also apply to the Indian Navy and Air force. The Pakistan Army is capable of launching limited offensives and using a well-developed network of obstacles, stalemating any Indian offensive for a period of time.

The Pakistan Navy fields 10 submarines of which seven are armed with USGW's — mainly the Harpoon system. Four of its eight frigates are also armed with Harpoons. Some of its MR aircraft are also capable of mounting Exotect anti-ship missiles. The Pakistan Navy is capable of interfering with India's SLOC's to the Gulf as well as launching surprise attacks on offshore and shore installations using submarine launched missiles.

The Air force has 319 combat aircraft organized into 17 squadrons. These are equipped with a mix of French aircraft (Mirage III's and V's), Chinese derivatives of the Mig 19 and 21 and some 25 F16's. Further F16's were on order but supply was frozen in 1990 when US military aid was suspended. The Pakistan Air force inventory seems to be a bit dated. It has been working with China to develop a modern fighter but with little progress reported till now.

The threat posed to India by the Pakistan military build-up is manageable as long as India maintains a quantitative and even more importantly a qualitative edge over Pakistan. Pakistan's economy is finding it difficult to sustain its current military establishment, leave alone to modernize and expand it. While not triggering an arms race, as long as India keeps to a steady and continuous path of modernization of its military assets it will eventually force Pakistan to realise the futility of trying to match India. After its experiences in 1965 and 1971 Pakistan is unlikely to launch a conventional offensive against India and will remain on the strategic defensive while using unconventional methods such as proxy war to keep the Indian Army occupied.

SOUTH EAST ASIA

South East Asia has been, for some time, the second largest importer of arms after West Asia. This is a reflection of the insecurities felt in the region due to both the rapid modernization of the Chinese armed forces and the gradual reduction of US military presence in the area. The booming economies of the early nineties made funds available for arms acquisitions, however, the financial crisis of 1997 meant that some of the plans, particularly of Indonesia, Thailand and Malaysia had to be put on hold. The revival of some of these economies will lead to a renewal of arms purchases.

Once more, the idea is not to carry out a detailed survey of every country or even cover all the countries in the region but to concentrate on those who can impinge on Indian security.

MYANMAR

Myanmar is of particular interest to India as we have common land and sea frontiers. Myanmar has for long been a sanctuary for militant groups operating in the north-eastern states, particularly the Nagas who have fellow tribesmen across the border. Sanctuary has not been a government policy, it is just that the terrain along the Indo-Myanmar border allows easy infiltration and exfiltration. Myanmar has itself faced various insurgencies throughout its recent history and that has meant that it has had to maintain a fairly large army. The army has also run the country for many years. The Myanmar armed forces total some 4,25,000, the bulk of these being in the army. The Army with strength of 3,25,000 is basically an infantry army with some 245 infantry battalions organised into a number of light divisions. Constant operational employment has meant that the Infantry is well trained and tough. Myanmar has a small navy, major combatants being 2 corvettes and 6 missile craft. The air force is reported to have 5 combat squadrons equipped mainly with Chinese aircraft.

The armed forces of Myanmar by themselves pose no threat to India; it is the close links, which they have developed with the Chinese armed forces that need watching. This is particularly true of Chinese activity in the areas bordering the Bay of Bengal. The Chinese have built a signal monitoring station in the Coco Islands and are also reported to have improved some of the naval bases in the mainland. They are also reported to have opened up the old Burma-China road as well as developing the Irrawady River for traffic. The Chinese Navy could use Myanmar as a base for operations in the Bay of Bengal and the Malacca Straits. China could also threaten India by land through Myanmar particularly if Myanmar does not actively oppose it.

However, Myanmar having now joined ASEAN, it is likely to be a little more circumspect in dealing with China. India too has taken the pragmatic road and though it may continue to deplore the lack of democracy in Myanmar it has decided to deal with its military regime as far as security matters are concerned. These military-to-military contacts need to be pursued vigorously and we must revive the earlier system of training Myanmarese personnel in our training institutions. We may also consider joint Naval exercises as a means of improving military-to-military ties and for confidence building.

INDONESIA

Indonesia is the largest and most populous country in South-East Asia; it is also the world's largest Muslim nation. However, Islam in Indonesia, at least up to now, is uniquely tempered and influenced by the country's past Hindu and Buddhist culture and traditions of which all Indonesians are very proud. It is also one of India's nearest neighbours, only 25 miles separating India's southern most point — Indira Point on Great Nicobar Island from the nearest Indonesian island. Indonesia is important, not just for its size and resources but also for its strategic location, lying athwart the sea-lanes leading from the Indian Ocean to the Pacific Ocean.

Indonesia has always paid attention to military strength right from its founding and even more so when the army under Suharto took over and continued to rule for years. It was however, hard hit by the 1997 financial crisis and has not yet really recovered from it. Political uncertainty and unrest in various parts of the country have further put back planned military modernisation, particularly of the navy. Given that Indonesia is a country of some 17,000 islands, the navy plays a very prominent role in its security considerations.

Indonesia's defence budget for 1999 was $ 1.498 billion and with this it maintained an armed force of 2,98,000 personnel. The bulk of these are in the Army, which has strength of 2,30,000. The army is largely infantry oriented with a small armoured component equipped with light tanks.

The navy has a strength of 47,000 and amongst its major assets are 2 submarines, 17 frigates and some 28 LSTs. However, one report suggests that only 20 to 25 % of its inventory is operational. The Wahid government had planned to increase the strength of the navy to 67,000 over the next 5 years. The plans called for purchase of maritime helicopters, modern corvettes and expansion of the marines. It is to be seen as to what the new government does with this plan.

The Air force fields 91 combat aircraft organized into 6 squadrons. One of these squadrons is equipped with 10 F16s, more were to be procured but financial and other reasons intervened. The serviceability of the aircraft is suspect.

Indonesian armed forces appear to require considerable modernization and reorganization. They have, however, been in more or less constant use dealing with internal strife and can be considered fairly well trained. Properly equipped and organized they can play a major role in policing and keeping the sea-lanes open. On the other hand if political instability continues or increases then it could affect the safety of the sea routes, which already suffer from piracy. India needs to work with ASEAN to see how it can help Indonesia to cope with its problems. It can also offer help train Indonesian forces particularly the navy and air force.

SINGAPORE

The city-state of Singapore is surprisingly the largest spender on defence in South-East Asia. Its 1999 defence budget was $ 4.2 billion, two and a half times more than that of Malaysia and three times more than that of Indonesia. Its armed forces total 73,000 of which 50,000 are in the Army, which is fairly mechanized, both with tanks and LCV's and very modern artillery systems. It is actually the Singapore Navy and Air force, which are of interest. The navy has 3 submarines with a fourth under delivery, all acquired from Sweden since 1995. It also has a number of patrol and coastal craft, many manufactured locally. Singapore seems to have concentrated on the sea denial role for its navy. The air force has 8 Fighter Ground Attack squadrons, 3 of these being equipped with F16s.

The reasons for Singapore's build-up appear to be a sense of insecurity sandwiched as it is between two large neighbours, Malaysia and Indonesia. It has also the finances to be able to afford the most modern equipment. Whatever the reasons for Singapore's military build-up it could play a significant role in any South-East Asian military alliance to resist outside interference in the area.

MALAYSIA

Malaysia, in common with other ASEAN nations, has also been gradually building up and modernising its armed forces. This process however suffered a setback after the 1997 financial crisis and is yet to regain momentum. Malaysia's 1999 defence budget was equivalent to $1.62 billion. It maintains an armed force of 1,05,000, the bulk of these, 80,000 are in the army. The army has both armoured and infantry units with the emphasis as far as mechanized forces are concerned being on light tanks and APC's. Major naval units are 4 frigates and about 40 patrol and coastal craft. It has been shopping around for submarines and has expressed interest in acquiring two of these for a start. Its air force has mainly American aircraft but in 1997 Malaysia purchased 17 Mig 29 aircraft, the first South East Asian nation outside the Indo-Chinese states to buy Russian equipment. Malaysia's modest arms build-up poses no threat to India and to the extent it bolsters South East Asian ability to withstand Chinese pressure, it is an advantage.

THAILAND

In common with other South East Asian nations Thailand has also been strengthening and modernizing its armed forces. However, again like other countries in the region, the 1997 financial crisis has hit planned acquisition and expansion. The Thai armed forces are, after Vietnam, the largest in the area totalling about 3,00,000. The defence budget in 1999 equalled $ 2 billion. The Army, as in all the countries in the region is the largest component, fielding 19,00,000 men and about 1500 armoured vehicles, mainly light tanks and AFV's.

It is the Thai Navy, which is a mater of interest. Much larger than the other navies of the area it is the only one to have an aircraft carrier in its order of battle. It also has 14 frigates and some 88 patrol and coastal aircraft. The naval air arm consists of 8 Harriers carried on the aircraft carrier and three P3 Orion maritime reconnaissance aircraft.

Thailand has also modernized its air force and two of its five fighter squadrons are now equipped with F16s. Thailand with its navy and air force working in coordination with other forces in the area can play an important role in controlling the sea-lanes in the region.

VIETNAM

The largest armed forces in the area and probably the most experienced are those of Vietnam. It has 4,84,000 personnel under arms. The army has a strength of 4,12,000 and fields nearly 12,000 MBTs, mainly T55 and T62's and about 600 light tanks.

The Vietnamese navy has a strength of 42,000 and major combatants include 2 submarines and 6 frigates. The air force has approximately 190 combat aircraft, a mixture of SU22, SU27 and Mig-21 bis. Vietnam also has fairly extensive air defence set up with about 66 SAM sites equipped with a variety of old Soviet systems.

Its importance to the region lies not just in the size of its armed forces but their comparatively better knowledge of the Chinese forces, having initially been trained by them and then having fought them. Integrated in to an ASEAN defence system, they could be invaluable in a warlike situation.

PHILIPPINES

The eastern most of the ASEAN nations, Philippines, was for a long time a major base for the US forces in the area and its armed forces had close links with them. The US forces were, however, withdrawn from the Philippines in 1992 and the links since then have weakened.

Philippines have faced a long running insurgency firstly by the Communists and now by Muslim militant groups. Its armed forces have, therefore, been kept fairly active since its independence. Its defence budget for 1999 was $ 1.4 billion. Its armed forces total 1,10,000 with an Army of 73000, Navy of 20,500 and Air force of

16,500. The navy is basically a coastal navy, the only major warship being 1 frigate. The air force fields 6 fighter squadrons. The Philippine military build-up has been modest in comparison to the other countries in the region. Given continuing political and financial uncertainty, the future build-up is also likely to remain modest. Recently the US has sent troops and equipments to help Philipine armed forces to deal with Muslim militant groups.

INDIA AND SOUTH EAST ASIA

South East Asian military build-up in no way threatens India, and to the extent it hinders Chinese expansion westward into the Bay of Bengal and the Indian Ocean, it is to our advantage. What is important is that we be prepared to play a quiet, but proactive military role in the region. With ASEAN not being a formal military grouping, military-to-military contact will need to be developed on a bilateral basis.

India already has a defence pact with Vietnam, which includes joint training and cooperation in the design and manufacture of conventional armaments. But there are opportunities with other countries also. Writing in the Asian Defence Yearbook 2000-2001, Prasun Bannerji states, "But what will cement the bond is the effort by the Indian Armed forces to assist in training and servicing indigenous militaries. There are a number of such programmes afoot. Thailand is looking to the Indian Navy to help integrate its lone light aircraft carrier purchased from Spain into its order of battle. The Republic of Singapore Air force is keen to utilise the vast Indian airspace to train its combat aircraft pilots just as the Royal Malaysian Air force hopes that the Indian Air force will help in maintaining its Mig 29s."

While they will not openly say so, Chinese military build-up and its aggressive claims over islands in the South China Sea, worries the nations of South East Asia. They are no longer sure of the American commitment to the area and given their memories of World War II, may not welcome a Japanese military presence in the region. Suspicions of Indian Navy build-up have been assuaged and it is time now for

India to build enduring military ties with the region starting with n,aval cooperation in dealing with piracy in the area.

India will need, however, to keep a wary eye on nascent fundamentalist Muslim movements in Indonesia and Malaysia. Both Muslim nations have till now had a very tolerant version of Islam, tempered in both cases by their earlier Hindu and Buddhist cultural heritage. Any change to an aggressive Islamic identity could prove unsettling to the whole region and would add to our security concerns.

EAST ASIA

In addition to China we will consider only two of the East Asian nations, Taiwan and Japan. Neither of them has a direct bearing on India's security, but both of them impinge on Chinese security perceptions and to that extent can influence the way China uses its military might in areas of particular interest to India such as South East Asia, South Asia and the Indian Ocean.

TAIWAN

Taiwan is a state, which is not a state, in that very few countries in the world now give it formal diplomatic recognition. Even the USA, its most staunch backer officially recognises it as part of China. Taiwan along with Japan was the first bastion formed by the USA to check the eastward expansion of communism and ever since the remnants of the Koumintang retreated to the island after the Communists took over Mainland China, the USA has guaranteed Taiwan against an armed invasion by China. It has continued to arm it in spite of vociferous Chinese objections. Taiwan, therefore, fields a fairly formidable and well-equipped armed force. With a defence budget of $10.9 billion (roughly the same as India) Taiwan has an armed force of 3,76,000, of which 2,40,000 are in the army. The army is basically designed to defend and is therefore Infantry heavy, but has mechanised forces including armour to be able to launch counter attacks against any beachheads an enemy might seize. The basic threat to Taiwan being by a sea-air invasion, both the navy and air force have equal importance. The navy's major combatants are 4 submarines, 16 destroyers, 21 frigates and a number of patrol and coastal craft. The USA has recently offered 4 Kidd class guided missile destroyers in lieu of the more advanced Arliegh–Burke class that Taiwan desired. The USA has also offered to supply 8 modern diesel submarines. Basically the Taiwanese Navy aim to deter amphibious assault by China as well as to prevent blockage of the island. The air force has 22 squadrons of which 7 are equipped with F16s and 3 with Mirage 2000s. The air force is capable of providing air defence to the island. While the Taiwanese forces may not be able to prevent a determined Chinese assault in getting ashore, they could cause heavy casualties and delay such an attack thus giving time to US forces to intervene. President Bush has pledged that the USA would come to the aid of Taiwan if the island is attacked by China.

Regaining Taiwan is one of China's main concerns at present. While it does not appear as likely to use armed forces to re-conquer what it considers a break away province, it does periodically indulge in sabre rattling including military exercises and missile firings. To substantiate its threat China maintains fairly large forces opposite Taiwan, and therefore, Taiwan reduces the amount of Chinese forces available for use elsewhere.

JAPAN

The severe losses of men and material in World War II and the horrors of Hiroshima and Nagasaki led to a strong pacifist lobby in Japan. This was reinforced by the new US drafted constitution that outlawed war as an instrument of policy for Japan and banned the raising of any armed forces. However the advent of the Cold War, the communist take over of China and the Korean War soon led to a revision. Japan was allowed to raise armed forces for 'self defence' and the Japanese armed forces are even now termed as the Japanese Self Defence

Forces (JSDF). What ever they may be called, Japan has one of Asia's most modern armed forces. While Japan spends just about 1% of its GDP on defence, given the size of the GDP this translated in 1999 to a defence budget of $41.1 billion, i.e. 4 times that of India.

Given the island nature of the country and its dependence on SLOC's for both its trade and supply of oil, Japan has concentrated on its Navy while not neglecting its ground and air forces. The total strength of the Self Defence Forces is 2,36,000. The Ground Self Defence Force totals 1,45,000. The major formations are 1 armoured division and 11 infantry divisions. These forces are designed basically for defence and have very limited offensive capabilities.

The Maritime Self Defence Force has some 43,800 personnel. The major combatants in the force are 16 submarines, 9 destroyers and 46 frigates. Given its long naval tradition and ship building skills, Japan builds all its war ships and its naval forces are organised both for sea denial and limited protection of its SLOC. Japan has accepted that it will operate to a limit of 1000 miles from its shore, which is in fact quite a reach. What it lacks in reaching out further are aircraft carriers and foreign bases.

The Air Self Defence Force has 12 fighter squadrons as well as AWAC and EW aircraft. It has, however, no long range fighters and no mid-air refuelling capabilities and is basically organised for air defence. The air defence is further strengthened with a strong ground air defence system, which among other items includes 120 Patriot air defence units.

There is also a very strong US armed presence in Japan. Some 40,000 US armed personnel serve in Japan, the largest being a contingent of 19,000 marines. The US 7th Fleet is also headquartered in Japan.

Japan faces a dilemma. Its nearest neighbour, China, is rapidly modernising its armed forces and has made it quite clear that it intends to be a superpower in its own right and to eventually challenge American supremacy in the area. Relations between China and Japan have historically been one of confrontation. Japan has had and still enjoys American protection including a nuclear umbrella. However, within the country there is growing unease on this dependency on the US and a feeling that Japan must have independent capabilities. Yet Japan also knows that major military build-up, particularly any ability to intervene overseas will raise hackles both in China and South East Asia and may be even in the US. It appears to be in Japan's best interest to link up with South East Asia and India to keep a check on aggressive Chinese aggression either into the South China Seas or into the Indian Ocean.

CHINA

Of all the countries in Asia, China is the most keenly watched, not just by its neighbours but also by the world at large and more particularly the USA. This is not just because of its growing economic strength but more so because of its single minded pursuit of military modernization. Military modernization was one of the four modernizations propounded by Deng Shao Peng in the 1970's and since then has remained as one of the focal points of all Chinese 5 Year Plans. The Gulf War in 1991 brought home to China the vast technological gap that existed between its armed forces and the western armies. Since then it has made concerted efforts to introduce high technology weapons systems as well as modernise its C31.

There have been various pronouncements by Chinese sources on the aim of China's military modernisation. These vary from "the ability to win local wars under high-tech conditions" to "the goal of defence modernisation is to develop a nuclear weapons capability and space technology not inferior to any super power and to have conventional military that matches that of any global power". Explaning an increase of 17.7% in the defence budget for 2000-2001, the finance minister Xiang Huaiching stated that the increase was required "to meet the need to raise salaries and the need to adopt to critical changes in the military situation in the world and prepare for defence and combat given the conditions of modern technology specially high technology".

Estimates of China's military expenditure vary considerably. China's official defence budget in 2000 was $14.5 billion and this went up to $17.05 billion in 2001. However most observers believe that the official figures are an understatement and that the actual figures could be about three times higher or about $50 billion or so. With this expenditure China maintains an armed force of 24,80,000 personnel with a fairly balanced mix between the army, which is the largest component, and the navy and air force.

China's modernization and military build-up has concentrated on the navy and air force. It has a large submarine force of some 71 submarines of varying vintage as also one nuclear submarine. It is trying to modernize its conventional submarines and design and build better nuclear submarines. A fleet of 53 surface combatants also form part of the navy of which the most modern are 4 destroyers on order from Russia. China is slowly expanding into a blue water Navy, however, the lack of aircraft carriers could limit its range of operations.

The Chinese Air force is receiving new SU27 aircraft from Russia and has an agreement for licensed production of these. It has also placed an order for 40 SU30 aircraft. Reports suggest that during the period 1992 to 1999, China placed orders for arms worth $10.9 billion on Russia and has already received equipment worth $ 5.9 billion. As regards the 18,30,000 strong army, the emphasis has been on reorganization and training it to fight a combined arms war under modern conditions. The army has been reorganised into 21 Integrated Group Armies (equivalent to our Corps). Of these 2 are deployed in the Chengu military region, which covers the area of Tibet. In addition to its purchases from Russia, China has a well-developed military - industrial complex and manufactures its own war ships, combat aircraft, MBTs, artillery pieces and missiles of various types. Most of these are copies of earlier Soviet equipment, updated to an extent by indigenously designed systems. China has made good use of its military production to gain influence over other countries particularly in South Asia and Africa by supplying military hardware at prices, which are cheaper than those from other sources.

With the collapse of the Soviet Union and the settlement of the border dispute with Russia, China faces no armed threat to its home territories. Chinese military thinking sees no global threat but only local ones along its borders, particularly those with India and Vietnam and the sea borders in the South China Seas. Chinese military modernization is therefore not for self defence but power projection, initially in its own neighbourhood and then further a field. It sees itself as the only country capable and willing to challenge the USA's sole superpower status. It realises that it cannot do this immediately and that it must first dominate Asia if it is to eventually challenge the USA's worldwide power. Within Asia it sees only two challenges, Japan economically and India as a potential economic and military rival with the population and natural resources to compete with it if India can put its act together. China has systematically tried to hedge India in and to keep it occupied in South Asia. It has done this by encouraging Pakistan to be a rival and has been its major arms supplier including aiding its nuclear and missile programmes. It is also Myanmar's main military supplier and has also supplied military hardware to India's other neighbours Nepal, Bangladesh and Sri Lanka.

To India, the Chinese military build-up poses two threats. One is direct to our northern borders using the unsettled Sino-Indian border dispute as a pretext. China has considerably improved its military infrastructure in Tibet, by constructing some 13 air bases and laying the Gormo-Lasha oil pipeline that eases its problem of supplying fuel to its forces in Tibet. The problem of supply will further ease with the construction of a rail link to Lasha on which work is reported to be in progress. China's growing influence in Myanmar opens another possible thrust line to the North-East states. One of the constraints China faced in operating from Tibet was that aircraft taking off from high altitude airfields in Tibet were restricted in the amount of payload that they could carry. With tanker aircraft now available to China this would no longer be a constraint as aircraft could take off from airfields in the mainland with full loads and still reach targets in India. The greatest advantage India has, however, is that the terrain favours the defender and with the army having learnt their lessons after 1962, any Chinese offensive is unlikely to make much progress. This, of course, is dependent on our not letting our guard down in a euphoria of another "Hindi-Chini Bhai Bhai" syndrome. We will also need to improve our early warning assets along the Sino-Indian border so that we are not caught by surprise.

The second, more insidious and longer-term threat lies in China's effort to become the sole Asian power. Much of this will depend on China's ability to modernize and field a true blue water navy with power projection capability. It does not have such a capability as yet. One of the essentials for such power projection would be the acquisition of bases to support such an effort. These could be in South East Asia, Myanmar or even Sri Lanka. It is this that we must keep an eye on and pre-empt basically by diplomatic effort. We will also need to work with all the nations in the region, Japan, ASEAN, Australia and the USA to contain China. Efforts must start now and not wait till China actually poses a threat.

The Chinese military build-up is one manifestation of its overall aim of attaining superpower status. At some stage this will lead to a clash with India unless we are prepared to accept Chinese hegemony. The clash may not necessarily be military, especially if we have built-up sufficient deterrence capability either individually or in alliance with other like-minded countries opposed to such Chinese hegemony. Such deterrence would force the competition to be non-armed and to be one of economics and political ideologies.

EXTRA REGIONAL POWERS

In addition to the Asian nations whose military build-up can impact on India's security, there are other countries outside Asia who also have a military presence in the region and its periphery and can have an influence on the security of the region. These are South Africa, Australia and the global powers with a presence in the region, the UK, France and above all the USA.

REPUBLIC OF SOUTH AFRICA

South Africa is strategically located athwart the SLOC's linking the Atlantic and Indian Ocean. It is the largest and most prosperous nation in Southern Africa. As it consolidates its internal political situation it will have a desire to play a greater role in the region and the Indian Ocean.

Presently it has modest armed forces equipped and trained for internal security duties. The current strength is about 63,000 personnel of which nearly 43,000 are in the Army. The navy with a strength of approximately 5,000 personnel has two submarines and six patrol craft. The air force has two squadrons of FGA's. The arms embargo during the apartheid years prevented RSA from buying military hardware from the international market and it was forced to design and manufacture its own military stores. This has given it a reasonable military industrial base, particularly in the manufacture of light armoured vehicles and artillery. RSA has however realised that it needs to modernize its armed forces particularly its navy and air force. Plans in the pipeline call for the purchase of three modern diesel submarines and four corvettes for the Navy; 28 JAS Grippin aircraft from Sweden and 24 Hawks from the UK. It is also to purchase A119 helicopters from Italy. These purchases show a definite intent to play a role in the Indian Ocean and its vicinity. India will need to work with RSA as far as protection of the SLOC's passing through the Indian Ocean.

AUSTRALIA

Australia has recently carried out a review of its defence needs in a white paper entitled "Defence 2000: Our Future Defence Forces". This paper advocates that the main focus of Australian military should be towards contributing to stability in the Asia-Pacific region. Its top priority will be its neighbours, an arc of islands stretching from Indonesia, Papua New Guinea, the South West Pacific and New Zealand, where it will build capability to protect its interest and foster stability. Its second priority is South East Asia and the third is East and North Asia. While the white paper does not call the major increase in military personnel, it calls for considerable modernization and replacement of current equipment. Defence spending is to increase by a total of US $ 12.7 billion over the next 10 years.

The armed forces of Australia total 55,000 personnel on active duty and reserves of about 28,000. The Army has strength of about 25,000 and can field the equivalent of two brigade groups. Plans call for the Army to be so structured that it can sustain a brigade on operations for extended periods and at the same time maintain a battalion group available for deployment elsewhere.

The navy will be a major component of Australia's ability to project forces into the areas of its top priority. Its submarine fleet will reach the planned figure of six by 2001-2002. It is continuing with the production of the Anzac class of frigates of which two are in service and six more to be built. It has the ability to lift and support a brigade group. Major assets of the air force are two squadrons of F 111's and three of F/A 18's. It also has two MR squadrons with 19 PC3 aircraft giving Australia a very good capability to keep a watch on the seas around it.

Australia sees no threat to its territory and sees its role as an agent of stability in its neighbourhood, particularly South East Asia. Its military build-up is with that aim. To the extent that stability in South East Asia is of common interest to both India and Australia, this military build-up poses no threat to India. The doubts once expressed by Australia on India's naval expansion and its strong condemnation on India's nuclear tests seems to have dissipated. It should now be possible for both countries to work out joint strategies to ensure stability in South East Asia, particularly Indonesia.

THE UNITED KINGDOM

The United Kingdom maintains a very modest presence in the Gulf region consisting of a small naval flotilla, the Armilla Patrol of two destroyers/frigates and a support ship. It also deploys a squadron of 12 Tornado aircraft based in Kuwait as part of the UN mandated Southern Watch to reinforce the no fly zone over southern Iraq. The UK presence in the Gulf region is purely in support of the US deployment in the area and it does not have any independent role or policy. The UK presence in the region has increased as part of the war against the Taliban in Afghanistan. It now has a carrier group deployed in the Arabian sea and provides the minimum compliment of the international security force deployed into Afghanistan.

FRANCE

France surprisingly has a larger presence than that of UK in the region. Its main component is a brigade-sized force of two marine infantry regiments and a support battalion based on the island of Reunion. Based also at Reunion is the Indian Ocean squadron of 1 or 2 frigates, patrol craft and two LSM's. This French presence is basically to look after its interests in ex French colonies in Africa. It also contributes a flight of five Mirage 2000 fighters based in Saudi Arabia to the Southern Watch.

THE USA

The USA has a major presence in Asia, particularly West and East Asia. West Asia falls under the US Central Command, headquartered in the USA but with the primary responsibility for West Asia and parts of East Africa. Since the Gulf War the USA has maintained a fairly strong presence in the West Asian region. The backbone of this presence is the US 5th Fleet based in Bahrain. The 5th Fleet consists of a carrier battle group, an underway replenishment group and two mine counter measure groups. The Fleet is a formidable force capable of launching both nuclear and conventional attacks using aircraft and ship borne cruise missiles. In addition to the 5th Fleet the US has some 3,500-ground troops based mainly in Kuwait and Saudi Arabia. There are also some 7,000 air force personnel with a varying number of combat and EW aircraft deployed in the area, again the major bases being in Kuwait and Saudi Arabia. The US has also pre-positioned equipment for an armoured brigade each in Kuwait and Qatar. In addition to these forces the US has, based at Diego Garcia, five ships carrying equipment for a marine expeditionary brigade. Thus, the US could in short order build-up to division strength of troops by just flying in the men and using the pre-positioned equipment. With the Cold War having ended the US can also quickly move forces from those located in the NATO area into West Asia, particularly the 6th Fleet operating in the Mediterranean.

The September 11 attacks on the World Trade Towers and the Pentagon and the consequent decision to launch operations to destroy the Taliban and Al-Qaeda in Afghanistan has led to an increase in the US forces in the region. It has now forces deployed in Afghanistan, Pakistan as well as some of the Central Asian Republics. Much will depend now on how long these forces stay in the area and the role they perform. Presently their presence helps to stabilize Afghanistan as well as caution Pakistan. This is all for the good. However, we need to recognize that as long as US forces are based in Pakistan any outbreak of Indo-Pak hostilities which may jeopardise US forces is likely to draw strong US response particularly against the side seen as the initiator of hostilities.

In East Asia, in addition to the forces deployed in South Korea, the major US presence is in Japan where it has some 40,000-armed personnel. The bulk of these are a marine expeditionary force located in Okinawa, with 13,000 airmen manning the US 5th Air Force as well as the US Navy's 7th Fleet in this area. The forces in Japan come under US's Pacific Command whose area of responsibility covers all of Asia, less West Asia and includes the Indian subcontinent less Pakistan which is grouped with West Asia under Central Command.

India has often been critical of the US military presence in Asia, particularly that in the Gulf region. Part of the criticism stems from the US use of the 7th Fleet to try and intimidate India in 1971 and the perceived US tilt towards Pakistan till the 1980's. The end of the Cold War, the increasing US economic interest in India and the down grading of the relationship with Pakistan has led to a reassessment by both countries of each others legitimate interests and role in the region. India now recognises that the USA has an interest in stability in Asia in general and West Asia in particular. It also has legitimate interests in the safety and freedom of the SLOCs through the Arabian Sea, Indian Ocean, Malacca Straits on to the Pacific. There seems to be a greater understanding in US circles of India's genuine security concerns vis-à-vis Pakistan and China and the collaboration between the two. Both countries are wary of China's efforts to increase its military capability and the uses to which the capability may be put to. This convergence of interests means that instead of viewing the US military build-up as a threat India can now look at it as something with which it can work to further its own interests in stability in West and South East Asia as well as in containing China. While there is no need for a formal military alliance between India and the USA, a system of consultation and coordination of common security considerations can be worked out.

NUCLEAR ARMS BUILD-UP

In addition to the conventional arms build-up in the area of our interest, there has also been a build-up of nuclear weapons in the region. China has been a nuclear weapons state since the 1960's, India achieved the capacity by the mid 70's and Pakistan probably by the mid 80's. Both India and Pakistan, however, became overt nuclear weapon states in 1998 after a series of tests by both countries. Iran and Iraq are two other countries believed to have nuclear ambitions but there is no hard evidence to show that they are actively pursuing such a programme. South Africa had achieved nuclear weapon capability but has voluntarily abjured it. Japan has the scientific and technical capability to develop nuclear weapons if it ever wishes to; presently being under the US nuclear umbrella satisfies it. There is also, of course, the US nuclear presence in the region. Discussion, however, is confined to the Chinese and Pakistani nuclear build-up and its effects on India's security.

China is estimated to have about 400 warheads ranging from 5Mt to low Kt warheads. It is also believed to have achieved the ability to deploy MIRV payloads, having clandestinely obtained the technology from the USA. It has tried to achieve the full triad of delivery systems, air, land and sea but basically depends on its missile forces. It has a wide range of missiles from the 158 Km range CSS-8 weapons systems to the CSS-4 with a range of 13,000 Km. Barring the short-range missiles, China is estimated to have 128 missiles in the IRBM/ICBM range. Of these the 40 CSS-2, introduced in 1971 are being slowly retired. The mainstay of the missile forces are the 20 CSS-4 ICBM's and the 48 CSS-5, IRBMs with a range of 1,800 Km. The only nuclear capable aircraft in the Chinese Air Force are the aging H-6 bombers (a copy of the Russian TU-16) with a range of 3,800 Km. China has tried to develop a submarine launched nuclear capability, has one nuclear submarine, and has built 12 SLBM's (the Julang, with a range of 1,700 Km). However, reports indicate that neither the submarine nor the missile have been a success. It is believed that China is constructing a nuclear subniarine and also a new SLBM based on the DF-31 missile, which itself is under development. The low Kt warheads, of which China has approximately 120, could be delivered by the shorter-range missile systems such as the M-9 (600Km) and the M-11 (300 Km), which could be used as tactical delivery systems. Incidentally, China has supplied the technology for both the M-9 and M-11 to Pakistan.

China's nuclear build-up is part of its overall drive to be reckoned as a superpower. The initial impetus was the break with the USSR in the 1960's and a requirement to have an independent nuclear deterrent against both the Soviet Union and the USA. China believes that even with just 20 ICBM's capable of reaching mainland USA it has achieved deterrence against the USA and would thus be able to withstand any US pressure.

It is difficult to visualise the situation where China would use its nuclear weapons against its Asian neighbours except as an instrument of threat and blackmail. This, however, would sit ill with its declared policy of "no first use". The only possibility of China actually using its nuclear weapons would be if it finds its conventional forces facing a humiliating defeat in any future conflict, an unlikely scenario. For India the basic requirement is to develop a sufficient nuclear force to convince China that any nuclear attack on India or its forces would lead to retaliation and unacceptable damage to vital Chinese targets. The essential for this is to have the delivery means to strike targets in the Chinese mainland.

While China's nuclear build-up has a wider aim, Pakistan's has been from the beginning purely Indo-centric. The defeat in 1971 shattered the myth that India could be defeated by a smaller Pakistan and it realised that in a purely conventional conflict India would always eventually turn out the victor. Pakistan's development and deployment of nuclear weapons, aided and abetted by China, is therefore basically to counter what it perceives as an Indian conventional superiority. It is for this reason that Pakistan cannot give a "no first use" pledge, as if it does so then the nuclear arsenal cannot be used to deter a conventional attack. This is in contrast to the Indian policy the Indian nuclear deterrent is only to deter a nuclear attack against India, and conventional aggression will be met conventionally.

Details of Pakistan's actual warheads and delivery systems are difficult to come by. It is estimated that Pakistan has some 15-20 nuclear warheads as on date. The basic delivery systems are the Ghauri I (range 1,300-1,500 Km) and the Ghauri II (2,000-2,300 Km) missiles, both based on the North Korean Nodong missile system. Pakistan also has the Chinese M-9 and M-11 missiles but it is not clear whether these are nuclear capable. The F16 aircraft is also a nuclear capable system and Pakistan would have modified these to carry a nuclear payload.

For India, the Pakistan nuclear build-up poses two challenges. The first is to be able to use its conventional superiority to deter Pak aggression, including proxy war, without escalating such an operation to a nuclear exchange. The second challenge would arise if a radical Muslim group was to come to power in Pakistan, for such a group may act irrationally and may compel India to look at a pre-emptive strike to remove the nuclear threat either on its own or in concert with other powers.

SUMMARY

Reviewing the overall picture of military build-up in the region of interest to India, what is noticeable is the increase in military spending over most of Asia, particularly West Asia and South East Asia. This increased military spending is not, except in the case of China, with any aggressive intent. In most cases the increased military spending is a consequence of a feeling of insecurity and is therefore defensive in nature. The insecurities arise both from intra-regional rivalries as well as internal dissent and unrest. As a result the military buildup in these regions does not pose a direct threat to India and in fact to the extent that India can work with these countries to promote stability in the region, is to India's advantage. India needs to improve military-to-military contacts with all the countries in the region so as to be able to dispel any fear they may have of India's military build-up. We need, however, to be wary of the possible rise of Muslim fundamentalism in West and South-East Asia as this combined with a military build-up in the regions could pose a threat at some time. Pakistan's military build-up has peaked and unless its economy improves dramatically or the international situation changes radically, it can only decline. It is a threat that India can manage and must not be over played.

The only real external threat to India comes from China's military modernization and build-up. China brooks no rivals and India is a potential rival. The Chinese have been conscious of this, ever since the 1960's, hence their close alliance with Pakistan and their efforts to gain influence with India's smaller neighbours. The unsettled boundary question provides China with a readymade excuse for military intervention at a time of its choosing. There has often been criticism, in certain circles in India, when China has been described as the number one threat to India, but this is a fact and must not be glossed over. In fact, one could say, that China is the only military threat to India. While India cannot and must not attempt to match China quantitively, it must always strive to attain qualitative parity if not superiority over the Chinese military. It must also be able to achieve parity, land, air and sea in any area where China attempts to physically threaten India. Such a demonstrated capability is the best deterrent.

As far as the nuclear build-up is concerned, till China, India and Pakistan can achieve a mutual nuclear restraint regime, India must continue to develop and deploy a credible minimum nuclear deterrent. Numbers of warheads are not the most important element of such a deterrent, what is important is the ability of all elements of a nuclear force, the warheads, the delivery means and the command and control systems to survive the enemy's first strike and be able to launch a retaliatory strike capable of causing unacceptable damage to the attacker. To be an effective deterrent, this capability of being able to survive and launch a retaliatory strike must be open enough to be able to convince the adversary of its credibility. India needs to build towards such a capability at an early date, concentrating initially on its missile capability till such a time that it develops a full triad of delivery systems.

FOUR

Conflicting Scenarios — An Indian Perspective

INTRODUCTION

Earlier in this study there was a previous chapter on "Technology and Security" covering the possible impact of technology on security and conflicts. The aim here is not to discuss theoretical aspects of the future of warfare but to examine the types of armed conflicts that India may find itself involved in the next decade or so. Even so, theoretically, given the military situation in the region particularly the Sino-India-Pak military equation, one could say that a future conflict could run the whole gamut from all out nuclear war, to a limited nuclear war, to an all out conventional war, to a limited conventional war, to externally aided low intensity conflict (LIC) to a purely internal conflict. There is a need, therefore, to briefly examine these before taking a more detailed look at the likely scenarios.

NUCLEAR WARS

Ever since nuclear weapons came into being much has been written about the use of nuclear weapons and about nuclear war fighting, all of it in the theoretical field, because there has never been a nuclear war, total or limited. The reason for this is, that even before President Reagan postulated that, "A nuclear war cannot be won and therefore must never be fought" the basic truth of this had been recognized by both the US and USSR in spite of whatever rhetoric they may have exchanged. This applied equally to the various theories of limited war and graduated response. Both sides realized that once a battlefield nuclear exchange started, command and control of these weapons would be lost and inevitably one or the other could be forced to escalate to a full blown nuclear war. While President George Bush may now condemn the theory of mutual assured destruction (MAD), the fact is that it was the fear of MAD, which kept the nuclear peace and still does.

It some times appears that in Asia, China, India and Pakistan have not fully grasped the import of acquiring nuclear weapons and the restraints and responsibilities it implies. China talks of fighting on a nuclear battle field using tactical nuclear weapons discounting the fact that if the adversary possesses nuclear weapons the next step could be an exchange of nuclear weapons targeting value targets and thus leaving no winner and only losers. Pakistan threatens a nuclear holocaust every time there is tension with India without seeming to acknowledge that a nuclear response would devastate Pakistan itself. The world is now beginning to get used to Pakistan's nuclear sabre rattling. Pakistan will soon realize that while its nuclear deterrence may prevent an all out conventional attack on it, it is unlikely to prevent limited military action. Eventually the realization has to come to all three countries that nuclear weapons can and should only be used if and when the very existence of the state is threatened. Even such use would have to be with the understanding that while it would ensure grievous hurt on the adversary, the inevitable retaliatory strike would, in the bargain, lead to its own destruction. Once this is understood then the true value of nuclear weapons would be realized, which is, to deter an unbridled conventional conflict keeping it below what is generally termed as the "nuclear threshold".

To ensure that a nuclear war does not confront India, one of the essentials in addition to conventional restraint, is the acquisition of a credible minimum nuclear deterrent. The credibility of a nuclear deterrent does not depend on the number of warheads held, particularly if deterrence is based on MAD. It requires not more than 10 to 15 warheads to destroy five major targets; what is crucial is the adequacy and survivability of the delivery means and the command and control arrangements. This is what India must strive to achieve. Once the adversary knows that however strong a first strike it may launch, India will be capable of launching a crippling retaliatory strike, this is what will provide the deterrence. This factor implies that a nuclear strike will only be as an act of desperation. It would then be up to us to ensure that the adversary does not reach this stage of desperation.

Given these facts, a nuclear war involving either China or Pakistan and India does not, in spite of western soothsayers of "doomsday scenarios", appear a possibility in the foreseeable future. Given the military balance between India and China, China is unlikely to face a situation vis-à-vis India where it will feel that it must use its nuclear weapons. As regards Pakistan, the only situation in which it might genuinely feel that it needs to use its nuclear weapons is if conventional attack by India threatens to break up the country. As this is a very unlikely Indian aim, the circumstances for use of nuclear weapons by either should not arise. The only development that could change this forecast would be the rise to power of a militant fundamentalist regime there. Such a regime could act irrationally, however, even in such a situation a clear statement that retaliation would be quick and severe, if there is any nuclear misadventure, should deter even the most rabid of militant groups.

CONVENTIONAL WARS

The last two decades of the 20th century saw a significant change in the manner in which conventional wars would be fought. These changes have been brought about by the applications of new technologies to war fighting leading to now what is commonly called "the Revolution in Military Affairs" (RMA). RMA has been extensively discussed in another part of the study, therefore, these will be only briefly mentioned to bring out the conditions under which India would fight a conventional war and the limitations that such a war imposes on the participants.

A major characteristic of this new warfare is the increased speed and lethality of such a war. This comes about by a combination of improved Reconnaissance, Surveillance and Target Acquisition systems (RSTA) that allow precision guided munitions (PGM's) to be accurately delivered to targets in the order of their priority, the whole linked by automated command and control systems using the power of the computer. In such an environment the electromagnetic spectrum becomes of vital importance and to a large extent, victory will go to the side that can best use this electromagnetic spectrum while denying its use to the adversary. The other notable point is the increasing importance of the air space as most of the systems used for RSTA would be space or air borne, as would be many of the launch pads for the PGMs. The land battle will be a land air battle and the side that can best combine and co-ordinate its land and air forces is the one that will gain success in battle. In the maritime field navies can be more autonomous than forces fighting on land, particularly if they have sea-borne air capability.

High technology warfare however also poses certain limitations. The first of these is the high cost of acquiring and fielding such modern systems. The result is that most armies can afford only a limited number of such systems as thus a long drawn out war with high technology weapons could be difficult for most medium sized powers including China, India or Pakistan. The increased lethality of these weapons systems would also tend to reduce the duration of wars. Another factor, which may come into play in the sub continental context, is that many of these systems have not proven themselves in mountainous or jungle terrain. Such terrain tends to make both acquisition of targets and guidance to them difficult. This particularly applies to India's land borders as much of it lies in inhospitable terrain: Indo-Myanmar, 1643 km, mountain- cum-jungle; Sino-Indian, 2410 km, mountainous including high altitude areas and the LC in J&K, 850 km, mostly mountains. Thus, when looking at high technology systems, we need to relate these to the terrain and conditions in which they will be used.

We can now look at the type of conventional war that India may get involved in. We will first examine an Indo-Pak conventional war looking basically at the land aspect of it. A historical fact to be taken note of is that both the 1965 and 1971 Indo-Pak conflicts were of short duration and objectives, other than in erstwhile East Pakistan in 1971, were limited. The short duration of both wars were due, to a large extent, to the immense pressure brought to bear on both countries by the Great Powers for an early cessation of hostilities. This pressure was aided by the inability of both sides to logistically sustain a long drawn high intensity war. To these two factors two more need to be added. The first is, that the international community is opposed to change of recognized boundaries by force and territory so gained would have to be returned to its erstwhile owner. The Kargil conflict, in fact, extended this even to de facto boundaries such as the LC in J&K. The second is of course, the nuclear dimension. This implies restraint in the objectives of a conventional war lest it degenerates into a nuclear exchange if it crosses the threshold of an adversary's ability to withstand an unfavourable situation.

One thus comes to the conclusion that a conventional war between India and Pakistan would be a limited one, in duration as well as objective. In fact, in the context of the international alarm, which is likely to be triggered by open Indo-Pak hostilities, it may be necessary to expressly state the limited objectives to allay misgivings. Kargil 1999 was an example; The GOI and Army Headquarters, both stated clearly that the operations had the limited objective of forcing Pakistan to withdraw to its side of the LC. India may be compelled to launch a limited conventional offensive, basically in J&K, to capture and temporarily hold areas through which major militant infiltration takes place. Such an offensive would need to be accompanied with a clear statement that such occupation would be vacated once the threat is eliminated. An action of this nature would either be on India's own initiative or as a reaction to a Kargil type intrusion. A similar limited objective could be set to the air force to strike militant bases and training camps in POK. Such strikes would have to be one off, as repeated strikes would definitely lead to resistance and escalation of the conflict. These strikes would use PGMs launched possibly from stand off distances or even beyond visual range. In any case escalation should be expected and anticipated. The escalation may take the form of Pakistan intrusions across the IB into J&K or even into Punjab and Rajasthan accompanied by air strikes on Indian air bases and ground forces. The Indian reaction could be across the IB to secure areas that would provide a cushion to some of our vulnerable cities that lie close to the border, e.g. Akhnoor, Jammu, Pathankot etc. and communication links that pass through and to other parts of J&K.

In the context of such limited wars we may need to re-examine organizational structures and strategies. The army may need to examine the quantum of mechanized forces required if deep penetration is no longer a viable objective. In the case of a short war, offensive air support demands on the air force would be considerable. Similarly for the navy interfering with Pakistan's sea lines of communication may really not give much dividends in a short war. On the other hand, drawing the Pakistan Navy out and then causing serious damage to it may have a great psychological impact. Defence of ones own VAs would of course be one of the primary tasks of the navy and air force. In such limited operations with a nuclear backdrop, limitation of the conflict becomes an objective by itself and not just victory. In any case victory in a limited war would only be relative.

A conventional war with China in the decade under consideration appears unlikely. China would not like, at present, to get involved in a war. Its focus would be on its economy and the modernization of its military. The military focus of China will be on Taiwan and on asserting its rights in the South China Seas. India would be on the periphery of this scheme of things. However, while not being a major focus of attention, China would do all it can to hedge India around and keep it occupied and confined to South Asia. This, it would do by continuing its aid and abetment of Pakistan's nuclear and conventional build-up, increase its influence in Myanmar and try to increase its influence in Nepal, Bangladesh and Sri Lanka. The attempt to increase influence would be both by economic and military means and by playing on the fears of India's smaller neighbours of its overwhelming presence in the region. Two developments that should be of particular interest to India are the rise of the Maoist movement in Nepal and the reported efforts by China to obtain facilities for its navy in Sri Lanka. While the Chinese moves will need to be met mainly by diplomatic efforts, the Indian military can play an important role by increasing military-to-military contacts and by offering not only to train personnel but to supply military hardware including tanks, aircraft and ships. Arming one's suspicious neighbours is one way of allaying their fears of any aggressive intent by India.

China would only initiate hostilities with India after it has consolidated its current military modernization and it has improved its logistic capability in Tibet. The aim of any Chinese offensive into India would be to inflict another humiliating defeat like the one in 1962, thus tearing to shreds India's pretence to be a world power. Such an offensive would only be launched if China feels that India is close to becoming a competitor. However, China is well aware that today's Indian Army is not that of 1962. It has seen, most notably during the Wangdung incident, that India is prepared and ready to stand up to it. It is also aware that India has improved its logistics and communications all along the Sino-Indian border. It also knows that in any future conflict, the Indian Air Force would now take an active part and is capable of effective interdiction of lines of communication in Tibet. Chinese military planners would, therefore, be aware that 1962 cannot be repeated and would be chary of being involved in a stalemate. To get over the difficulties of a direct attack on India, the Chinese may be tempted to consider an attack through Myanmar, thus threatening the current Indian defences in the eastern sector. There may well be a need for us, therefore, to look at our defences on the Indo-Myanmar border and to keep an eye on Chinese activities in Myanmar.

If hostilities do break out both sides would have limited objectives. The limitations are imposed both by the terrain that makes any deep penetration costly and time consuming and the danger of igniting a nuclear war. However, in the Sino-Indian context, the nuclear threshold is likely to be higher than that in an Indo-Pak conflict as none of the vital areas of either country lie close to the borders. The Chinese aim would be to repeat the 1962 offensive and they would consider it a victory if they were to penetrate as deep as they did at that time, particularly in the eastern sector. The war in this sector would however include Sikkim, which was not a theatre in 1962 and also as discussed earlier portions of the Indo-Myanmar border. India's aim would be to stall the Chinese offensive as close to the existing LAC as possible and then launch limited offensives to secure the Chinese launch pads, cut off Chinese ingressing forces and destroy them by a combination of ground and air action. Both air forces are likely to play a major role, particularly in interdiction of lines of communications and hitting reserves as they move into battle. Given the more open terrain of the Tibetan Plateau, compared to the rough and forested terrain on the Indian side of the border, the Indian Air Force should have an edge in delivering precision attacks on enemy targets. Any Chinese offensive is capable of being halted by India providing it continues to maintain its current posture along the border, continues to improve its communications and logistics and deploys effective RSTA assets including space-based to achieve early warning of a Chinese build-up. During this decade the Chinese Navy is unlikely to be able to play a major role in a Sino-Indian conflict unless it rapidly improves its capability to deploy forces at a distance from its bases. However, we will need to maintain surveillance on the SLOCs leading from the South China Seas into the Indian Ocean so as to be prepared to meet any Chinese threat, particularly to our island territories in the Bay of Bengal.

Examining the emerging scenario, the conclusion is that any conventional war that India may get involved with either Pakistan or China, will be a limited war, limited both in duration and in the depth of the objectives. The limitation as discussed comes both from the nature of modern war and the nuclear background under which the war will be fought. While the wars may be limited they will, for the duration they are fought, be intense. In fact, the very short duration of the war will mean that both sides will fling in everything they can to achieve the maximum gains in the shortest time so as to be at an advantageous position when the war ends. The result of this will be that casualties and attrition rates are likely to be high, and both sides will attempt to degrade the others electronic systems. Armies will have to be trained to withstand the intense strain and be prepared to take the initiative in the face of disruption of communications with higher headquarters. Victory will not necessarily go to the bigger battalion but to the one with a qualitative edge will depend in military hardware and before deciding even more on the quality of its manpower. These are factors that must be considered the future shape and size of the armed forces, the choice being quality over quantity, both in weapon systems and the men to man these. The other aspect that will need to be developed for success in any future conventional war is complete unity in doctrine, planning and execution between the land and air forces; this is vital.

LOW INTENSITY CONFLICT

Nuclear deterrence, the cost of conventional wars, even limited ones and an international climate that frowns on open warfare between nations has led to an increase in what can best be described as indirect armed aggression. Such aggression takes the form of instigating a portion of the target states population to take to arms to redress perceived grievances with training, arms and guidance provided by the instigator. In many cases the instigator infiltrates own personnel in the guise of volunteers, freedom fighters, jehadis and the like. J&K is a notable example. These forces use the tactics of terrorism and guerrilla fighting to achieve their objectives. Such type of conflict is now generally termed as Low Intensity Conflict (LIC).

There is a need to distinguish between an internal security situation, that may also include an insurgency, and the foreign sponsored and directed low intensity campaign. The former is an indigenous armed movement and is a purely internal matter. The internal security situation in the country is being discussed separately. What we are concerned with is external aggression in the guise of freedom fighters, etc. This is the situation we face in J&K. It needs to be recognised that it is not just an insurgency but Pakistan aggression using irregular forces, trained, equipped and guided by it, fighting the Indian State in the guise of so-called freedom fighters. This is the Pakistan option to achicve its aim without an open conventional war. It has the advantage of keeping the Indian Army tied down and the added advantage of deniability when accused of committing aggression. The Indian Army is therefore likely to remain committed to such operations for some time to come. The recent terrorist attacks on the US and the subsequent US pressure against states that sponsor terrorism may force Pakistan to reduce its arming, training and infiltration of the jehadis into J&K. There is, therefore, a glimmer of hope that the LIC in J&K may gradually die down.

LIC of the type being fought in J&K is in some ways a misnomer. The conflict is in fact of considerable mental and physical intensity for the men involved in it. There are no safe areas, there is a need to be ever alert and there is very little let-up in the operations. To add to the intensity, the insurgents are well armed, often better armed than the security forces. The militant has not just modern small arms but is equipped with a range of man portable surface-to-surface and surface-to-air missiles, machine guns, mortars and sophisticated communication equipment. The army thus faces a well-equipped adversary. The problem of LIC for an army is that it is a war of small detachments, of an ambush here, of a raid there and a cordon somewhere else. It is also fought under the rules of aid to civil authorities, which lays down the use of minimum force. All this adds to strain on the army.

The Indian Army has considerable experience in LIC, although, there is a reluctance in army circles to accept the fact that LIC is the type of war it will be increasingly involved in. Once this fact is accepted then the army will learn to treat LIC as one of its primary tasks, as important as fighting a conventional or nuclear war. It will then prepare, train and organize itself for the long drawn out nature of an LIC. This is one of the dilemmas an army preparing for both conventional war and an LIC faces. As brought out earlier, conventional wars will be intense, but of short duration; the quality of manpower and weapons and not their quantity will be important. In contrast an LIC is always of lesser intensity but of longer duration and in addition to quality the quantity, particularly of manpower, becomes important. LIC is manpower intensive. The Indian Army has to reconcile to both these requirements, those of LIC and those of conventional war. One solution tried has been the raising of special forces for counter insurgency operations such as the Assam Rifles and the Rashtriya Rifles. It is, however, a very expensive proposition to have a completely separate force for LIC operations and a separate army for conventional war that may or may not occur. The Army will therefore, continue to be involved in LIC, especially in areas such as J&K, where there is a large element of foreign involvement and support.

Successful conduct of LIC requires close cooperation between the military, law and order forces and the civil administration including the political regime in the area of operations. There is, therefore, a requirement to work out a broad national doctrine for LIC that allows for such coordination to be established in a formal manner. There is also a need for a joint forces doctrine for LIC, particularly for a joint land-air doctrine. While the major responsibility for the conduct of LIC will be with the army, the air force can play a role in providing surveillance, early warning and in the movement of Army Quick Reaction Teams, particularly in remote areas. The air force can also provide offensive air support in areas where civilian collateral damage is likely to be minimal, using attack helicopters and training aircraft suitably armed. There is a need to work out procedures by which army requests for offensive air support can be quickly met and do not need to be referred back to Air Headquarters, the Joint Chiefs or the Cabinet Committee on Security. LIC is a "dirty war" and the army does not like it. However, it is the type of war that the army is involved in today and is likely to remain involved in for the next decade. The army therefore needs to refine its LIC doctrine to cater for a long duration involvement in this and to examine how it can keep troops fresh in such an environment, be ready for limited conventional war and yet provide enough time for rest, recreation and training for its force.

The Indian armed forces are also likely to be involved in LIC operations as part of their commitment to UN operations that increasingly are changing from peace-keeping to peace-making. They have already been involved in such operations in Somalia and Sierra Leone in the recent past. LIC may also need to be fought in case India is called upon to intervene in any of its smaller neighbours. However, such intervention should generally be at the invitation of the neighbouring country and for limited objectives and periods. What ever the circumstances, LIC is the type of war that the armed forces, particularly the army and Air force are likely to be involved in for the foreseeable future.

CONCLUSION

Examination of the type of conflicts that India could be involved in, in the near future, reveals that the most likely is Low Intensity Conflict with a strong foreign support and instigation. Such an operation is already in progress in J&K and is likely to continue as long as Pakistan feels that it can sustain it and withstand international pressure to curb militant activities from its soil. This pressure is increasingly beginning to tell on Pakistan. Pakistan is also realising that instigating militant activities is a double-edged weapon as these militant groups then feel that they have a right to interfere in the internal affairs of the country. Pakistan now finds that such groups are affecting its own internal security. Pakistan's future policy in fostering terrorism in Kashmir would depend, to a large extent, on the US view on this in the light of terrorist strikes in New York and Washington and the US pledge to fight terrorism worldwide. There can be two scenarios, one that the US calls on Pakistan to disband all terrorist camps on its soil and stop the proxy war in Kashmir; the second could be that Pakistan as a quid-pro-quo for supporting US actions in Afghanistan gets the US to turn a blind eye to its activities in J&K. However, Pakistan would have, by now, realised that the proxy war is unlikely to force India to concede Kashmir to it. As support to such activities becomes increasingly counter productive, Pakistan may be induced to call off its proxy war in J&K. Such a denouement would be speeded up if we were able to take advantage of the war weariness of the Kashmiri people and induce them to stop supporting militancy and use peaceful, democratic means to obtain redress for their grievances. Such an outcome would be greatly facilitated if we were able to win the battle for the hearts and minds of the people. This requires concerted and co-ordinated efforts by both the armed forces and the civil administration. However, all this will take time and the armed forces, particularly the army will remain committed to LIC operations. There is a need, therefore, to formulate national, joint services and army doctrines for LIC.

China may also instigate LIC in the north-eastern states if it feels that the situation is ripe for such a move. It might consider this as a low cost option to keep India militarily engaged without having to commit its own forces. We need to solve the problems leading to insurgency in these areas expeditiously to forestall any Chinese move into these areas.

The other type of war that we may be involved in is a limited conventional war with either Pakistan or China and in certain circumstances with both simultaneously. The limitations on conventional wars rise from a number of circumstances. The cost of a high tech conventional war, the high casualty and attrition rates make a long war prohibitively expensive. The possession of nuclear weapons by all three protagonists also puts a break on an unbridled conventional war due to fear that if it goes out of control it would lead to a nuclear exchange.

While the three protagonists may not be able to field state-of-the-art weaponry comparable to those of the western powers, they will nevertheless have systems one generation below. All three are likely to be at the same level with China and India having a slight edge over Pakistan in the quality of equipment. The likely short duration of the war will mean that the war will be intense for as long as it lasts, with both sides aiming to be in a position of advantage by the time the war ends. The intensity of the war and the improved lethality and accuracy of the weapons systems implies that casualties would be high as also the attrition on equipment would be substantial. The Indian Army needs to get used to fighting on a dispersed battlefield with subordinate commanders trained to act independently. It must also develop the resilience to accept heavy casualties and yet be able to regroup and complete its task.

An Indo-Pak limited war may break out as an extension of the proxy war in J&K and may initially start with incursions across the LC and then extend to hostilities all along the IB. While the air forces of both countries may attempt to strike deep in to each other's territories, the land battle is likely to be fought close to the LC and IB. Both sides will generally be on a strategic defensive, offensive action being basically to unbalance the others' offensive forces.

A Sino-Indian conflict is likely only if China feels that India is reaching a stage of economic and military development to challenge it. It may then decide that a war may be one way of hindering India's development. China is likely to be aware that it is unlikely to succeed in imposing a resounding military defeat on India and will realise that if it does not it will lose face. Given the situation, China is unlikely to initiate a conflict, at least not till it has consolidated both its economy and its military modernization. The war would be limited and basically confined to disputed areas. It may however last a little longer than an Indo-Pak conflict as the terrain along the Sino-Indian border imposes limitations on the development of the full combat potential of both protagonists.

The escalation of a conventional conflict to a nuclear one is a very remote possibility in the Indo-Pak or Sino-Indian contexts. What the nuclear build-up of the three countries does is to limit the scope of conventional conflict and make LIC the most attractive option. Nuclear asymmetry may, however, lead to attempts at nuclear blackmail. It is therefore necessary for India to build and maintain a credible nuclear deterrence capability. Simultaneously we must work with China and Pakistan to initiate nuclear restraint and confidence building measures. The eventual aim should be for all three to forswear use of nuclear weapons against each other.

FIVE

The Role, Size and Shape of the Army

INTRODUCTION

While national security now covers a much larger gamut and not just the territorial security of the nation, maintaining the territorial integrity of the nation still remains one of the basic aims of a nation's security apparatus. Territory, after all, is what finally gives shape to a national entity. The defence of the nation's territorial integrity from armed threats to it whether external or internal is the primary task of a nation's armed forces. Territory is defined as positions in land, therefore the defence of the nations territory falls basically on its land forces ie., the army working in close cooperation and coordination with the other two services. The primary role of the army is therefore to protect the territorial integrity of the nation from external aggression. Given however, the increasing use of subversion, proxy wars and the like, maintenance of internal security of the nation is now an equally important part of the army's role.

The size and shape of any army is governed by a few basic factors, viz. the land threat the army has to prepare to defeat, the national military strategy to meet these threats, the resources, men, material and financial available to equip the army and most importantly the length of the borders to be defended and the nature of terrain along these borders. Land is the crucial factor for after all an army's primary task is to defend the land from an invasion. The terrain along the borders dictates the nature of threats that can develop across them as well as the strategy and tactics to deal with these threats. It is necessary therefore, to examine India's land borders and the terrain along these before one can come to a conclusion on the size and the shape of the army. It is important to remember that all armed invasions in India have come across its land borders.

THE LAND BORDERS

India's land borders stretch for 14,100 kms and touch six countries. Bangladesh (4,351 kms), Myanmar (1,643 kms), Bhutan (699 kms), Nepal (1,751 kms), China (2,410 kms) and Pakistan (3,244 kms including the LoC in J&K). Obviously along such a long border the nature of terrain will differ. It is however not necessary for to study these borders in detail but only look at their major characterstics and their affect on the army.

The first characteristic that stands out is that nearly 5200 kms of these borders, those with Myanmar, China and the LoC in J&K lie in mountains cum jungle or high mountainous terrain. Such terrain is most unsuitable for use of mechanized forces and therefore great deal of reliance has to be placed on Infantry. On the Indian side of the border lateral movement along the border is difficult if not impossible. Movement of reserves from one sector to another is time consuming and hence each sector needs to have its own in-built reserves. All this makes defending these borders a manpower intensive task. On the other hand the nature of the terrain also has an affect on the type of operations. While infiltration by small bodies can be carried out anywhere along the borders, largescale incursions would be confined to areas where the road communications of each side meet or can be easily linked. This limitation would equally apply to any counter offensives we may wish to launch across the borders. Thus, a careful study of terrain would indicate that the border need not be held in equal strength all along its length and the total quantum of forces required to hold these borders can be judiciously reduced by holding the likely routes of ingress strongly while deploying light forces in other areas. Another factor that impinges on the type and quantum of forces required in the Sino-Indian border is that while the approach from the Indian bases to the border is through difficult terrain and time consuming, on the Chinese side, the Tibetan plateau is less rugged making movement easier. Thus while China can keep forces further back from the border and move them quickly to man the border, India has to maintain comparatively larger forces on or close to the borders.

The bulk of the 4,000 odd km border with Bangladesh lies in riverine terrain and some of it in jungle covered hills areas, not very suitable for mechanized forces other than those based on light amphibious armored fighting vehicles (AFVs). The numerous rivers lay a premium on bridging resources and heliborne forces to speed up the rate of an advance in such terrain.

It is in fact only the 2,100 kms of the IB between Pakistan and India which lies in the plains and deserts that is to an extent suitable for large scale use of mechanized forces. Appreciating this, both countries have attempted to build a series of defences based on artificial articles such us canals and ditch–cum–bunds (DCPs) along the border in the areas of Punjab and northern Rajasthan. Further south the Thar Desert while suitable for tracked vehicles poses problems for re-supply based on wheeled transport.

Another characteristic of India's borders is that many places of strategic and historical importance lie very close to the borders. To take just a few examples, Tawang, Gangtok and Leh on the Sino-Indian border; Kargil, Uri, Poonch, Akhnoor and Jammu to the LC; Pathankot, Gurdaspur, Amristar, Ferozpur and Fazilka on the Indo-Pak IB. The result of this is that along large stretches of the border one cannot fight the classic mobile defence battle where space is traded for time, the enemy drawn in and then destroyed. The battle has to be fought in the forward zone and little if any loss of territory can be accepted. This is further compounded by the probability that most future conventional wars are likely to be short and it may not be possible to regain lost territory before the war ends.

The implication of the nature of our borders and the terrain along it is that the army will continue to be a basically infantry oriented army and will continue to require large man power resources with its implications on expenditure on pay, allowances and other related matters. Methods of allocation will need to be worked out and will be discussed later.

LAND THREATS

Armed threats across India's land borders can come only from two sources, China and Pakistan. The Myanmar border may however be activated if China were to use this area to strike at India and turn our defences along the border with Tibet.

As discussed elsewhere future conventional wars in the Indian context are likely to be limited wars, limited both in time in space. Nevertheless, while such wars may be limited they will be intense and given improved accuracy and lethality of modern weapon systems, attrition both of men and material will be high. The short duration of the war implies that there will not be the time to call up reserve personnel and integrate them into units and formations. Once commence the war will have to be fought by forces in being and therefore as long as a threat of war with Pakistan or China or both remains India will need to maintain a large standing army. The short nature of war also implies that there will not be time to recoup losses in men and material by new production during the course of the war and therefore, adequate reserves need to be part of the army in peace time.

The other threat which the Indian army faces and needs to be prepared to keep facing is that of low intensity conflict or irregular wars. Some of these can be of purely indigenous origin, or at the maximum of getting some material assistance from other sources. The other is targeted intervention by a neighbouring power using not only dissatisfied elements of the indigenous population but also mercenaries/ volunteers from its own population or even from a worldwide network as for example the mixed nature of fighters found in the Taliban ranks in Afghanistan. We are faced with such a threat for a long time and while there are many in the army who feel that such threats should be handled by police type forces, the fact remains that worldwide when such threats become so serious as to threaten the integrity and security of the nation it is the army which has to face the problem. Therefore, till such time as we continue to face such threats the army must be prepared and organized to face such a threat in addition to be in prepared to counter conventional threats simultaneously.

There is a tendency to raise a number of a specialized forces to deal with terrorism and insurgency. One is not sure that this is the best way. A regular army unit has the flexibility to switch from a CI role to a conventional one quickly. Specialized units such as the Rastriya Riffle battalions may not be able to do so. On the other hand special forces such as Para Commandos, the NSG, etc. do need to be strengthened and equipped to take on carefully targeted strikes on terrorists hideouts, training camps and the like. Counter terrorism and counter insurgency are manpower intensive tasks. While counter insurgency particularly in the border areas will necessarily need the army to be deployed, terrorism, particularly in the other parts of the country should basically be treated as a law and order problem to be dealt by police forces.

As this is being written one is not sure what effect the USA's war on terrorism will have on the situation in J&K. Currently there is no let-up in terrorist activities and in fact there is an apprehension that Taliban who escaped from Afghanistan into Pakistan may be diverted to J&K. This of course would increase the intensity of insurgency in J&K. On the other hand if the USA is serious about eliminating terrorism and brings strong pressure on Saudi Arabia to stop financing organizations and countries who encourage terrorism and pressurises Pakistan to stop sponsoring and instigating terrorism one may find an easing of the armed conflict in J&K and a chance for a political process to get underway.

INDIA'S STRATEGY

India's strategy for dealing with threats across its borders, basically those from China and Pakistan can best be described as one of dissuasive deterrence. The strategy has two legs. The first is to deploy strong defensive forces along or close to the borders during peacetime so as to be able to man prepared defences at short notice and blunt any enemy offensive close to the border and limit penetration. These defensive forces have inbuilt reserves to launch counter attacks to destroy enemy penetrations. In the plains such reserves are based on mechanized forces. The second leg is based on strong theatre reserves capable of launching offensive into enemy territory and carrying the battle to him. This strategy is basically a reactive one. It waits for the enemy to launch the first offensive, depends on the defensive forces to hold such an offensive and then strike back with its own offensive. The strategy has the advantage of laying the onus of starting hostilities and being branded the aggressor on the opponent. The presence of strong defensive forces, deployable at short notice or already deployed on the border is aimed to convince the opponent that his offensive will not succeed and only lead to loss of life and material of his forces, thus dissuading him from starting hostilities. This dissuasion is further reinforced by the presence of strong offensive forces aimed at sending a message that not only will the attack be blunted but the war will be carried deep into his territory. However, as the enemy has the initiative in such a strategy and can choose when and where to start the war, India is compelled to maintain a strong standing army to cover all possible areas of enemy ingress. As regards fighting a simultaneous war on two fronts i.e, China and Pakistan, the strategy calls for remaining on the strategic defensive against China while taking offensive action against Pakistan to compel it to call off its attack before switching forces on the Sino-Indian border.

India has also remained in a reactive mode even as far as the low intensity conflicts in various parts of the country are concerned. The country is content with fighting the insurgents once they have crossed into its own territory with no effort to strike at their bases across the borders. This increases the strain on the army which bears the major burden of these operations. At some stage a reappraisal of this strategy may be needed. There will be a need to formulate a proactive strategy for selected aims and targets.

FINANCES

The army already reccives the largest share of the defence budget, nearly 55% of it. There are two reasons for this apparently skewed allotment to the army. The first is the army's large manpower partly explained by the imperatives of terrain and threats discussed in the preceding paragraphs. The other is the fact that large portions of the army are engaged in active operations and the army budget has to cater for this. The army of course feels that even this allocation is too little and it needs more funds. However, at some stage the army has to realize that it cannot continue to have such a large share of the budget and modernization of the other two services, which are capital intensive, is also a national imperative.

Considering all the factors examined above certain conclusions can be drawn. The first, that due to the terrain along our borders and the nature of threats across these India will continue to require to maintain a large standing army with an emphasis on infantry. The possibility that future conventional wars will be of limited duration and will be fought over limited depth means that the mechanized forces may not be able to develop their full potential. The army also needs to take into account the fact that it is likely to have to continue to deal with the low intensity conflicts for some time to come. The army must therefore be organized to face both conventional and LIC simultaneously and be prepared to do this even while receiving a diminishing share of the defence budget. It is with this background that we will consider the course the future developments in the army should follow.

FUTURE DEVELOPMENTS OF THE ARMY

The Indian Army presently has a strength of 9,80,000 personnel, i.e., just little under a million strong. With this strength the army is able to field a force of some 35 divisions, three of which are armoured. There are also a number of independent armoured, infantry, artillery, air defence and engineer brigades. This is a formidable conventional force. The army, therefore, is capable today of facing any conventional threat from its likely adversaries and of carrying the battle to the enemy.

However, as discussed previously in this study, even conventional war today makes use of a variety of high technology weapon systems and very responsive and speedy command and communications systems. It is this particular area, that is of making sure that the army does not find itself left behind in the Revolution in Military Affairs (RMA) that the army should focus on over the next decade. The main areas to be focused on are discussed below.

Reconnaissance Surveillance and Target acquisitions (RSTA): Future wars will be won by the side which wins the information war. One of the essentials of winning the information war is the ability to gain accurate intelligence of the enemy and this is what RSTA provides. The Indian army presently has a long way to go in this field. It needs to acquire at short notice the whole gamut of RSTA assets from airborne sensors mounted on helicopters or UAVs to ground based sensors of all types of radar, thermal imaging, night vision devices and the lot. This is not the place to discuss details of equipment but some which are of vital importance are gun location radars for the artillery and squad and individual night vision and surveillance equipment for the infantry.

Precision Guided Munitions (PGMs): Targets having been acquired must be destroyed and for this a number of new precision guided munitions are available and must increasingly be part of the army's inventory. These will need to include guided weapons fired from helicopters as well as from tube and rocket artillery. Improved air defence weapon systems and anti-tank guided weapons of the fire and forget variety will also need to be inducted.

Electronic Warfare Equipment: At the heart of most modern weapon systems and equipment are electronics, whether it is in detection and surveillance, whether it is in guidance or in command and control. It has been stated by many military thinkers that the next war will be won by the side that best uses the electro magnetic spectrum and denies its use to the enemy. There is therefore the need to build up assets to cover the whole spectrum of electronic warfare, from electronic support systems to electronic counter measures to the new field of electro-optic counter measures and electro-optic counter counter measures. While building up this capability the army must not ignore those deployed in the mountains; the need here is for lightweight easily transported systems. The army also needs to look at its communication equipments particularly the wireless sets, which must be both light and secure.

C3I: To manage all the high technology systems, whether in the field of RSTA or EW or PGMs there is a requirement for a robust and well-established C3I system. Though the army has been at it for some time a system does not yet seem to be in place. It appears that in the search for a perfect solution the army is delaying the fielding of at least an embryo system. This may require to be relooked into and it may be worthwhile to use the enormous expertise available in the nations IT industry to help find solutions. Also use of commercial hardware should be looked at not all hardware needs to be ruggedised.

FORCE STRUCTURES

The strength of the Indian army is more than adequate and needs no augmentation. However, certain reorganization would strengthen the efficacy of the current forces. The major recommendations are discussed below.

Mechanized Forces: While there are a sufficient number of the armoured regiments which as they gradually get to a mix of T-72, T-90 and Arjun Tanks are well equipped. It is felt that instead of a number of the independent armoured brigades these could be grouped together to form at least two more armoured divisions. This reorganization would enhance the offensive options in a war in the plains and force Pakistan to exercise even greater caution in launching its own reserves.

Airborne Forces: Our frontiers along the mountains pose a major problem in the quick movement of reserves from one sector to another because of the terrain and because most of this movement is against the terrain of the country. This forces the piece meal deployment of reserves. One way of improving mobility in the mountains is by the use of the air, basically helicopters for quick movement of men and material. It is recommended that each corps operating in the mountains have on its orbat an air-mobile brigade. This brigade is to be found by converting the independent infantry / mountain brigades on the army's orbat. These air-mobile brigades would be supported by a helicopter force with the mix of light, medium and heavy helicopters capable of lifting one battalion group at a time. This airlift capability would need to be included in the IAF airlift plans. This would give enormous flexibility to the corp commander to quickly reinforce a threatened sector and also open out offensive possibilities into enemy territory. In addition to these air-mobile brigades there is a requirement to relook at the proposal to raise an air- assault division. This was to be done by converting one of the existing divisions with the Para-brigade amalgamated into it. This division would be equipped and trained for carrying out paratroop and heliborne assaults as well as air landed operations. Such a division would be a potent force as an army reserve capable of being moved rapidly to reinforce either an offensive or defensive operation. It will also be an ever present threat to the enemy while kept in reserve forcing him to deploy troops to guard rear areas. This division could also form the core of the army component of a national Rapid Reaction Force (RRF)which we should raise to be able to assist a friendly country or to take part in UN operations.

Amphibious forces: We have over a period of time practiced in a desultory manner amphibious operations without seriously contemplating a permanent force fully trained and equipped for such a role. There is a requirement for a minimum of an amphibious brigade for the A&N Islands and one more located on the main land to be able to reinforce this if required as well as provide for the turnover of units. These brigades again can be found from the existing orbat but must be specially organized, trained and equipped for amphibious operations. They will require special equipment such as amphibious armoured vehicles, engineer support vehicles and the like and above all constant training in their role and not an odd exercise. These forces could also be part of a rapid deployment force in conjunction with the air assault division discussed above.

FINANCIAL SAVINGS

The major limiting factor to achieving either the required level of technical sophistication or the force levels discussed above will of course be the availability of funds. Even though as the economy grows there would be a proportionate increase in the defence budget even if allocation remains constant in percentage of GDP terms, this will still not be sufficient if a large portion of it continues to be utilized for pay allowances and pensions. Yet, as discussed somewhere in the earlier paragraphs, the tasks the army is faced with make it man power intensive. Saving must therefore be found by innovative means.

One of the problem of army manpower is that most army personnel rank and file as well as officers are regulars with a long term of engagement. This means that the army has to carry them through for a long time as well as pay them a pension. This is in contrast to the state in most advanced armies where the bulk of soldiers, both officers and men, enlist for a limited period of time before moving out to the civil stream. We need to move towards such a system. With the economy opening up and expanding, employment opportunities in the civil stream should improve. However, a more immediate solution could be the oft discussed proposal that of moving of personnel out of the army and into the central police organizations after they have done a tenure in the army. Basically this means that all recruits to these forces including officers, would first do a tenure in the army before joining their parent organization. Such a system would ensure that the army retains a youthful profile and the CPOs get trained persons and the lifetime costs of personnel are shared between the army and the CPOs.

The army must also look at manpower reductions. These may be difficult in the fighting arms but an increase in the use of TA units could lead to some reductions; in defensive formations one out of three battalions of a brigade could be a TA battalion. Such a TA battalion must be locally raised and have a limited liability. For example, the brigade tasked to defend say Gurdaspur would have two regular infantry battalions while the third would be provided by a TA battalion located and raised in Gurdaspur with liability to be embodied only if Gurdaspur is threatened. Of course the battalion would be embodied every year for annual training and exercises. The TA concept can be extended, for example, to TA transport companies who carry out their normal activities in peacetime but are embodied in times of emergency to support the army. These are only some examples. One is aware that certain studies on this have already been carried out in army headquarters, it now needs implementation.

The other area of manpower savings would come from privatizing some of the static support units. Thus, for example, base workshops other than those dealing with specialized and imported equipment, could be privatized. In fact, as far as Indian manufactured equipments is concerned the concept should be that the manufacturer would be responsible for maintenance support through the lifecycle of the equipment. For example, if Telco supplies trucks to the army, Telco would be responsible to establish workshops at selected points to carry out third line and base repairs of these trucks and this would be built into the contract. The army would only carry out running repairs. Considerable savings both in manpower and establishments costs would occur if such measures were to be implemented.

WAR WASTAGE RESERVES (WWR)

One other area which could lead to financial savings is a close look at the scales of ammunition and equipment held as war wastage reserves in the light of the expectation that war will be limited both in area and in time. The period therefore for which reserves need to be held could be reviewed. However, while carrying out such a review few factors need to be kept in mind. These are:

- While future wars may be of short duration they will be intense. Attrition of equipment and expenditure of ammunition will be heavy and the WWR must cater for this .
- WWR is not just to meet expenditure during war but also to ensure that at the end of the war losses can be recouped quickly.
- The short duration of the war will imply that it will be difficult to make up losses from fresh production during the course of fighting and probably impossible to makeup as far as imported equipment and ammunition are concerned.

Therefore one may need to have two separate scales, one for indigenously produced items and the other for imported items. The stocking of the indigenously produced items may be at a lesser scale while for imported items these would need to be higher. A fifteen day intense and thirty days normal scales for indigenously produced items may serve the purpose while for imported items this may have to be at thirty days intense and sixty days normal.

SUMMARY

The type of terrain and the nature of threat that the army has to be prepared to combat makes it imperative for India to maintain a large standing army. The current strength of the army is sufficient to deal effectively with any threats which may rise in the near future. There is a need however for a concerted effort for technological upgradation particularly in the fields of RSTA, EW and C3I.

While the force levels are sufficient certain amount of redeployment may be needed. This would include reorganizing the armoured assets and raising of air mobile formations for the mountains and also the raising of a quick reaction force consisting of an air assault division and amphibious brigade, to function in conjunction with appropriate naval and air assets.

Greater use of the TA concept and privatization of some of the support functions could lead to financial and manpower saving which in turn would provide the wherewithal for modernization.

Revising the WWR scales to cater for shorter but more intense wars could help achieve some financial savings.

SIX

Maritime Dimensions of India's Security

Maritime dimensions cover a vast spectrum ranging from maritime assets, energy exploitation, the exclusive economic zone and its resources; issues concerning maritime boundaries as well as specific subjects such as merchant shipping, ports and harbors, fisheries, Antarctica expeditions and oceanographic research; maritime accidents, environment and pollution etc. It is intended to deal more with the security aspects of the maritime dimensions than with specific areas of the dimensions themselves.

The Indian Ocean comprises a fifth of the water surface of the earth, peopled by a third of the world's population. India has been a great maritime nation with a strategic geographical position in the Indian Ocean. The Indian Peninsula juts into the Indian Ocean, astride the major shipping lanes of the world, which provide the shortest route between the Atlantic and the Pacific. India's place among the great maritime nations was well recognized by our ancestors.

Instances are replete in history where India's benevolent influence spread to the East and the West through our seafaring people and the medium of the oceans. It was with the coming of the Mughals, the landlocked tribe of Central Asia, that importance of the seas was forgotten. India paid a heavy price for it by becoming an easy prey to the advancing maritime colonial power. These lessons are etched in our psyche and never again should India become weak at sea inviting aggression. Strength of India derives from being strong at sea. India is perhaps the only country whose name has been attached to a great ocean. We also have maritime boundaries with seven nations in the Indian Ocean. Its geographic position with a long coastline and Island territories provides India with a great advantage in the maritime field.

India's strategic position in the Indian Ocean is clearly evident when seen in the context of the massive flow of trade through the sea-lanes of communications, which join the major regions of west and east. Seaborne trade passing through Indian Ocean in 1993 was over half trillion dollars, nearly 15% of entire world trade. 200 ships crossed Malacca strait everyday. 28 passed through Strait of Hormuz, carrying nearly 17% of the world trade in volume. Over half of United States requirement of oil passes through this route. One-third of the total ships in the world and over half of the entire world shipping capacity takes passage through these choke points. The economy of the eastern Asian nations that is Japan, ASEAN and China is closely interlinked to the energy resources in the Persian Gulf and Central Asian Region. Any obstruction in the flow of oil will have serious repercussion for the consuming countries.

India's vast maritime interests, it's geography, trade, the Exclusive Economic Zone which is nearly as big as the land mass and millions of sea faring people who live on the coast and in the Island territories make the country a great maritime nation. It is these compelling imperatives and the growing importance of the seas to which India would turn to in years ahead which make their security vital for our very existence. Our growing energy needs would be obtained from offshore oil reserves as well as imports by sea. The sea-lanes of communication and our merchant marine would be vital to our growth, as would be the ports and harbours that are the gateways connecting the country to the global village. It is for good reason that the present century has been called the century of the seas. As resources deplete on land, man's attention would turn to the unlimited riches beneath the seas, an area in which India is already ahead, being a pioneer investing nation with mining rights allotted in Central Indian Ocean. We have to gear ourselves for this stupendous task of harvesting the power of the oceans. There are vast, virtually limitless resources, living and non-living, minerals, oil, gas, food, etc which, could be tapped from the seas. Oceans are also source of energy.

No nation that aspires for greatness can neglect the maritime dimension. The US, Russia, China, France, Britain and Japan, have all developed maritime infrastructure and have large and technologically advanced navies. The navies are not only instruments of power projection but have the added advantage of unobtrusive presence, flexibility and rapid response. They are all capable of acting swiftly and silently in the borderless oceans, both on the littoral and at sea during peace or war. The navies are also ideally suitable for the strategic role. Nations with extensive maritime interest must have large navies capable of oceanic role and greater reach with sustaining power to conduct operations far away from their mainland. In essence, therefore Indian Navy has been and will continue to be regional in reach, oceanic in outlook and proactive in scope. Smaller nations with limited maritime interests could make do with coastal navies since they do not have to depend on the seas. Let us now examine the maritime interests of India in some detail.

Our merchant shipping consists of 480 ships at about 7.05 million GRT. The Indian tonnage ranked 17th at 1.27 % of the world's tonnage is still very meager. Countries like Greece have 13.7%. Shipping made tremendous strides till mid 70s but its growth stagnated in the next twenty years. China in comparison in the last 25 years increased its gross tonnage from 3 million to 20 million tonnes. Since the rejuvenation of the economy and emphasis on export-led growth, the importance of this sector has been realized and it is anticipated that the tonnage would grow to 9 million GRT by the early 2000, the aim being to carry about 30 to 35 % of our trade in bottoms of Indian flag. Percentage share of Indian flag in foreign trade rose from 29.7% in 1995 to 30.5 % in 1998-99, as against 41% in 1987-88. This trend must be reversed. The estimate share of foreign trade by sea is 65.4%. Another aspect is the age of the Indian shipping fleet, half of which is between 10-20 years old and nearly 15% above twenty years old. Apart from this there would be a need to expand the capacity to transport LNG for India's future energy requirements. Another area would be the expansion of coastal shipping and inland waterways. The augmentation of merchant shipping so vital to the sustained growth of the economy is likely to take place at a faster pace in the future adding a modest 2 million tonnes every five years. Protection of SLOCs would, therefore, become a major task.

In the 11 major and 184 intermediate/minor ports, a total of 287 MT of cargo was handled in 1998-99. This is likely to rise to 415.4 MT by 2002. If the economy grows at 6-7% annually, it is estimated that this figure could increase by nearly 3 times to 1273 MT in 2020. Ports and harbours are the gateways to the rest of the world. There has been a growing awareness of the shortcomings of infrastructure and its critical role in sustaining high economic growth. Installed capacity must be augmented with special emphasis on containerization and automation so that the turn around of ships could be faster. There is also a need to attract private capital in the modernization of the ports as well as to privatize the operation of the ports themselves. Ports and harbours could be closed by threats and this would have adverse effect on economy. Their security is therefore essential.

India has an EEZ of 2.02 million square km, which is 66 %of the landmass of the country. Her coastline is 7,615 km long with 1,197 Islands. The extension of the continental shelf from 200 to 350 kilometers by 2004 would enhance the EEZ by a further 1.5 million square kilometers. Her status as a pioneer investor in seabed mining has been recognized by UNCLOS III by the allotement of 1,50,000 sq.km of area in central Indian Ocean for this purpose. Our main interests in the EEZ would involve exploitation of living resources for purposes of food, exploitation of non living resources as our alternative to the fast depleting land-based resources, development of ocean related industries, extraction of oil and pursuance of independent ocean policy. India must be able to exercise fully her sovereign rights over this extended area including rights over laying pipelines and submarine cables.

India's offshore reserve of oil and natural gas estimated in 1980 is one billion tonnes and 660 bcm of natural gas. In addition to the seven fields off Bombay basin, natural gas has been discovered offshore in Andaman and Nicobar Islands, Gulf of Cambay and Kutch and basins of Brahmaputra, Godavari and Cauvery. The gap between production and consumption is 1:1.3 approximately. Faster economic growth would entail increased demands on energy. Offshore sector contributes nearly 65 % of oil and 70 % of gas. Huge platforms, structures, pipelines, etc., have been created with an investment of over Rs.20,000 crores. Though at present the main activity is focused on the West Coast, in years ahead, such platforms would spring up on the East Coast and the A & N Islands. This has been borne out by the recent reports of oil having been found in the Godavari basin, which is likely to be of the order of 5.7 to 10.4, million metric tonnes. The existing production capacity of 40 million tonnes of crude oil is likely to be stepped up to meet the growing energy demands of the country. The energy demand of crude oil is expected to rise to 122 MT by 2002, 190 MT by 2012 and 365 MT by 2025. Demand of coal, oil and natural gas is likely to be 770 MT of oil equivalent. As compared to this, crude oil self- sufficiency has fallen from 63% in 1989-90 to 32 % in 1999-2000 with import standing at 64 MT. In the next 5-7 years energy dependence on sea would increase from 80% to 90%.

According to an estimate, Indian EEZ has a potential to yield 2,000 billion tonnes of mineral nodules and every million tonnes of nodule is expected to provide 15,000 tonnes of nickel, 12,000 tonnes of copper, 15,000 tonnes of cobalt, 60,000 tonnes of manganese and large quantities of gold. The minerals of the continental shelf consist of heavy placer minerals ferriferous ones like magnetite and diamonds. Phosphorite and gluconite along with gold have been found in the submarine placers. In addition, marine chemicals such as magnesium, sodium phosphate and bromine could be extracted from seawater. Tapti and Narmada rivers into the Arabian Sea carry nearly 20 tonnes of uranium annually.

Assuming that 15 % of the Indian population of one billion lives in coastal areas, about 150 million people are directly dependent on the sea for their livelihood. Most of the fishing activity being non-mechanized, is confined to the territorial waters and the annual catch is only about 2.7 million tonnes against the sustainable 4 million tonnes. Presently due to lack of resources, fish contributes less than 5 % of protein to our diet. However, there is tremendous potential in this area to feed millions, since fishery resources are renewable, in abundance and easily accessible. Our export of marine products could be greatly enhanced if modern and mechanized methods are adopted for deep-sea fishing beyond 100 meters. Chartering of foreign vessels could also be considered. An area that requires urgent attention is measures against poaching in our waters. A large number of fishing vessels from neighbouring countries especially in the Bay of Bengal carry out poaching of fishes. The coast guard has apprehended nearly 600 foreign vessels. However, this represents only a small fraction of the poachers that got away.

Smuggling of gold and silver is a traditional activity between the Persian Gulf and the western coast of India. However, this took a serious turn with a transhipment of explosives and small arms in the early 90s especially in the Bombay blast case and exposed our vulnerability. Over the years the nexus of narco terrorism has gained considerable proportions with operations ranging from the LTTE in the south, the Golden Crescent in the west and the Golden Triangle in the east of India. The vast unguarded coastline of India with its island territories provides an ideal place for the nefarious activities of the ISI.

India took a far-reaching step in 1981, when it decided to undertake expeditions to the Antarctica. Among the 45 signatories to the treaty, 26 including India have consultative status enabling them to participate effectively in the negotiations. To date 19 expeditions have been mounted. In 1996 India ratified the protocol on environment protection wherein all treaty parties agreed to prohibit mineral resource activities for a period of 50 years and accorded priority to scientific research. India's "Maitri" station is among the few permanent stations in Antarctica with its nearest neighbour South Africa 800 km away. India's consultative status must be reinforced with renewed emphasis on research in disciplines such as earth sciences, bio-science, remote sensing and oceanography. India's oceanographic activities are driven by a quest for scientific knowledge since it is a monsoon dependent country. New discoveries and inventions in ocean sciences would also have economic benefits. Our presence in Antarctica should therefore be seen as a national effort to promote greater scientific knowledge.

India has maritime boundaries that required delimitation with seven states. Of these, with sustained diplomatic efforts we have reached 12 maritime boundary agreements resulting in virtually completing the task with Indonesia, Maldives, Myanmar, Thailand and Sri Lanka. The two cases that have yet to be settled are with Pakistan (Sir Creek) and Bangladesh (New Moor Island). Disputes of this nature do not by themselves cause serious concern. However, when added to other territorial disputes, the situation could become complex causing unnecessary irritation in bilateral relations.

The navies of the Indian Ocean are being modernized by almost all the maritime nations of the region. Indonesia plans to build a 120 ships navy with 25 frigates and large amphibious elements. Similarly Singapore, Malaysia and Thailand are also building hightech navies with missiles, subsurface and amphibious capabilities. Thailand has acquired an aircraft carrier and Knox frigates from United States and Jianghu Class frigates from China. Bangladesh, Myanmar and Sri Lanka have small navies mostly acquired from China. During the Cold War, the Indian Ocean has seen the presence of nearly 100 warships. This has declined and very few Russian ships are permanently based though the presence of United States Navy subsequent to the Gulf War has become a permanent feature. The navies of the Indian Ocean region, though small would be equipped with high technology anti-ship missiles and subsurface forces along with force multipliers.

As far as Pakistan is concerned, the size of its navy is far greater than its maritime interests. Its Navy is India specific and it has followed the strategy of sea denial with main emphasis on submarines and shore aircraft. It is likely that Pakistan Navy would maintain a force level of 6-8 submarines, 8-10 destroyers/frigates, 10-12 missile craft and a few support ships. They would also have a strong maritime reconnaissance capability with air- to-surface missile carrying aircraft and helicopters. Pakistan is reported to be modernizing and building 2-3 more ports to provide necessary flexibility in operations. These ports at Gawadar and Ormara will provide her with defence in depth as well as for interdicting sea-lines of communication in the Gulf. China has ambitions to become equal to the US. These are clearly indicated by its thrust for a strong blue water navy. Its defence budget is increasing at an average rate of 12%. It has a credible nuclear deterrent to strike far away from homeland. Broadly speaking, there are two components of the Chinese maritime strategy, to move eastwards and southwards. The Chinese PLA Navy has a force level of approximately 60 destroyers and over 100 submarines. There are plans for building two aircraft carriers. Their subsurface forces are being modernized with the induction of type 093 and 094 submarines. Each of the strategic submarines would be armed with DF-31 missiles of a reported range of 10,000 km. The conventional submarine forces are also being modernized with the induction of Song class and Kilo class submarines. Russia has been assisting the PLA Navy in the induction of high technology weapons, warships, aircrafts and submarines. In the next 20 years the presence of the Chinese Navy is likely to grow in the Indian Ocean with bases acquired from Myanmar and Thailand and close cooperation with Bangladesh, Sri Lanka and Pakistan.

In the light of the developments, which are taking place in our region and taking into count our national interests, our maritime strategy should aim at meeting threats from Pakistan in the short term and China in the long term. Specific maritime threats to our naval forces and merchant shipping operating in the Arabian Sea would range from anti-ship missiles, which could be launched from submarines, ships and aircrafts as well as information denial and electronic warfare. Our offshore assets and coastal region in the north Arabian Sea could also be targeted. The main objectives of our maritime strategy should be the defence of the mainland and islands territories, security of our maritime interests and maritime cooperation among friendly neighbours. The navy has to be built to have an intervention capability against any threat posed at sea by extra regional navies. It would also have to ensure maritime surveillance and presence in areas of our interests with sufficient reach and staying power. The area of operations would at least cover the Arabian Sea and Bay of Bengal from the Straits of Hormuz and Red Sea in the west to the Malacca Straits in the east. Occasional forays into the Pacific Ocean, East Asian rim and South East Asia would be necessary. It would be regional in reach, proactive in scope and oceanic in outlook. The navy would also provide a bridge between friendly neighbouring countries to enhance maritime cooperation. A strong navy would act as a source of stability in the region bringing peace and prosperity, thus enabling the country to concentrate on its economic growth.

India's draft nuclear doctrine is based on "no first use" principle. Under this condition, the deterrence must work to prevent a conflict from escalating into a nuclear holocaust. The deterrence would work when the adversary realizes that the response to his first use would invite instantaneous and one hundred percent credible nuclear strike devastating him. How could one achieve this capability with technology, laying bare installations on the surface of the land? The best way would be to deploy the nuclear deterrent from below the impregnable reaches of the oceans. It is here that the needle in the haystack is impervious to detection, especially when one does not know where the haystack is! The SSBN submarine armed with nuclear tipped Submerged Launch Ballistic Missiles would provide India the strategic sea-based deterrent. The invulnerability of the nuclear submarine makes it an ideal platform, especially in our scenario with our declared nuclear doctrine. The suitability of the sea-based deterrent has been accepted by all nuclear weapon states and more than half of the US and Russian missiles are carried in their SSBNs. India in any case, has no option but to develop this capability, in view of its declared "no first use" principle. This is one of the way in which the nuclear deterrence would work with our adversaries, thereby preventing war and ensuring peace and stability.

A look at the emerging maritime warfare in the major navies of the world shows that with the availability of high technology sensors and weapons, the reach of the maritime forces has increased considerably. As far as the major navies of the West are concerned, with the end of Cold War, sources of threats at sea has reduced. In future it is anticipated that wars would be fought along the littoral, an area around 200 miles off the coast and a similar area inland. The United States Navy is being shaped to play an important role in the littoral warfare by projecting power ashore on land. In their view operations would be conducted under four basic areas, first being the dominant maneuver where forces are concentrated from all parts of the globe to bear upon the operational area. This is followed by the second phase in which precision engagement is carried out from platforms at sea on targets on land. In this scenario, the forces at sea have to be fully protected through what is called full dimension protection in all the three dimensions. Operations of this nature cannot be carried out without focused logistics. In general, missions of the navies would most likely continue as at present with emphasis on sea control, presence, blockade, support of land operations, sea based deterrent, power projection as well as peace-time missions of peace-keeping, disaster relief, anti-piracy, maritime cooperation, etc.,

Having briefly stated the emerging trends and their implications, let us now turn to technology that is reshaping maritime warfare. The first of these is stealth. In military combat, the initiative tends to rest with the one who detects the other first. "Stealth" has therefore become a matter of survival for any modern weapon/weapon delivery system/platform as the technology for detection has made rapid advances. In its widest sense, stealth covers not just reducing the chances of detection but also the ability to confuse the enemy to obviate identification of specific targets and masking the true role of the mission. Each element, which provides the enemy with some form of detection and classification must be considered and fully understood if stealth is to be effective. The characteristic signatures of any naval platform which makes it identifiable are, acoustic, radar cross section (RCS), infrared, magnetic, hydrodynamic, wake and extra low frequency electrical (ELFE) emissions amongst others. The platforms, on which any weapons systems are mounted, therefore, need to be designed to have maximum possible stealth features. The next important feature is the Unmanned Air Vehicles (UAVs). The potential of Unmanned Air Vehicles to provide reconnaissance and as a force multiplier would be exploited more and more in future. Such air vehicles could be made smaller and carry all types of radar, IR and other sensors. Similarly the next logical step would be to make these vehicles with stealth features and ability to undertake air-to-attacks. Another area of technology, which has impacted warfare, is the area of ammunition and other disabling mechanisms. The main object in this area has been to increase the destructive power and accuracy of the delivery of the ammunition. Thus, laser- guided bombs were largely used in the Gulf War against Integrated Ground Air Defence Systems. However, their actual probability of kill turned out to be considerably less than what was initially announced. Nevertheless, increase in accuracy and destructive power would enable forces to require much smaller stocks of ammunitions in their inventories in the future. The next generation of "smart" ammunition and missiles are likely to undertake target recognition, identification and assessment in a dense EW environment and counter measures deployed by the target against the attack. In addition to the lethal ammunitions non-lethal or less than lethal weapons are another category of successor generation imposition techniques. Finally we have sensors and related situation awareness aids which have now the capability of providing the commander at sea with the comprehensive view of the tactical situation. These systems are based on extremely high- resolution mapping and weather sensors. Space-based and ground display systems in combination would also allow worldwide monitoring of weather. In addition, major break-through has been achieved in enhancing capabilities of sensors mainly through high speed processing. Such systems would also include not only threat related data but information on one's own ships, aircraft and submarines operating in the same or nearby theatres. Information about the enemy of any type from any source would be compared with the database of the enemy's information procured during peacetime. Information dominance would play a crucial role in war at sea.

What are the implications of these technologies and what would be their affect on force levels in general? As far as numbers are concerned, size of most navies would reduce though combatants, as individual units, would have far greater capability. Most of the development would be budget driven. The main emphasis would be in downsizing manpower and reducing lifecycle costs. Due to increased level of threats, surface combatants would need to have greater survivability. There would be increased emphasis on the sub-surface element of the force structure though surface ships would continue to have their importance from the point of view of visibility. The future warfare is also likely to be conducted with greater emphasis on joint operations. It would not be a farfetched scenario where a submarine or a ship at sea under the directions of an airborne early warning and control aircraft operated by the air force is deployed for striking a land target in support of army operations. In addition, with greater access to information, the side that has dominance of information will gain. The re-projection time of force levels for operations would also be minimized.

In the area of research and development, our emphasis would need to be placed on acquiring such technologies, which are not likely to be made available to us through normal means. Due to obvious reasons, access to these technologies would be restricted and in some critical areas it would need indigenous effort to develop them in-house. The first task effort would be to identify technologies specific to naval applications, which would be needed in the future. The system of developing indigenous weapons and sensors is too time consuming. Advances in technology are so rapid that most of the time obsolescence overtook our projects. Our system would have to change to adapt to such challenges. It would also be necessary for us to invest more in R&D in-house. While doing so we should not hesitate to exploit such off-the-shelf technology, which meets our requirements. The defence production in the future would need to be taken up as a national effort in partnership with the private sector.

The main effect of Revolution in Military Affairs on maritime warfare would be in the field of Information Technology, which would dominate the concepts and tools of warfare. Maximum effect would be felt in the areas of force multipliers such as the man behind the gun. In addition there would be a need to maximize situation awareness through information dominance. To exploit full potential, all maritime forces operating on surface, below and above surface would have to be networked with space and shore. In the field of weapons, trends indicate that capability of forces at sea is being augmented to enable fire support from sea. Air-surface attack capability of aircraft, operating from aircraft carriers, would also be made available to ships and submarines by a family of precision guided munitions systems. Such weapons would be interchangeable from one launcher to another. In addition, most of the weapons would be carried in vertical launchers inside the ships. In the area of anti-missile defence, protection would be enhanced through signature reduction and anti-missile missile systems. For the design of production of platforms, the main thrust areas are reduction in cost through improved operating, manning and support systems along with series production and modular construction. Their manning levels would also be reduced and condition based monitoring systems would be inducted to improve reliability.

The surface platform would have multi role capability. Other important features would be in the area of electric driven propulsion, open architecture and modular replacement of systems, improved survivability, reduced signature, automated damage control with intelligence sensors and actuators and use of composite materials. Electric propulsion is being favoured since advances in gas turbine technology have reached their saturation. This type of propulsion also enables reduction in noise signature. The aircraft carrier might well be without a catapult with greater emphasis on STOL and VTOL aircraft of improved performance. Mine warfare has also gained considerable importance. It's cheap and poses great obstacle to shipping entering harbours as well as in amphibious operations. This type of warfare is extremely important in our case as our western adversary has limited ports and could be effectively contained bottled inside by mine warfare.

Some factors that should be kept in mind while planning force structure of the navy would now be examined. The capabilities of the force structure would depend on the quality and type of information available to the force structure. The battle of the future would be dominated by information and we must prepare to induct systems, which provide this capability in the force structure. All force levels are likely to be networked with each other as well as with the shore and space thus drawing on the strength of the structure as a whole. The subsurface element would continue to receive greater priority though a reasonable balance would be maintained in the types of dimensions. The force would be equipped with the family of missiles having improved response time and accuracy, greater volume, longer range and low cost of weaponry. The platforms would have stealth futures and operate UAVs to obtain not only tactical reconnaissance but in near future, air-to-surface capability. To counter threats posed by submarines, there would have to be strong ASW counter measures and capability with air element. Intelligence about the enemy would be an essential feature provided to the forces in real time. For this long range maritime surveillance would be critical to fleet operations, both in offence and defence. The force structure would take into account such defensive measures to counter its vulnerability to space-based surveillance systems, information warfare, which can disrupt flow of information; smart missiles and strong NBCD counter measures. Other factors affecting the force structure could be briefly stated as follows:

- Force mix would be based on types of missions and tasks expected.
- Integral air capability in Fleet operations would be crucial for surveillance, strike, defence and anti-submarine operations.
- Space would have to be exploited to enhance capability, especially for reconnaissance and intelligence gathering purposes.
- Balance between dimensions would be maintained with slight shift towards subsurface.
- Number of small ships might have to be reduced by taking full advantage of the force levels of the coast guard.
- As budget tends to constrain development, over all numbers may get reduced but capability as a whole would be enhanced through networking and acquisition of force multipliers.
- Survivability of the surface element would need to be specially catered for.
- Affordability would become an important consideration.
- Ability to carry out joint operations with the army and air force must be built into the force structure.
- Force structure would have appropriate mix of space based surveillance systems, real time and secure communication systems, stealth platforms, UAVs , smart ammunition and information technology.
- Sea based nuclear deterrent would be the only viable strategic option of the future.

It is our view that indigenous warship building would gain momentum in the future and the capital budget could rise to nearly Rs17,000 crores in 2020. We must be fully prepared to enhance the ship-building and ship design capacity to meet the requirement of the future. A 10-15 years ship building plan must be put in place. This imposes serious responsibility on maritime community as a whole, who would have to spearhead such a growth. We have been unique in having achieved an in house design capability. We must build on these foundations laid by our worthy predecessors. The quality of design work must also be improved and should include a research and development element in platform design, hull forms, hydrodynamics, structures, materials etc. In this scenario building indigenous capability to meet the entire spectrum of naval weapons and equipment would not be easy. Under these circumstances we would have to fall back on our strength of innovation and integration of systems from various sources. The platform designs of the future must provide greater multi role capability, improve stealth, higher speed, greater survivability and weapon load. The new designs would have to focus on ergonomics, friendly operator/maintainer features, lessons learned from previous ship construction projects especially the experience of operating in Indian conditions. The designers would also have to focus on new materials and learn from previous designs. Our shipyards have achieved considerable growth in the past decades. However, we must accord greater priority to reduce build time in ship construction programmes, experiment with new types and methods of construction, design to cost and decrease re-work and overheads. If we are to succeed in our export drive, our shipyards would have to become more competitive and build ships to international standards. Naval architects have great responsibility in this endeavor through warship overseeing teams. The quality, productivity and reliability of the output of the shipyards must improve so that the navy obtains best value for its money. Shipbuilding has to be given the rightful place of a strategic industry in the country.

Development of the Indian Navy has shown that there was a high growth phase in the 50s, perhaps on the advice of our erstwhile rulers who understood the importance of sea power far better. This was despite the fact that in their view the Indian Navy was to perform a secondary role to that of the Royal Navy. In fact, the first fifteen years after Independence saw as many ships added to the fleet as in the next three decades. There was a slump after 1962. This was mainly due to country's preoccupation with the land borders. However, to some extent it was also due to the fact that the navy did not exert itself in the conflicts of the 60s. The political leadership either did not know what to expect from the navy or thought that it would have an insignificant role to play in the event of a conflict. But everything changed in 1971. The Navy did the nation proud. Its bold initiative of taking the war to the adversary's citadel, the choking off of the Pakistani fleet in the west and cutting off of all aid to the eastern wing of Pakistan as well as Pakistan army's retreat from Bangladesh are now a matter of history. Since then, slowly but surely the importance of the maritime dimension in national security has been accepted as an essential ingredient. Deploying the eastern fleet on the western sea-board with the western fleet had a salutary effect during the Kargil operations.

Navies, world over, have long gestation periods. In our case it takes a bit longer but the Indian Navy's faith in self-reliance has paid rich dividends. Considerable resources have been wisely invested in warship design and building. We have the capability, the expertise and infrastructure. We need to improve our efficiency. The neglect of the 1985-95 decade seems to have ended. We do not need much more resources than what have been allocated but we do need the will to carry it through the next decade or so. Finally, if we wish to play our rightful role in the comity of nations, we must stand up and be counted. For that, both economic and military strength is necessary and the navy an ideal instrument. The essential prerequisites to be powerful at sea in the new century would be the mastery of technologies to harness the power of the oceans. Work on this cannot be delayed and the foundation of our sea power should be laid in our Research Labs and Technology centres.

In conclusion it can be said that India has all the attributes and can become a great sea power. It must organize itself to look at the oceans, encompassing exploitation of the maritime resources, enacting legislations, development of infrastructure and appropriate technologies and addressing political, economic and other dimensions of maritime security in a holistic manner. If India visions itself to be regional power, it will have to be a strong maritime power. It will have to allocate sufficient resources to the maritime sector and create a more coordinated and effective management structure at the apex level. There is an urgent need to establish an ocean commission which can coordinate the maritime aspects of some 13 ocean related ministries.

With the spread of globalization maritime security is becoming more crucial to the development of the nation. Maritime trade and transportation is assuming greater importance in view of their central role in economic growth of nations. While there will always be a certain amount of competition in international relations, common threats are compelling nations to find new ways of cooperating in the maritime dimension. India will emerge as an important player in the Indian Ocean in the future and she is geographically well situated to influence the trade routes. She would therefore be in an ideal position to ensure that good order continues to prevail on the ocean routes. It will be in the interest of maritime nations of the Indian Ocean as well as in the rest of the world, that their trade continues to flow without hindrance and interruption. Either alone or in company of like-minded nations as a coalition, India could ensure that sea lines of communications, from Gulf of Hormuz to Malacca Straits are kept safe and secure through the deployment of her naval strength by undertaking joint patrolling. Here, it would be necessary to emphasize the benevolent nature of Indian political thought. The growing strength of Indian Navy should be seen more as a sign of stability in this region rather than means of establishing hegemony. Threats posed by terrorism and piracy at sea affect all maritime nations and would therefore need to be responded to collectively on a regional basis. Before such arrangements take shape, it is necessary that political hurdles be removed. This is not an easy path since Asia is politically, ethnically and economically disparate. Yet for the well-being and greater good of people, individual political objectives may get submerged in the larger good and nations may increase their economic cooperation. Once economic ties strengthen, political differences can be more easily bridged and a new framework of maritime cooperation and security established. The Indian Navy in the future is expected to provide the bedrock of stability in the Indian Ocean region.

SEVEN

Role of Air Power

INTRODUCTION

The Gulf War in 1991, the use of NATO air strikes in Kosovo and the highly successful air campaign against the Taliban in Afghanistan, have focused attention on the criticality of air power as an instrument of national security and achieving international military/security objectives.

The military aim of the Gulf campaign was to liberate Kuwait and force the aggressors back to Iraq. Overall, the Coalition air campaign accumulated a total of 109,876 sorties over the 43-day war. Iraqi air defence, command and control systems and air assets were targeted at the beginning of the campaign. Thereafter, the entire campaign was conducted under conditions of air superiority. Nearly 60,624 tonnes of ordnance was dropped over a one and a half month period. After a 38-day air campaign, the ground offensive began with the ground forces

1 Indian Nuclear Doctrine by NSAB.

over-running the Iraqi Republican Guards within 100 hours. Today's operational planners will appreciate the complexity of prioritization and planning an air campaign consisting of nearly two and a half thousand sorties per day operating from different airfields thousands of kilometers apart located in different countries, differnent aircraft carriers and interspersed with cruise missile attacks! This was possible using modern day C4 assets, an integrated planning mechanism and the concept of a single component commander for all air and space assets.

The recent US led campaign against Taliban forces in Afghanistan has once again demonstrated the vital role of air power in modern day warfare. Even while many traditionalists were deliberating on the limitations of air power, the Taliban collapsed under the sheer weight of incessant air assaults. Undoubtedly, as in the case of the Gulf War, the final task must perforce be accomplished by forces on the ground, but this only when air power has ensured that the cost of committing ground troops is minimal.

The earlier NATO air campaign in Kosovo is a contrast. When the threat of use of air power did not result in President Milosovich backing down, an air campaign was launched. The objectives set out by NATO for the air campaign were political rather than military since the US President had ruled out the use of ground troops. This clearly put air power in a solo performance role, one for which in spite of its great potency, it is not ideally suited. With over 1,000 aircraft committed, the campaign lasted for nearly 11 weeks somewhat longer than anticipated.

Undoubtedly this was an air campaign that excelled in its precision, compelled, as it was to ensure as little collateral damage as possible. Infrastructure targets in the midst of cities were engaged and destroyed and while some 30 cases of collateral damage were recorded, in the overall context this figure is low. The sheer intensity of NATO air power did finally result in a political agreement. Whether or not this was cost effective use of air power is a debatable point. There is, however, little doubt that the political objectives set out by NATO were achieved.

In 1998 when two embassies of the US were targeted by terrorist bomb attacks in Nairobi and Dar- e- Salaam causing considerable loss of life, the US responded with cruise missile attacks against targets in Sudan and Afghanistan. This was a new determinant in the use of air power. The significance of these attacks in politico-military terms is that it was the first time that unmanned air power had been used to engage targets across international frontiers in times of peace. It was also the first instance of selective use of air power to engage terrorist targets perceived to be against a nation's interest. While peacetime use of unmanned vehicles for reccee purposes across international frontiers has been a common practice, it is for the first time that unmanned strike vehicles have been used. A window has been opened to suggest that air power can be used in peace time across international frontiers to further perceived national security interests. It would appear that in circumstances such as these, cruise missiles have been placed in a threshold lower than manned fighters and surface-to-surface missiles.That such missiles can be launched from land, sea and air gives them unfettered reach and operational flexibility.

INDIAN PERSPECTIVE ON AIRPOWER

A new chapter has opened up in the security calculus of India with the country opting for a policy of nuclear deterrence. It naturally follows that air power is destined to play a predominant role, if this policy is to enhance rather than reduce national security. Considering that Indian security planners have traditionally failed to understand the strategic and tactical potential of air power, it is worth looking at India's past record.

In the first Kashmir war with Pakistan soon after independence, the IAF was used. Fighters provided support and transport aircraft opened new frontiers of high altitude operations with the Dakota. The IAF was small and air power as is presently understood still in a nascent stage. Reaction to a desperate situation rather than any philosophical approach to air power determined its use. Even then, air power made a crucial difference to the defence of the Kashmir Valley.

In the 1962 Indo-China conflict, air power was not used for fear of widening the conflict. An ideal opportunity for use of air power was lost out of sheer ignorance of security matters. With IAF air-bases close to the ground fighting, vulnerability of Chinese logistic lines and the distance and altitude limitations of Chinese airfields, the IAF would not only have pulverized the PLA forces, but perhaps brutally undermined the confidence of PLA for decades to come. Historically this marks the start of a cautious philosophy by the Indian establishment towards use of air power, a mindset that continues to haunt the Indian security establishment.

During the post 1962 period, the IAF was still in the process of being augmented when the Ind-Pakistan war of 1965 commenced with PAF's surprise attack on India in September. India, including its Air Force were not ready for such an attack. As reported by observers, the IAF lost more aircraft than the smaller Pakistan Air Force and there was considerable comment on the lack of coordination between the ground and air force.

In the Indo-Pakistani conflict of 1971, the IAF outnumbered the PAF in the east and neutralized it, thereafter supporting the Army and contributing to its success. In both east and west, the IAF went to great lengths to meet all army requests, and in some cases complained that the army asked for air support when it could have done the job itself. The 1971 war was probably the high point for the IAF.

Between 1987-1990 the IAF participated in the 'Indian Peace Keeping Force' in Sri Lanka. While transport aircraft ferried troops and logistics in support of the operation, it was the helicopters, which were integral to the army's operations including providing fire support. This major contribution has surprisingly not been given credit either by the army or the IAF resulting in the absence of use of IAF helicopters in the decade old low intensity conflict against terrorists in J&K.

In 1988, when rebels attempted to overthrow the government of Maldives and the latter approached the Indian government, it was the

IAF's strategic heavy lift capability that enabled a battalion of troops to retrieve the situation.

Pakistani intrusion into the Kargil sector went unobserved primarily because the IAF was not integrated into peacetime operations towards border management, a task left solely to the BSF and the army. Once again, there was clear reluctance towards employing air power during the initial stages of ground operations. Had this not been the case, army casualties would certainly have been minimized.

Historically, the Indian security establishment has to this day not comprehended the value of air power in contributing to enhanced national security both in defensive and offensive terms. This in turn has left various instruments of national air power divided and the IAF in particular under- funded far below the potential that national security compulsions demand. With the nation having declared itself a nuclear weapon state with a commitment not to resort to first strike, the primary responsibility of protecting the nation from nuclear attacks, both missile or aircraft borne and to protect the second strike forces falls squarely on the doors of air power. From all accounts, this urgency does not appear to be shared by guardians of the Indian security establishment.

INDIAN AIR FORCE-DOCTRINAIRE OVERVIEW

Since the Indian Air Force is the primary instrument of national air power, it is worth exploring what its own contribution has been towards enhancing national security and enabling air power to be given its rightful place.

Longterm planning has been one of the strong points of the IAF. While few in governance and indeed sister services, have understood the far-reaching impact of air power's military potential, the IAF has steadfastly displayed vision, in anticipation of potential national security needs. In the fifties and sixties, the IAF could boast of Mysteres, Hunters, Canberras and Gnats in its armoury. These were contemporary weapon systems of the time. At the time, India was one of the few countries developing an indigenous fighter (HF-24). The IAF was well established in north-eastern parts of the country well before the 1962 Chinese invasion, though the decision not to commit the IAF was not of it's choosing.

In the seventies and eighties, major modernization took place with the IAF inducting the Jaguar as a deep penetration strike aircraft and Mirage 2000 a multi role fighter (both with in-flight refueling capability), the IL 76 and MI 26 as strategic lift transports/helicopters respectively and the Mig 25 strategic reconnaissance aircraft. Strings of FBSUs along the entire border were set up to enable rapid response 'close air support' to the ground battle. The phased Air Defence Ground Environment System (ADGES) plan was nearing completion in the west, north, east and island territories, with the peninsula to follow. Looking deeper into the future a Southern Air Command was formed with emerging air power needs across the oceans and island territories in mind. A proposal to build a new fighter base at Andaman and Nicobar Islands was approved by the government and work started before it was halted, leaving only Carnicobar. On the missile front, while much credit has been given to the scientific community, it was IAF's formal Air Staff Targets for the Prithvi and Agni missile systems in early eighties that gave birth to the Integrated Guided Missile Development Programme.

Indian Air Force's vision of the role of air power into the future as also its potential at the time was far ahead of contemporary thinking on national security. As an example, crucial and timely support to Maldives would not have been possible without the IAF heavy lift response.

As aerospace and avionics technology has moved forward, application of air-power assets in the hands of the other services as indeed even police forces has become inevitable. This has not only resulted in blurring of boundaries of roles and missions amongst the three services, but also resulted in institutional rivalries. Recent reports of the long-range Agni being put under operational control of the army merely confirms the confused strategic logic within the Indian security establishment.

The IAF has also not fared too well with Hindustan Aeronautics Ltd. (HAL) and Defence Research and Development Organization (DRDO). It fully supported programmes like the HF-24 and Ajeet and sponsored the LCA in furtherance of indigenous aerospace capability. Yet as a matter of fact though not policy, the IAF was kept out of the LCA programme resulting in a state where the programme's very viability is today under question.

National security is paying a heavy price for such institutional rivalries. Lack of clarity on service roles and missions without an integrated approach to national security results in overlap, under utilization and wastage of scarce defence resources. Also serious operational gaps occur as happened when in mid -eighties, an IAF proposal for additional strike aircraft was countered by a DRDO study, which proclaimed surface-to-surface missiles to be more cost-effective. This was actively supported by the then Army Chief. The IAF lost valuable years in winning this futile argument. Recent press reports have quoted the erstwhile Scientific Advisor to the Government stating that Unmanned Air Vehicles will begin to start replacing fighter aircraft by 2010. One is not privy to IAF's response in this regard, but one thing is sure, it has a battle on its hands for future aircraft inductions! History repeating itself with the exception that these are not actions befitting a nuclear power.

Analysts have long argued about whether the IAF is a tactical or strategic force. To its credit the IAF has never indulged in this theoretical debate. Its Balanced Force concept evolved in the fifties is still the backbone of its force planning. More recently, with rapid advances in aerospace technology and consequent escalating cost of airborne platforms, the IAF has also introduced a philosophy of an optimum blend of high tech/high cost with relatively modest tech/lower cost aircraft. The LCA was conceived in the latter category though later hijacked by the technology hungry scientific community to the former category. A fatal change that may well result in the project's demise.

The core philosophy of the IAF is that flexibility in time, space, reach and firepower are its hallmarks, not any straitjacket definitions or roles. The Balanced Air Force is equipped, trained and adequately innovative to undertake any mission that the call of national security may demand. That the national ethos is one of reluctance to use air power and if forced, only in a limited role is a reflection of the lack of both doctrinaire and operational understanding of air power's potential and role in the minds of the security establishment. With India having declared itself a nuclear state, the doubting Thomas's can no longer confine the IAF to the tactical backyard.

This historical overview is a pointer to the severe institutional contradictions retarding an air force that was well on its way to becoming a truly national security asset in an otherwise deteriorating nuclearised security environment. Much needs to be done to redress some of these imbalances if air power is to play its rightful and indeed central role in the security of a nuclear-armed India.

INDIAN SECURITY MANAGEMENT — WEAKNESSES

"The IAF is a large and professional force. But as reflected in its performance in internal budget battles and the wider political debate, it does not seem to have developed an air doctrine that articulates the importance of air power to the defense of India. Nor has the IAF developed and publicized a concept for the greater employment of air power in the defence of India, which would seem to be a prerequisite to gaining a larger voice in the allocation of resources." This conclusion from a RAND Corporation study aptly sums up the lack of appreciation of the potential of air power within the Indian security establishment. However, the fault is not that of the IAF but the flawed and archaic higher defence organization whereby the services are not included in policy making in matters of defence and security. With authority solely in the hands of non-professional bureaucracy and with the political leadership taking only peripheral interest in matters of defence, those who make policy have just not understood the long-term importance of air power with all its ramifications. Not willing to commit the IAF in 1962 and doing so with some hesitation in Kargil are mere operational manifestations of this weakness.

Worse have been the continuing erosion and parceling out of scarce airborne resources without any operational- analysis and cost-effectiveness criteria.Military strength and the way it is integrated into the decision- making process denote both national deterrent capability and the nations potential to safeguard sovereign interests. This will not be feasible unless the Service HQs are integrated with the Ministry of Defence (MOD) and a Combined Defence Staff concept responsible for integrated operational planning and execution constituted. While inter service/institutional rivalries may still surface, these will then be tempered by professional audit and accountability in the decision making process. This will also obviate weaknesses such as reluctance to commit air power; something that was done in 1962 and nearly happened in the Kargil conflict.

From all accounts available, the recent reorganization attempted appears to be both half hearted and incomplete. While appointment of the CDS is on hold, integration of Service HQ with the MOD has been ignored.

SUMMARY

The over riding philosophy enjoining credible nuclear deterrence with no first use, is the nation's ability to survive a nuclear first strike and retaliate with an effective response, backed by strong conventional air power. These are military roles that fall under the purview of its air force. Effective deterrence means that potential adversaries need to be convinced of survivability of India's retaliatory and response capability including the Command and Control structure. It follows that the potential of the IAF to back this policy must not only exist, but be seen to exist.

It is well known that India's past approach to management of national security and integration of institutions of defence, more specifically those relating to air power, has not necessarily been based on professional security considerations. Unless India is seen to be making radical departures from this approach, countries not favourably disposed will perceive windows of opportunity.

Areas that need a major change are summarized below:

- The recognition that with the nation having declared itself a nuclear weapon state with a commitment not to resort to first strike, the primarily responsibility of protecting the nation from nuclear attacks, both missile or aircraft borne and to protect the second strike forces falls squarely on the doors of air power.
- Formation of an IAF Strategic Command.
- Formation of an IAF Aero Space Command.
- Rationalization of IAF force levels using scientific analytical methods.
- Enhancement of IAF's Information Warfare capabilities.
- Formation of a Joint Air Space Management Agency under control of the Air Force to monitor air space and objects in space.
- Formation of a National Air Guard towards smooth integration of civil air assets during contingencies.
- A review of manpower policies within the air force towards greater operational integration, higher teeth-to-tail ratio and meeting the needs of changing technology.
- Modernizing the IAF with force multipliers and smart systems, including priority towards indigenous development of cruise missiles.
- Tranquility on the Indo-Chinese border or resource constraints must not delay programmes for infrastructure augmentation/build up in the North-East, peninsular India and Island territories, as these are insurance against security challenges of tomorrow.

EIGHT

Internal Security

GENERAL

Internal Security (IS) environments have changed beyond recognition in the post-Cold War period, but the general perception regarding internal security has remained unaltered. Internal Security now encompasses both external and internal threats to a country, besides law and order problems. Time has come not only to redefine the term but also to enlarge its scope to include all the elements which endanger internal security in the present conditions. In the current environment the term internal security should encompass the following:

- State-sponsored and domestic terrorism
- Insurgencies and guerrilla warfare
- All armed movements, indigenous or sponsored
- Narco-Terrorism and connected smuggling activities
- Gun running and illegal manufacture of arms or ammunitions

- Corruption and misgovernance at various levels of administration
- Nexus between politicians and criminals
- Caste and communal politics, which generates internal conflicts
- Deliberate attempts to destablise the country politically and economically, by a hostile country or its surrogates
- Organised Crime in its various manifestations
- Cyber terrorism
- Employment of weapons of mass destruction by terrorists

The ability of a hostile country to mobilise forces, taking advantage of ethnic or religious cleavages, to undermine and destroy the socio-economic infrastructure of a targeted country, without directly using its armed forces, should be considered as a grave security threat. This form of aggression may not be immediately recognized, and remain unchecked till it assumes dangerous proportions. This kind of threat can assume many forms, ranging from attempts of social and political disruption to insurgent-terrorism and armed movements by highly trained surrogates. This type of aggression can prove very effective in destroying the physical and the institutional assets of a state, specially if internal dissensions already exist in its society.

In this paper threats to the internal security of India will be examined in their various manifestations. It is evident that we have largely failed to manage our internal problems efficiently because of lack of political vision and will to deal with the problems. A periodic assessment of means and methods available to the country and their efficacy, is necessary for effective planning. Factors that have direct bearing on the internal security situation and which require immediate attention have been discussed in succeeding paragraphs.

INFRASTRUCTURE

The existing infrastructure is inadequate to meet the current and future challenges posed to our internal security. The law and order keeping agencies are not appropriately organized, they are by and large inefficient and are prone to corruption. A reorganisation of our police forces, changing of archaic laws and review of our judicial system has been long overdue. These aspects must receive immediate attention.

EFFECTIVE INTELLIGENCE

The ability of the modern criminal, militants and insurgents to strike suddenly and then disappear or melt away, can only be countered by a highly efficient intelligence system. An effective intelligence system cannot be established without costs or dedicated men. For effective intelligence operations, the system has to be modernized and manned by highly efficient and dedicated personnel. The intelligence system should be able to anticipate the likely designs of our adversaries and subversive elements operating within the society. Detailed analysis of intelligence reports and coordinated efforts to decipher signs of adverse developments is absent in our system. Despite the reforms suggested by the Group of Ministers on the subject, there are few signs of improvement on the ground. The delays in implementation of reforms should not be accepted.

MORAL AUTHORITY

The moral authority of a government or the legitimacy of its policies has a direct bearing on internal security problems. Principles should not be compromised for the sake of political expediency. To be acceptable to the people, it is necessary that the government retains moral high ground. A government must be able to convince people that its stand on various issues is not only legitimate and honest but is also meant for the general good of the people.

INFORMATION MANAGEMENT

Dissemination of authentic and accurate information to the public and the media is absolutely essential to counter disinformation and false propaganda. Free and fair dissemination of information is vital for establishing the legitimacy of the government's actions.

Planned management of information will involve focused political, economic and ideological thrusts to change the attitude of the people towards important issues. If accurate information is made available to the people, they will come forward to support the national effort. A change is required in the government outlook in the age of electronic media. Reactions, attitudes, behavior and emotions largely depend on the images created by the media. If the media is kept in the dark, it takes recourse to unauthorised sources and dubious means to keep the public informed of various important developments. The consequences are generally damaging for the government and the country.

THREATS TO INTERNAL SECURITY

Terrorism

Terrorism poses the most serious threat to our territorial integrity and internal security. We must recognise this threat in all its manifestations. The modus operandi of terrorist groups, the impact and the consequences of their actions need to be understood fully to defeat them. A national effort is essential in this direction.

The circumstances surrounding cross-border terrorism, narco-terrorism or jehadi terrorism in the current environment and the likely future activities of these organisations have to be anticipated to deter and control terrorism in all its manifestations. If the national goals are clearly enunciated, effective operational plan will be easier to evolve. Various contingencies, which may arise in the future, should be assessed with cogency. We seem to have no central authority to manage counter-terrorism policies or to take a longterm view of terrorism.

Terrorist attacks are becoming increasing lethal, and they now aim to kill maximum number of people. This trend reflects the changing motivations of terrorist groups, and easy availability of sophisticated weapons, around the world. We should develop means and organisations for formulating suitable policies to counter these threats. Acts which are calculated to undermine the confidence of the people, in the government and established institutions of the country, must be resisted with great determination.

Massacre of innocent people is considered perfectly legitimate in the current terrorist ideologies. The targets are chosen for their symbolic value, the assassinations of political opponents or the massacre of the innocent women and children, witnessed in the US, were calculated to spread anger and despair through out the world. India has yet to adopt effective policies to counter such terror tactics. Presently we tend to resort to knee-jerk reactions without cogent planning.

Many terrorist groups are in a position to use biological, radiological or nuclear weapons. These weapons of mass destruction can cause very large number of casualties, immense material damage and can even lead to political destabilization of a targeted regime. Use of a chemical weapon against civilians by the Japanese religious cult 'Aum Shinrikyo' is an example of this kind of attack. A threat of this type can be expected from jehadi terrorist groups operating from Pakistan or Afghanistan. Nuclear blackmail can prove a potent weapon in the hands of a terrorist group to drive a hard bargain and make a country bend to its demands.

Terrorist activity, which is calculated to undermine national will and a government's credibility, when supported or sponsored from another country would require a strong national response. No single ministry or national agency can handle such a challenge in isolation, as it can take varied forms, from random terrorism to mass scale destruction, from jehadi terrorism to narco-terrorism and so on.

As the primary aim of jehadi terrorism is to destabilize and overthrow an incumbent regime and establish an Islamic state in its place, isolating and alienating selected segments of the population generally precede this movement.

The main aim of narco-terrorism is the "use of organized terror to secure control over a state by another state or an organized criminal network to achieve predetermined political, economic or social objectives, through organizational and financial empowerment through drug trafficking".

Both jehad and narco-terrorism attack the socio-political system. High monetary returns enable their organizations to buy government servants, political leaders, even members of the judiciary. They hoodwink people by initiating welfare measures, ostensibly, for the common good of the people. Orphanages, hospitals, schools, even housing schemes for the poor, form part of their tactics to delude the authorities. They field candidates in elections and ensure that some of them enter the government of the country.

State sponsored terrorism involves external terrorist groups, who operate from safe bases established in the sponsoring state. Both indigenous elements and mercenaries are deployed together to create a high level of terror and chaos. In J&K, Pakistan has been sponsoring terrorism through highly trained jehadi groups, who operate from safe bases located in Afghanistan and Pakistan.

Pakistan also trains a number of Kashmiri youths, mainly from the Valley, for terrorism and subversion. Terrorist operations in J&K have acquired the shape of a mini-war, which has no front or rear. The sponsored terrorists are armed with high calibre, state-of-the-art, weapons which include anti-aircraft missiles and rockets. The main thrust of Pakistan-sponsored terrorism in J&K has been to:

- Employ fanatical jehadi–mercenary groups, who are well armed and motivated to attack the Indian Army and the paramilitary forces.
- Indoctrinate Kashmiri youths to raise the banner of Islam and fight against Hindu domination.
- Provide arms and training facilities to the Kashmiri terrorist groups.
- Employ terrorism, in selected parts of India, to divert critical human and material resources from constructive programmes.
- Attack economic infrastructure, across the country, to disrupt industry and trade.
- Instigate religious strife to create chaos and break the political and social cohesion between diverse elements of the Indian society.

- Involve Indian armed forces in tackling internal problems, almost on a permanent basis, to disrupt their training for war

Terrorism when employed as a lethal force targeting the military, socio-political and economic infrastructure of a country constitutes a safe method of waging a war in the nuclear era. The ultimate aim is to upset the regional balance of power by a process of attrition. We should consider operations by highly trained groups, which are employed for long term political objectives of destabilizing and weakening India as acts of war, not merely law and order problems. The immediate objective of the sponsored forces is to gradually erode the authority of India over J&K. In this proxy war, Kashmiri's are being used as gun fodder. India has yet to develop appropriate tactics to deal with this kind of aggression. We still do not appreciate fully the enormous capabilities and resources available to the jehadi forces. Our anticipation of the Pakistani designs has been woefully slow and we are still groping for an effective political and military response.

The government should realise the grave nature of the threat that the country is facing. It should first muster all the national resources to sort out the internal problems of J&K. Once internal problems are out of the way, we can concentrate on external issues more effectively. Pakistan and other jehadis must be considered as one entity in the joint jehadi venture in Kashmir. Their terrorist bases and training establishments must receive due attention of the Indian might in cooperation with the international community. Jehadi terrorism should not be allowed to go on unchallenged, both overt and covert means should be used to attack it. A unique opportunity has presented itself, after the devastating and brutal terrorist attacks on America, to advocate raising an international task force against terrorism.

Insurgencies

In the last three decades threats of insurgencies have increased in our country. These threats have been aggravated due to a peculiar geographic and demographic configuration of the country and its immediate neighbourhood. The ethnic and religious affiliations of the population along the international frontiers facilitate infiltration across the borders. Major disparities in economic conditions and the resources of various countries of the region have led to rivalries and search for methods to achieve equality, even if unfair and unethical methods have to be employed. Our neighbouring countries have often provided arms to the separatists groups in India for weakening India.

Insurgency is the most effective form of armed struggle against an established authority or ruling elite. Insurgents use all possible means, political resources, propaganda and foreign assistance as means of spreading violence against the targeted political system, which they disapprove or consider illegitimate.

Insurgents generally employ terrorism combined with guerrilla warfare to demoralize and harass the government forces. Insurgencies have been categorized according to their political or socio-economic objectives by various scholars. The most common categories are:

- **Secessionist:** The objective is to opt out of the existing political arrangements, religious or economic system. The aim generally is to establish a separate independent state.
- **Reformist:** Their aim is to obtain a larger slice of the economic cake and a higher social status or more political benefits. The reformists, however, do not aim to overhaul the system.
- **Restorational:** An insurgent movement with the aim of restoring the prevailing political or economic system, which according to them has been distorted or disturbed by a ruling elite.
- **Reactionary:** Insurgents who want to hark back to an imagined, golden past. They generally seek to revive the old religious, political or economic practices and systems.

The jehadi movement radiating out of Afghan-Pakistan region defy normal classification but they have borrowed much from the communist revolutionary movements, substituting religion for communist dogma. However they have created a new insurgent terrorist culture, which has caused much blood shed. This movement uses terrorism as the cutting edge to overawe their adversaries, passive spectators and non-conformists.

Guerrilla Warfare

Guerrillas employ highly mobile, lightly equipped groups to confront the superior numbers and better equipment of the governmental forces. To succeed against modern and well-organized armies, guerrillas must acquire popular support and sympathy of the people. Guerrilla forces need favorable terrain to evade superior forces and avoid pitched battles. Guerrillas, unlike the insurgent-terrorists, do not attack common people because their support is important to them. They employ hit and run tactics, to harass and tire the opposing forces, which they cannot hope to defeat in battle. Mountains, fast flowing rivers, deep gorges that do not provide easy access to the regular armies help the guerrillas to keep these forces at bay.

We are mainly concerned here with the guerrilla tactics, which have been used by the insurgents in the North-East and some parts of J&K. In Indian conditions no guerrilla force, even with external support, can pave the way for a political change. Experience of last four decades indicates that insurgent and guerrilla forces have not been able to bring about any political changes in any part of India. However, guerrilla tactics when combined with terrorism often lead to the collapse of the local administrative system. Religious politics, combined with transnational terrorism and guerrilla warfare, can pose serious challenges to the security forces in J&K. We should employ special forces with good knowledge of local conditions, religious and cultural susceptibilities of various regions in J&K to combat this type of enemy.

Armed Movements

Armed movements trigger off religious extremism, terrorism and ethnic conflicts. These movements assume dangerous proportions if they are supported by external forces.

Armed movements lead to internal instability, economic stagnation and ethno-religious strife. They can develop into prolonged "uncomfortable wars" if sophisticated weapons, training facilities and safe havens are provided to the groups waging the war, by a hostile state. Terrorism and illicit drug trafficking invariably follow in the wake of these armed struggles. Coercive violence, ethnic cleansing, displacement of large populations, complicate the internal security situation and the multi-dimensional nature of the conflicts make their resolution extremely difficult. Armed movements in various parts of India have the potential to destabilize the country.

Organized Crime

Organized crime usually encompasses the following activities:

- Narcotic trafficking
- Arms smuggling
- Criminal anarchy created by politico-criminal nexus, linkages with internal and foreign crime syndicates
- Subversion of the economic and financial institutions
- Promoting criminal activities and disorder through bribes and corruption
- Extortion, blackmail, abductions of industrialists and others
- Collaboration with foreign intelligence agencies for monetary benefits

Organized crime, subversive terrorism, and narcotic trafficking go together because there operations are closely linked. Political nexus with crime syndicates are the fountainhead of all corruption and most criminal activities in India. Crime syndicates have established networks all over the country. They have close links with international intelligence agencies, as arms smuggling, subversion and manipulation of financial institutions are some of the activities which are invariably linked with subversive intelligence. Sophisticated means of communications and transportation have created formidable criminal edifices. The system of criminal investigation in our country is obviously not designed to act against this criminal monolith. Organized crime has to be tacked by an integrated system, which can infiltrate into these criminal organizations, anticipate their plans and eventually destroy them. Control of organized crime requires deployment of special agencies, which can cut off their financial support, attack their communication system and sources of weapon supply. A task force approach, dedicated to specified geographical areas may work better than the usual compartmentalized handling of various crimes. Targeting of drug trafficking syndicates or specific drugs, which generate very large sums of monies, must be given top priority.

The new generation of criminals use highly sophisticated methods for drug trafficking, money laundering and smuggling. Our security agencies and legal system have not kept pace with the new methods which are being adopted by organised crime syndicates and terrorists. Needless to say, sound and focused intelligence is the most important factor in the war against organized crime and its collaborators. Innovative concepts of intelligence sharing within the country and with the international intelligence communities are now absolutely imperative.

Criminal-political nexus leads to intimidation of officials and undermine the authority of the government. Corruption in high places and the nexus between politicians and criminals should be recognized as the most dangerous link in the crime chain, which subverts not only the government but most other national institutions as well. An apex body which can coordinate intelligence activities, formulate new procedures and oversee the financial institutions, enforcement and investigating agencies, would be useful to combat:

- Organised crime
- Narcotic trafficking
- Money laundering
- Criminal terrorism
- Gun running and smuggling operations

Caste Wars

Caste wars in Bihar and some other parts of India have degenerated into mindless bloodletting and ethnic cleansing. Murders and violent clashes between armed caste groups hold a new and dangerous threat to our society. The Brahmrishi Sena of the Bhumihars, the Loric Sena and the Srikrishna Sena of the Yadavs and some other senas continue to operate with impunity.

Caste divisions are rigid all over India and now various deprived caste groups have started demanding their rights by force of arms. The higher caste groups are unwilling to accept this situation and have organized themselves into *senas* (armies) to fight back with vehemence. The illegal arms in possession of these *senas* run in lakhs.. Whatever the causes, violence and large-scale disturbances generated by caste wars have disturbed peace in many parts of the country. Constructive programmes and schemes for the upliftment of the poor suffer as maintenance of law and order takes priority over development in these circumstances. The usual approach to use the police to douse the fires has proved ineffective, the friction continues despite all efforts. Caste problems require social reforms, that are long overdue, to reduce caste prejudices and internecine conflicts. The caste problem is gradually attaining dangerous proportions and if it is not controlled immediately it will bring socio-economic progress of many states of North India to a standstill. Caste wars are likely to spread and take the form of a civil war in the next few decades.

Religious Conflicts

Religious biases and communal tensions have increased lately. The rise of Muslim extremism and the communal politics of the radical Hindu groups are largely responsible for this state of affairs. The demolition of the Babri Mosque, the communal conflagration in its wake and the subsequent bomb blasts in Mumbai vitiated the atmosphere beyond redemption. The Temple-Mosque politics has spread communal poison far and wide. It has triggered waves of violence and spread mistrust among a majority of Hindus and Muslims. The declaration of the VHP to start the construction of the Temple in March 2002, on the same site, regardless of the court judgment and the *Chetavani Yatras* which are being organized, may disturb peace through out the country. SIMI, a Muslim youth group which was deeply involved in violent religious politics, has been banned only recently.

Whether it is caste or communal strife, the overall loss is of the country because the economy and the general progress of the country comes to a standstill during such conflicts. A market, or a house or a business premise cannot be categorized as Hindu or Muslim, it is Indian. Destruction of such material assets is always a national loss, not a loss of any caste or community only.

It is necessary to control caste and communal passions to safeguard our integrity and socio-economic well being. Communal and caste politics encourages terrorism and spreads lawlessness, which only helps our adversaries who want to take advantage of religious and caste cleavages to destabilize the country. Politico-social reforms (not only punitive action) are required to control divisive tendencies.

The Naxalite Movement

The Naxalite problem has assumed threatening dimensions in the last three years because of easy availability of sophisticated weapons. A nexus has lately developed between Naxalite groups of Andhra Pradesh, Orissa, Bihar and Uttar Pradesh. The People's War Group (PWG) and the Maoist Communist Centre (MCC) have also established links with the LTTE, Maoist Revolutionary Group of Nepal and some separatist groups of Assam and Nagaland.

The Naxalites groups have lately grown more brutal and bold. They have killed a large number of police personnel, high officials and ministers. They now hold people's courts, collect taxes from the rich villagers and levy fees on mining and forest contracts. A well-coordinated inter-state police operation is required to eliminate this menace, but an organized attempt is not in sight due to petty rivalries between the states and lack of an apex organization to coordinate efforts of various agencies.

Threat from the Air

In December 1995, an unidentified AN 26 aircraft which took off from Karachi, entered the Indian airspace in broad daylight, refuelled at Varanasi and finally dropped ammunition in Purulia (WB). It was intercepted five days later, when it was about to leave the Indian airspace. The hijackers of Indian airline flight IC-814 in December 1999, got out of the Indian airspace without even being challenged. These incidents indicate our vulnerability and a danger of "Twin Trade Tower" type of attack on our industrial towns or government complexes. Besides attacks by larger aircraft, possibility of micro-light attacks on VIP areas also exists. It is not quite clear who guards our inner airspace and how effective that organization is to thwart such attacks.

Weapons of Mass Destruction (WMD)

In the current environment, terrorists and their fellow travellers are making use of new technologies to attack the economic infrastructure of a country. This has been often called the "fourth generation warfare". As this kind of war is waged by non-state actors within a country, it can prove far more damaging than a conventional war. WMD can take many forms but the devices which are normally used are:

- Poisonous chemicals or gases
- Biological weapons, such as disease organism
- Radiation or radioactive devices

India is particularly vulnerable to WMD devices because of overcrowding in its towns, trains and places of worships and entertainment. Use of WMD, besides killing people in large numbers can trigger off political upheavals and lead to large-scale rioting and disorder.

Cyber Terrorism

In the modern age criminal syndicates, terrorists and other subversive elements can wage cyber or netwarfare. The principal threat from cyber-war is to our communication and information systems, particularly those which are used for controlling law and order situations. Netwarfare can be used to spread disinformation, disseminate subversive or communal propaganda. Cyber space management should, therefore, be considered an important component of internal security system.

Crime syndicates and terrorists have succeeded in targeting banks, stock exchanges, commercial and financial institutions in many countries by penetrating their computer system. This technique has helped them in demanding ransoms, blackmailing officials, and spreading other criminal activities through out the country. Trade, industry and markets have also been manipulated through cyber-terrorism in some countries.

NetWare, which is a comprehensive and sophisticated approach, will figure increasingly in promoting societal disorders and law and order problems. Cyber-wars and netwars can be mounted simultaneously and can pose the greatest challenge to our law and order enforcing agencies.

Disturbed Areas

A close watch has to be kept on politically volatile areas of the country. The Northeast and J&K, being the two most sensitive and volatile areas of the country, are discussed here briefly.

The North-East

The seeds of separation of this region from India were sown before Independence. The proposals of autonomous state comprising Lushai hills and Chin hill ranges in Burma were under consideration before 1947. Another proposal, called 'Crown Colony Scheme', joining the hill areas of Assam and Burma was also envisaged at one stage by the British.

The Nagas demanded independence soon after the British left the subcontinent. Intentions to solve the issue were not lacking but the tendency of the government to postpone the issues was apparent. The Nine Point Programme signed between the Government of India and Naga National Council was crafted to postpone the issue of the status of Nagaland for 10 years. The terms of the agreement were kept rather vague for this purpose. In 1956, Phizo announced the formation of a federal government, started collecting taxes from the people and raised a Naga Federal Army. A fierce and relentless struggle has continued in the east since then, in which Indian Army faces highly trained and motivated Naga guerrillas.

The problems of Manipur

In Manipur, UNLF demanded national self-determination in 1964. It established links with Naga and Mizo insurgents, formed *PREPAK*, an urban guerrilla force and started an armed struggle. A new dimension was added to it in 1992 with the fratricidal Naga-Kuki clashes. The disturbances regarding extension of the Naga ceasefire outside Naga areas was a problem of our own making, A clear evidence of our lack of understanding of the complexities of the situation in the North-East.

Militancy in Tripura

The insurgency in Tripura was triggered off because of large-scale influx of Chakmas from Bangladesh. Seng Krak (clenched fist), a tribal militant group was formed to oppose the influx. Later, Tripura National Volunteers (TNV) collaborated with MNF to escalate violence in the state and they specially started targeting the police and Paramilitary forces.

Turmoil in J&K

The first blueprint of waging a non-conventional war in J&K was drawn in 1947-48 by the Pakistan Army. When another determined effort in 1965 to annex J&K also failed, Pakistan embarked on a well-planned proxy war in 1989. The Pakistani designs would not have succeeded if there was firmness in India's policies concerning the political conditions of J&K. Lack of good governance, political ambivalence and corruption at various levels were the main reasons which gave Pakistan a chance to launch the proxy war successfully. Pakistan using its jehadi forces and the turmoil in Kashmir to great advantage is slowly turning it into a religious war. Illegal drug trafficking, arms smuggling, sectarian violence also go on unchecked in these circumstances. Cleavages among various ethnic and religious groups in J&K are some of the most dangerous by-products of this environment.

Army may not be able to restore peace or control the situation created by Pakistan's proxy war unless political and administrative problems are resolved first. It is evident that the improvement in internal situation in Kashmir depends on the following factors:

- Good governance
- A reliable intelligence system
- Efficient and well equipped police forces
- Control of corruption at all levels
- Curbing of drug trafficking and arms smuggling
- A long-term political solution, which satisfies all segments of the population
- Planned economic progress to reduce unemployment and improve the quality of life of the common people
- Effective counter-measures against fundamentalist and separatist propaganda
- Counter-mobilization of the population. This should have been attempted in J&K right from the initial stages of the separatist movement
- Raise consciousness of the silent majority about the futility of the struggle
- Ensure active participation of people in constructive projects
- Initiate widespread welfare measures for families of the victims of terrorism
- Counter separatist propaganda aggressively

THE ROLE OF SECURITY FORCES

The State Police

The primary role must be played by the state intelligence and police forces in maintaining internal security. Their training and the equipping policy, however, need to be standardized to improve efficiency. The present organizations are only suitable for tackling ordinary crimes and keeping an eye on the *goonda* element.

The state police forces are neither organized nor trained to confront the present day criminal elements or handle political or economic unrest. A large percentage of policemen should be armed with non-lethal weapons for crowd control under present conditions. Political leaders of all hues continue to hinder efficient functioning of the police, as long as the appointments and transfers of all ranks, including the IPS cadre, are in the hands of the state governments, this situation cannot be remedied. Senior police officers are generally rendered ineffective because of politico-criminal tie up in the state. The state police and intelligence agencies must be made more independent.

The Central Paramilitary Forces (CPMF)

Presently paramilitary forces are used in scattered sub-units on an ad hoc basis. This effects their efficient and effective functioning. Local authorities generally misuse them for VIP protection etc. There is need of a command authority, which can oversee deployment of CPMF units in various situations. Their strength and deployment should also be determined by this command authority. Their role and the period of deployment in various situations should be reviewed by a central authority and not left to the state administration. It is necessary to ensure proper relief of the units, adequate rest and recuperation, to increase their operational efficiency and discipline. Zonal headquarters can also be established on lines of "army areas or sub-areas" to oversee ground operations and administrative requirements of the CPMF.

The present organization of the Para-military forces is not suitable for counter-insurgency roles. Special Units trained for counter-insurgency operations in varied terrains are required in the North-Eastern theatre and J&K. There is a need to undertake an extensive reorganization of CPMF with a view to:

- Train all-purpose Rapid Action counter-insurgency forces for quick reaction in crisis situations
- Counter anti-national propaganda and carry out welfare work to win over locals and isolate the anti-national elements
- Counter terrorism in an offensive role, instead of manning static post and pickets
- Facilitate collection of real time intelligence in insurgency areas

It is suggested that a CPO or CPMF Forces Committee or Board be established at MHA. The senior most Director General should be the chairman of the joint staff. All policies concerning the role of CPMF in internal security duties should be decided by this committee or board. Rationalisation of procedures for deployment in various states should be standardized by this body.

The next level should be the Zonal Commands. The country should be divided in three or four security zones, accordingly certain CPMF units be placed under command. Allotment of forces on a zonal basis will provide better working conditions and help quick deployment and movement of forces to troubled areas. A joint doctrine for employment of the state police, RR. units (when deployed) and CPMF should be worked out by the MHA. Presently there are serious functional difficulties and avoidable friction. The senior-most officer, regardless to which cadre he belongs, should be in charge, if regular army has not been deployed for internal security operations.

The jurisdiction of the BSF to deal with illegal immigrants should extend to a specified hinter land, where they should be responsible for coordinating the law problem with the local police and civil officials.

Linear and static deployment of BSF units on borders needs to be reviewed. Better mobility and communication systems are required to be provided to the BSF to match their opposite numbers. Company-wise deployment of CPMF units for internal security duties needs to be reviewed as in the prevailing environments a company is no longer a viable operational unit.

The Army

Army has been involved almost on a permanent basis in internal security duties since the 1980's. There is a tendency to insist on the army's employment in restoring ordinary law and order situations, caste and communal disturbances. Army need not be employed for long periods when the civil administration is intact and functioning. Long drawn deployment of the army in insurgency areas may be only accepted in special circumstances, only if the situation and the conditions are not likely to improve because insurgents are too strong or well-armed to be tackled by the state police or the CPMF.

Army's assistance may, however, become unavoidable in the border states where the insurgents have external support and safe havens across the international borders. RR units working in conjunction with the local police or the CPMF should be able to bring most situations under control. The role of the army should be limited to remote jungle or mountainous areas where chance of collateral damage to the civilians and their property is minimal.

Internal security operations are manpower intensive. This necessitates deployment of large number of front line troops for operations. Raising more RR or paramilitary units can solve this problem. Experience shows that lightly equipped forces with local knowledge are better suited for counter insurgency and counter terrorist operations than the regular army units. The regular army units can be better used for blunting an offensive mounted by the insurgent forces.

Procedures and rules for calling out the army units should undergo a radical change. Large-scale deployment of the army should only be sanctioned by the central government for specified periods. Fresh sanction should be made mandatory after three months of deployment.

ROLE OF THE GOVERNMENT

Essential Counter Measures

It is necessary for the government to institute measures, which will assist in maintaining internal security and controlling the lawless elements. Some factors which require urgent attention are:

- Establishing good relations between the government and the people.
- Gaining confidence of the people by resolute and firm action against criminal and lawless elements.
- Constituting a single authoritative body which can take a holistic view of the internal security environment.
- Initiation of welfare measures, improvement in public works, health and education programmes, providing more avenues of employment to the people which will help in restoring peace.
- Taking effective steps to end corruption in public life.
- Showing political capacity for making far-reaching changes in procedures. Taking innovative political measures to improve the internal security environments.

EXECUTIVE SUMMARY

- Internal problems can endanger national security more critically than external aggression. Domestic problems affect a very large number of people. According to various reliable estimates more than 50 % of our districts are affected by some kind of organised violence and conflict or the other.
- The nexus between organized crime and politicians has grown by leaps and bounds over the years and now poses a grave threat to

the security, progress and economic well being of the country. This problem must be tackled on a war footing.

- Sharp decline in moral standards and gradual deterioration in administrative efficiency, increase in train accidents, cheating on a mass scale, which were never witnessed before in our country, have now become everyday occurrences.
- Caste, religious and ethnic conflicts must be controlled by creating mass awareness about the damage these conflicts are causing to the country. Religious fundamentalism has taken a new and more dangerous form. This trend should be curbed with an iron hand.
- Unconventional tactics, non-traditional policing methods are necessary to avoid harsh measures against the people. Laws should be tough but their applications must be fair and transparent. The legitimacy of the government and its intentions should never become suspect. The will of the government to maintain law and order regardless of the diverse pressures must be clearly demonstrated in all circumstances.
- Infrastructure required for combating terrorism, insurgencies and organized crime must be strengthened without delay. A country cannot contain internal threats without developing the required infrastructure for combating subversion, criminal activity, militancy, terrorism and insurgency.
- The proposal of setting up of a federal agency to deal with the offences which endanger national security must be pursued with some urgency in view of the grave terrorist threats which the country is facing today.
- Ability to anticipate events by reading the telltale signs which precede violent movements, insurgencies and terrorism should be developed as a special discipline, distinct from gathering of normal intelligence. The likely future actions of jehadis, and mercenaries must be watched carefully.
- In the present environments police alone cannot ensure security either of the human resources or the economic infrastructure of the state. A central task force, with specifically trained personnel

for the various tasks involved, should be made available to the states when required.

- The civil police and the armed police units in the states and their officers are generally under the influence of radical political parties or powerful political bosses. Their efficiency and discipline is poor because they are involved in local caste or communal politics. Frequent inspections by senior officers from the Center may help improve their morale, discipline, professional efficiency, training, and fitness for strenuous duties.
- The command and control of CPMF must remain centralized during internal security duties. Their employment should be decided by their own senior officers and not by the DG of the state where they are deployed. CPMF should only be employed when the state police has failed to control the situation.
- Presently the police forces are neither trained or equipped for their task. The present day criminals, insurgents, terrorists and mercenaries are far better armed and organized than the police forces. Special police units are, therefore, required to deal with these elements. In the prevailing circumstances controlling political violence and public unrest also require specialization to reduce civilian casualties.
- Well-trained, suitably organized, composite police forces of adequate strength should be raised in every state under a uniform policy agreed among the states and the Center. A longterm and holistic view of all internal security problems should be taken and procedures for coordination between CPMF, RR and other armed elements of the state police should be formalized.
- Raising of requisite number of RR and other Paramilitary units trained and equipped for counter insurgency and counter terrorist operations is necessary to free the army from internal security duties. Several rapid action units, trained to deal with crisis situations may be formed. High mobility and sophisticated communication network will be essential for these units.
- The situation prevailing in J&K, Assam and some other states in

the North-East demands well equipped and specially trained counter-insurgency-paramilitary contingents. These should be specially equipped, highly mobile, lightly equipped units, which can effectively combat terrorists and insurgents.

- It may be necessary to make a distinction between internal security and "Internal Stability Operations". In internal stability operations surrogates of a foreign power are invariably involved. internal stability operations should therefore be considered a separate category and not a part of an ordinary internal security situation.
- Unified commands have not functioned properly. Employment of senior military commanders as advisors diverts their attention from vital operational tasks, as witnessed in J&K. It may be better to establish joint operational headquarters functioning side by side rather than an ineffective unified command.
- The problems of the North-East and J&K have remained unsolved mainly due to insensitive attitude of the Centre towards these regions, besides bad governance and widespread corruption in these regions.
- The governments of the North-Eastern regions and the government of J&K have not been in control of the situation, being non-representative in character. Insurgency has also become a lucrative business for politicians and bureaucrats.
- The situation on the ground has taken a turn for the worse because government schemes have never been implemented properly. Many innovative schemes, announced by the Centre during the last decade, also did not work because of lack of proper implementation.
- Mobilization of people against insurgents has not even been attempted. Lack of clarity, gross inefficiency and mismanagement at the grass roots keep the pot boiling in the North-East and J&K.

DETAILS OF INSURGENT AND TERRORIST GROUPS ACTIVE IN INDIA

APPENDIX TO CHAPTER 8

PAK-SPONSORED GROUPS

Hizb-ul-Mujahideen (HuM)

- Year of formation: 1989
- Headquarters: Muzzaffarabad in Pakistan Occupied Kashmir(PoK)
- Supporters: Jamaat-e-Islami, Inter Services Intelligence Directorate, (ISI of Pakistan)
- Headquarters: Islamabad
- Aim: Merger of J&K with Pakistan
- Leadership: Maulvi Yusuf Shah and Syed Salahuddin

Lashkar-e-Taiba (LeT)

Militant wing of Markaz-e-Dawa-Wal-Irshad (MDI), it was formed during Afghan resistances in the 80s. The cadres mainly consist of Afghans and Pak nationals. The group receives funds from Saudi Arabia and was inducted into the Kashmir valley in 1994.

- Origin: Established in 1993
- Headquarters: Muridke near Lahore. It has 50 other offices in Pakistan
- Objectives: To establish the rule of Allah throughout the world. Fighting a holy war against India. Use J&K as a gateway into India for liberating the Muslims of India
- Supporters: Ahle Hadis and, ISI of Pakistan, Wahabi Movement of Saudi Arabia
- Leadership: Hafiz Mohammed Saeed

Harkat-ul-Mujahideen

- Origin: October 1993
- Main Offices: Islamabad and Lahore
- Leadership: Fazal-ul-Rehman and Abdul Rashid

Originally formed as Harkat-ul-Jehad-e-Islami in early eighties. The group split in 1985 into Harkat-ul-Jehad-e-Islami and Harkat-ul-Mujahideen. The two reunited to form Harkat-ul-Ansar, in October 1993. When banned by the US in 1997, it changed back its name to HUM. Maulana Masood Azhar formed Jaish-e-Mohammad as a splinter group of HUM in Jan 2002, after his release from an Indian prison in exchange for the hijacked Indian Airlines plane and its passengers who were held as hostages by Pak-based hijackers.

Al Badr

- Origin: Formed in 1998
- Head Office: Muzzaffarabad (PoK)
- Objective: Merger of J&K with Pakistan

The aims of all these groups are:

- To establish global supremacy of Islam
- Liberate Muslim majority areas of the Subcontinent
- Merger of J&K with Pakistan

OTHER PAK-SUPPORTED GROUPS ACTIVE IN J&K

- All Umar Mujahideen (AUM)
- Islami Jamaat-e-Tulba(IJT)
- Islamic Students League (ISC)
- Jamaat-e-Islami (JI)
- J and K Liberation Front (JKLF)
- J and K National Liberation Army (JKNLA)
- J and K Students Liberation Front (JKSLF)
- Muslim Janbaz Force (MJF)

- Op.Balakote a part of Muslim Mujahideen (MM)
- Tehrik-e-Jehad-e-Islami (TNJF)
- Dukhtran-e-Millat

Markaz-e-Dawa Wal Irshad (MDI) — A CENTRE FOR TRAINING JEHADIS

The center was established in 1987 in Muridke (Lahore) with an avowed objective of preparing a force to wage jehad against non-Muslims and supporting liberation movements of Kashmir, Palestine, Bosnia etc. The center was co-founded by Prof. Zafar Iqbal and Hafiz Mohammad Saeed.

ACTIVE NAXALITE GROUPS

Naxalite movement originated in Naxalbari (WB). Charu Majumdar was its main motivator. Currently there are at least 40 Naxalite groups active in the country. Among these, the PWG and the Maoist Communist Group (MCC) still adhere to the concept of annihilation of class enemies. Currently Andhra Pradesh is a major center of Naxalite activities.

The MCC was formed in the early 1970s in Bahragora (now in Jharkhand) close to Midnapore district. MCC is popular with the poor in the remote areas of Bihar and Jharkhand because of the total collapse of the social and administrative systems there.

Outlawed in mid-1987, following the massacre of 42 Rajputs in Delelchak and Baghaura villages of Aurangabad district in Bihar, the MCC has, however, established supremacy over other revolutionary groups operating in central and south Bihar. In the early 1990s, it had completely undermined the administration of Bihar's southern district of Chhatra.

The People's War Group (PWG), of Andhra Pradesh, was formed in 1975 by Kondapalli Seetharamaih. It has taken the name 'People's War' (PW) after its recent merger with the Communist Party of India (Marxist-Leninist) Party Unity.

PW faction of West Bengal is attempting to create a corridor of influence running through Chattisgarh, Andhra Pradesh, Orissa, Bihar and West Bengal to south Nepal, where the PW, MCC and the Communist Party of Nepal (Maoist) hold sway.

INSURGENT ORGANIZATIONS OPERATING IN THE NORTH-WEST

The ULFA — Assam

The birth of The United Liberation Front of Assam (ULFA) can be traced to the anti-foreigners movement led by the students of Assam under the aegis of the "All Assam Students Union" (AASU) from 1979-1985.

ULFA was established in April 1979 to wage an armed struggle to liberate Assam from the "exploitation by India" and to create an independent, socialist Assam. The founders of ULFA were Arbind Rajkhowa, Golap Barua (alias Anup Chetia), Pradip Gogoi and Paresh Barua (head of the armed wing).

UNLF — Manipur

Nearly two decades after Independence, in 1964, Arambam Somorendra formed the United National Liberation Front(UNLF) in Manipur to demand "national" self determination.

PLA AND PREPAK — Manipur

In 1978, Bisheshwar formed the People's Revolution Army (PLA) in Manipur. With the formation of PLA and the People's Revolutionary Party of Kangleipak (PREPAK), an urban guerilla force ('Clenched Fist'), violence escalated.

Tripura — URA — UPJATI JUBA SAMITI

TUJS aims to secure the creation of an autonomous tribal district council under the Sixth Schedule (by amendment of the constitution), restoration of tribal Lands alienated to non-tribals and recognition of

"Kok Borok" in roman script as an official language. In 1979 another group, the Tripura National Volunteers (TNV) began to indulge in violent acts. Two other organizations, All Tripura Tribal Front (ATTF) and the National Liberation Front of Tripura (NLFT) emerged in 1988. There was no ideological commitment, the main motivation being make quick money by extortion, kidnapping and highway robberies.

ALMA & HYNNICH ACHIC LIBERATION COUNCIL — Meghalaya

Growing corruption and unemployment has given rise to two militant groups, ALMA and HALC. Both these groups are accomplices of the NSCN (IM).

NSCN (IM) and NSCN (K) — Nagaland

The emergence of Bangladesh after the 1971 Indo-Pak war changed the course of the insurgency not only in Nagaland but in the other tribal areas as well. The rebels had lost their bases in erstwhile East Pakistan. The surrender of the splinter group headed by Scato Swu and Zuheto and the renewed offensive by the security forces forced a section of the underground Nagas to reach an agreement with the government. The outcome was the Shillong, Accord of 11 November 1975.

The agreement, however, failed to bring peace to Nagaland, mainly because it was signed by a segment that did not represent Naga National Council (NNC). The agreement was repudiated by the group led by Issac Swu and Muivah. Together, they formed a new party, the National Socialist Council of Nagaland (NSCN) in 1980. The NSCN split vertically eight years later after a bloody feud between the Muivah and Khaplang factions. The NSCN(IM) succeeded in securing fresh support from Pakistan's ISI in the 1990s but NSCN(IM) and NSCN(K) continued to clash. Lately both factions of the NSCN have agreed to a government-sponsored ceasefire and presently an uneasy peace prevails in Nagaland.

NINE

Indian Security Management — Need for Change

THE CHALLENGES

The Nuclear Dimension

- With India having declared a policy of "credible minimum nuclear deterrence with no first use", the defence management structure needs to be reorganized to deliver.
- The major impact of this development is on the air force.
- First, the air force must ensure a credible and rapid response air defence capability to act as a deterrent to any potential nuclear strike-missile or aircraft borne.
- Should deterrence fail, the IAF should have the potential to detect, identify and engage the hostile nuclear weapon system before it finds its target.

- These challenges demand an integrated and rapid response air defence system and not one with divided assets and diluted command and control.
- The final challenge is to retain the capability to absorb a nuclear first strike and then respond in "punitive retaliation with nuclear weapons to inflict damage unacceptable to the aggressor."[1] Considering that for India, submarine-based capability is still many years away, a credible force in the short and medium terms would have to be based on aircraft and missiles.
- The survivability and response capability of nuclear forces and their command and control network should be such that any potential adversary is convinced of the diversity, dispersal, hardness and response capability of the nuclear forces and the supporting infrastructure.
- This requires a strategic air command with the necessary infrastructure, C4I2, weapon systems, training and alert status to execute the tasks.

Revolution In Military Affairs

A combination of information revolution, rapid advances in weapon systems' technology, use of space applications and precision guided munitions all add to the generic RMA process.

- It is now possible to integrate vast amounts of inputs, from intelligence to real-time target information from sources on land, sea, air and space, process it and permit meaningful decision-making at the operational commander level to enable effective and timely response.
- In essence RMA will tend to push the conventional war concept towards prevention through deterrence.
- Yet when limited wars do take place they will be intensive with wide use of high technology weapon systems.
- Those armed forces that fail to keep up with technology will lose their deterrence and fighting edge.

- While the loss of nearly 1200 military lives during the IPKF operations caused barely a ripple in the national conscience, the recent Kargil skirmish saw the nation grieving for every coffin that was received. This was another facet of the information revolution. The lesson US learnt at great cost in Vietnam is only now beginning to unfold in India.
- The next battle will be seen in every drawing room and street corner and the dynamics of casualties and media handling by the services will sway national mood and politics.
- The armed forces can no longer be insensitive to this reality.
- Undoubtedly, this is another compulsion for integrated planning and efficient conduct of joint operations.

Unconventional Warfare

As the possibility of wider conflict recedes, unconventional threats have already begun to take their place.

- Proxy war, unheard of fifteen years ago, has tied up large number of ground forces in J&K. Ever since Operation Blue Star large numbers of army troops have been regularly employed in internal security operations in Punjab, Sri Lanka, Kashmir and Assam.
- Information revolution has opened opportunities for psychological operations.
- As drug trade supports arms for terrorist groups, counter-narcotics operations get drawn into national security planning.
- Most of these unconventional threats pose a direct challenge to the army and ground forces.
- The next area for unconventional warfare is clandestine use of airborne platforms and airspace. As the terrorist attacks in the US demonstrated, possibilities are endless. This has horrifying potential if weapons of mass destruction are added.
- Responses to unconventional threats need to be offensive and pro-active in nature, not defensive and reactive.

The Battlefield

Within the nuclear backdrop with the growing RMA and international sensitivity to potential nuclear flash points, any major conflict of the 1971 variety in the sub-continent now looks somewhat remote.

- Ultimately there may be localized conflicts aimed solely at altering border positions.
- Inherent in such a scenario is the assumption that future conflicts, if any, in the region will be limited in nature with adversaries attempting to ensure that the nuclear threshold is not crossed.
- The nation will need to contend more and more with terrorism and proxy war concepts on the ground, in the air and on the seas possibly with weapons of mass destruction.
- The nuclear dimension now places severe limitations on the strategic use of conventional IAF strike power in a limited conflict scenario. This needs centralized control.
- It will be incumbent upon the IAF and the other services to see that in the event of a limited conflict, the nuclear threshold is not inadvertently approached.
- These are challenges not just for the IAF, but also for national security management as a whole.
- Integrated warfare can no more be treated as a slogan, but an overriding compulsion.

The battlefield of even a limited war will, however, throw challenges not heretofore encountered. Air will be saturated with helicopters undertaking different missions. Air defence weapons from shoulder-fired missiles to long-range ones will be available both with the ground troops and the air force. Fighters providing close support, air superiority and those transiting for deeper strikes, will all wrestle for the same air space. AWACS attempting to exercise command and control will be hunted by enemy's long range SAMs/BVRs. Aircraft will be launched from bases far and wide, all heading for the same battlefield.

This dense air environment will pose serious challenges to the "identification of friend or foe" problem. The position of the ground forces will change rapidly and determination of "forward line of own troops" may not always be easy. Roles and missions will tend to get blurred and even overlap.

- This battlefield scenario poses a challenge to military planners. Vast volumes of information/data some in real time will saturate the command and control system if not channeled properly.
- It requires prudent decentralization and a broader based decision-making process to analyze and filter information for command decisions.
- Sophisticated planning and integration will be the key for best military results and to avoid incidents of fratricide.
- One positive lesson of the Gulf War is that it demonstrated sophistication of a high degree in being able to plan and execute a high intensity air campaign using both sophisticated and conventional weapons and command and control systems.
- Designation of a single commander for air resource applications under the overall task force commander was central to these air operations.
- In spite of this institutionalized approach, instances of serious conflict of approach in use of air resources belonging to different US arms like the AF, Navy, Marines and Army have been widely documented, pointing to powerful parochial interests even within an integrated approach.
- Within the existing single service organization in the Indian battlefield context, optimum and effective use of air power will pose insurmountable problems. Hence, the inevitability of integrated planning and conduct of operations.

Military Roles and Missions

Continuing erosion and parceling out of scarce airborne resources on a subjective basis without any scientific systems analysis and cost-effectiveness criteria merely dilutes overall defence capability. While many of the airborne and operational missions and roles are the preserve of the air force alone, air and space resources are today necessary for other combat arms as well. Faced with imperatives of security and development, the services must factor cost-effectiveness and affordability into their roles and missions. Rationalization should be on lines of specialization, combat effectiveness and cost effectiveness with the underlying philosophy that services retain core areas of competence while integrating core competence of other services in their plans.

In essence all airborne assets (except fleet-borne ones) should belong to the IAF. Similarly while AD assets could be with all the services, those over land and within EEZ must remain under the AD Commander in the Operational Command.

Any review of defence management must, therefore, encompass the following broad concepts:

- Rationalization of service roles and missions based on scientific operation system analysis such that duplication and wastage is avoided.
- Optimum utilization of air assets to benefit from economies of scale and specialization with the air force (with the exception of fleet borne operations).
- Recognition of army and navy's need for airborne missions and decentralizing operational command and control if it furthers operational efficacy.
- Integrated institutionalizing of and protecting national security as a result of Revolution in Military Affairs (RMA) and continuing resource limitations.
- Integrated institutionalizing in response to unconventional threats to national security like terrorism, proxy war, and drug trade, Psychological Ops (PSYOP), etc.
- The final aim must be to provide the nation with maximum operational value for defence investment, not single service-wise but overall militarily.

The Need for Change

This background enforces the need for an urgent change in the higher defence organization of the country. The change should aim to achieve the following:

- Looking at defence-wide solutions rather than viewing them from a single service perspective.
- Best value of security for given investments.
- Decentralization of operational, administrative and financial authority with corresponding accountability.
- Integrated service planning and operations.
- Retaining single service ethos, specialization and loyalties.

The last two decades have been ones of momentous change for militaries across the world. High technologies and corresponding costs together with the end of the Cold War and emerging unconventional challenges forced the armed forces in the industrially advanced countries to look at options for change. They were compelled to introduce tough measures. Recent conflicts have clearly demonstrated the complexity and inescapability of synergy in fighting a modern battle. The Indian armed forces cannot afford to resist change.

Potential of Air Power

It is air power that will deter potential violators of national sovereignty and it is air power in concert with other arms that will punish those who subvert territorial integrity. While the air force must remain the main instrument of air power, the latter constitutes many other facets like aerospace industry, aerospace R&D, civil aviation, the civil aviation infrastructure, resources of space and air arms of the other services.

The challenge to a developing country like India with its obvious security and development imperatives is to integrate, harmonize and deploy these resources for optimum and cost-effective security value, rather than to indulge in needless fragmented and institutionally driven objectives.

IAF Role and Missions

Of the three services, it is the air force that must introduce the most fundamental changes in its operational and organizational philosophy, now that the country has declared itself to be a nuclear state. One major role of the air force will now be to act as an instrument of strategic deterrence and failing this, offence- in a nuclear environment. With C4I2 centres becoming high value targets, air force's role towards Information Warfare also assumes crucial significance. For the policy of deterrence to succeed, IAF's capabilities must be substantial and transparent. Accordingly, the air force will need to rethink its priorities, organization, force structure, staffing, training and personnel policies. Even more crucially, however, the Indian security establishment must seriously introspect on whether past policies of fragmenting air power resources, maintaining an IAF budget share which has its roots in history rather than in overall security terms and generally glossing over air power becoming the predominant source of national security, are viable options any more.

The following have traditionally been designated air force roles. With evolution of technology and enhanced weapon capabilities, there is a tendency for roles and missions to overlap. It is for clarity in planning and cost-effective conduct of operations that the need to clearly define roles and missions is being proposed. The very spirit of the reorganization is to retain specialization within services while decentralizing command and control for operational tasks:

- Strategic Air Operations. nuclear, conventional and surface -surface missiles
- Strategic Reccee including space
- Air Defence control of Indian air space including the TBA and the EEZ
- Tactical Reccee including space manned and unmanned
- Airborne ELINT and SIGINT operations
- Airborne EW operations
- Airborne command and control operations

- Counter Air Operations (aircraft and missiles)
- Close Air Support and Battlefield Interdiction
- Maritime strike within the EEZ
- Strategic airlift
- Tactical and peacetime airlift tasks for all the Services including in the TBA (excluding fleet Ops)
- Management of military space assets with operational control decentralized with the respective users

Reorganization of the IAF

In order to effectively discharge the above designated role and missions, the following changes and additions to the IAF organizational and management structure become essential.

Strategic Air Command

A new Strategic Air Command must be formed as an Air Force Operational Command under the direct operational control of the political executive through the combined Defence Staff Organization. It should consist of long-range missiles, long range strike aircraft earmarked to it, the National Command Post, Field Command Posts and associated C4I2.The air force should be responsible to provide infrastructure, technical, maintenance, logistics and administrative support to the forces of this command. In addition, the air force should be responsible for training of the force to undertake its operational tasks. The majority of personnel would be from the air force, with suitable personnel from the army, navy and R&D to enhance the integrated operational philosophy introduced with the combined defence staff concept. Suitable changes may become necessary when SLBMs are inducted.

The primary role of SAC will be to ensure a credible and effective strategic operational capability, both nuclear and conventional, in order to deter a nuclear attack on India and its Island territories failing which the ability to absorb a first strike and respond with an effective and punishing second strike.

Its conventional roles will include pooling and operating all strategic airborne resources of the country including strategic reccee/lift/strike, ELINT, SIGINT, space borne platforms, conventional strike, AWACS, FRA, etc. both during peace and during war in furtherance of national war aims. Such airborne resources that are with RAW and other civil agencies will need to be absorbed within Strategic Air Command for optimum utilization and results.

The reasons for this to be primarily an AF command merit recording to prevent inter-service problems.

- Airborne strategic assets are limited in numbers, are high value and need protection in bases and while in the air.
- Conventional Strategic Air Operations are IAF roles.
- IAF operations depend largely on fixed infrastructure that is static and targeted. The IAF is geared to defend this from enemy attack.
- Being responsible for defence of air space, the IAF specializes in detecting, identifying and destroying hostile air elements in responses that are in minutes and seconds. Detection and identification of nuclear threats will be a vital input to strategic command for which suitable integration with the IAF air defence system will be necessary.
- Strike aircraft of the IAF by virtue of inherent flexibility, will form an essential component of conventional and nuclear deterrence/ strike.
- Once the decision to induct the SLBMs emerges, they will be controlled directly by the Civil Command Authority at the National Command Post. No change to the structure of SAC is visualized.

Aerospace Command

Much of today's operational command, control, communications, navigation, intelligence and surveillance capabilities are heavily dependent on space-based platforms. The role of space and space-based platforms is destined to increase manifold in the coming years. Countries that depend on others for space launches, platforms or space-based sensors are limited in their security options and freedom. While militarization of space is not a reality today, denial of navigation or communication data selectively is already a reality. For countries like India that need to maintain security independence in their national security options, it is vital to maintain parity in space technology. As ISRO and other agencies develop capabilities towards this, it is vital that the armed forces are part of their development programmes such that services staff requirements are an integral part of the design and development process.

Logically this should be done through an IAF Aerospace Command consisting of representatives of all user services, which can be tasked to interface with all agencies concerned with development of platforms and sensors and the operational aspects.

Information Warfare

The air force has some of the finest software specialists in the country and a Software Development Institute (SDI) tasked with the responsibility of developing, upgrading and maintaining software for C4I2 and weapon systems. With software becoming all pervasive, the role and complement of SDI needs to be expanded substantially to include software security in the operational environment along with a wider operational role towards Electronic and Information Warfare. This would entail operational wings of this development establishment to be based in operational commands with technical and R&D support originating from the SDI. The concept of a service organization encompassing activities from research to operations while being unique is an emerging necessity.

Force Levels

Force levels must be optimized for greater combat effectiveness. Considerations that could permit optimizing of force levels are as follows. Flexibility of deployment inter theatre, long ranges of aircraft extendable by flight refueling, large load carrying capability, enhanced accuracy of navigation and weapon delivery, availability of force multipliers and PGMs, enhanced role of surface –to- air missiles in air defence, combat capability of advanced trainer aircraft, potential of transport and helicopters to undertake offensive missions etc. All these add massively to air forces' offensive and defensive firepower. Rationalizing of force levels must be attempted through scientific tools for analysis.

The philosophy must now be to replace quantity with not only the quality of weapon systems, but also quality of tactical shrewdness and exploitation of air power in the field. A large part of the valuable infrastructure must be retained on a "care and maintenance" basis for exploitation, should the need arise. Tranquility on the Indo-Chinese border or resource constraints must not delay programmes for infrastructure augmentation/build up in the North-East, peninsular India and Island territories, as these are insurance against security challenges of tomorrow.

Rationalizing of transport and helicopter force levels for optimum peacetime utilization coupled with induction of civil resources along with National Air Guard pilots and crew in operational contingencies is the essence of cost-effective force planning. To maintain a lean transport force, routine peacetime communication and freight tasks should be contracted to the civil sector.

Missile systems, radars, control and reporting centres, command posts, communication networks, EW systems, PGMs and a host of other operational infrastructure vital to the operational potential of the air force has long surpassed the pure flying based squadrons in numbers. The contribution of these non-flying elements to the overall operational capability of the air force needs to be acknowledged in the future organizational and personnel policies of the air force including the vital command and career aspects.

Force Multipliers and Smart Systems

Absence of present day force multipliers does not befit an air force of a nuclear capable nation, as its deterrent posture will stand compromised. Past gaps need to be made up urgently. The surface-to- surface missile force must be complemented with cruise missiles. Indigenous development of the latter must be a mission-oriented priority as these are systems covered by denial regimes.

Human Resource Development and Management

As the air force becomes more dependent on space, automated C4I2 and software based systems; it is already moving closer to the realm of highly automated warfare. Those at the sharp end will then be highly dependent on the minds that drive the system and indeed much of the ability of the air force to maintain its strategic deterrence/ offensive capability will be driven by how uniquely and cleverly software and technology are handled and exploited. To sharpen and exploit this potential it is necessary to look at engineering and maintenance not as a support function, but as an operational element.

Such a philosophical approach would require the air force to undertake only first and second line repair capability farming out the deeper third and fourth levels to civilian repair depots/industry, where huge human and infrastructure resources are grossly underutilized. Once the majority of engineering and technical elements are integrated towards operational tasks it is from within these that intellect and knowledge will emerge towards developing firmware and software solutions for strategic, tactical and information warfare. Adoption of this philosophy alone will demand a major restructuring of how the air force of the future will look and work

Clearly there are two aspects to logistics, both requiring different knowledge, skills and priorities. The crucial one is operational logistics relating to operational capability. The other relates to administrative support that can be handled by the administrative system. To ensure high levels of weapon system availability in peace and war, at the lowest possible costs, the logistics system needs to be reorganized and specialized. Assured logistics will be the foundation of a potent air force of the future.

Air Traffic Controllers and Fighter Controllers are specialists very closely involved with operations. They must be brought into the operational mainstream if they are to display the agility and dynamism of the present and emerging aerospace operational environment.

The Air Force of the future must focus on quality of recruitment, training and performance, which is nothing short of exceptional. Leadership based on meritocracy and not seniority will be the key to a successful Air Force of the future. Authority and accountability must go hand in hand.

OTHER INTEGRAL COMPONENTS OF NATIONAL AIR POWER

R & D and Industry

Aerospace industry forms the bedrock of national air power. Its R&D drives technology and promotes self-reliance especially against denial regimes. Its exports support both R&D and the industrial base thus promoting affordable weapon systems for national security. While India possesses all the pre-requisites for a sound industry, its contribution to the building of the nation's air power has not been in keeping with this potential. Lack of an integrated and mission oriented approach is the cause. The only way to harmonize action towards achieving clear strategic goals is to set up an independent Aeronautics Commission working in close concert with Indian Space Research Organization. The commission should consist of technocrats and professionals tasked to steer the development of aeronautics and missiles towards clearly defined strategic goals and national requirements. The air force as the ultimate operator must be a key player in the Commission.

Rationalization of R&D must also encompass the following:

- DRDO must aim at pure defence research towards evolving materials/technology for future defence applications.
- Development of weapon systems must be within the purview of design and development departments of production agencies. The

domain of translating technology into cost-effective production methodology rests with them. Also it is they that will support the weapon systems in service by providing continuing modification and product support.

- Laboratories carrying out integration/application work for a service must come within the control of the service concerned.
- Finally, there must not be a civilian audit on military weapon system requirements/specifications, but a professional military one.

Rationalization of defence production must encompass the following:

- OFs/PSUs must compete for armed forces' requirements against the private sector
- Self-reliance cannot be a justification to promote OFs/PSU interest over pure military requirements. The former is a longterm ideal, the latter a security imperative
- Contracts must be awarded on fixed cost basis
- Managements must be freed from government interference
- Involvement of private sector needs active promotion for greater efficiency and professional management
- For survival in the market place strong investment in R&D, exports and economies of scale are pre- requisites
- This is only possible if linkages are established with similar industries of like-minded countries for a wider technology and market base and economies of scale

Civil Aviation

In a developing country, civil aviation including its infrastructure is a rapidly growing area. In many areas civil aviation is now a driving technology. Already in times of crises civil aircraft and helicopters can be deployed for military purposes. For cost benefit, the air force can scale down its transport/helicopter force levels and integrate civil assets of transport aircraft and helicopters along with manpower, into its contingency plans. Such philosophies will only work if the concept of a National Air Guard consisting of selected civil pilots, engineers, controllers and other support services were introduced. This approach will permit a leaner air force. With civil aviation also becoming target of hijackings and Purulia -type incursions, National Air Guardsmen within the civil establishment will promote a better operational ethic to tackle acts of air terrorism in routine peacetime operations.

Air Space Management

A crucial task of the air force is surveillance of national air space in peace and war. Space is already teeming with platforms and sensors that contribute significantly to today's operational capability of most nations. With ballistic missile trajectories taking them into space, monitoring and tracking space objects is now an operational imperative. Missile threats demand an organization that is capable of responding instantly in peace and war. A Joint Air Space Management Agency needs to be set up with the task of tracking and identifying all objects in air and space. This authority must function under the control of the air force whose central responsibility is to track, identify and if need be, engage hostile elements.

Air Resources of Other Services

While many missions and roles are the preserve of the air force alone, air and space resources are today necessary for other combat services as well. Faced with imperatives of security and development, India must factor cost- effectiveness and affordability into its force plan. The armed forces need to rationalize roles and missions relating to air and space resources for greater operational effectiveness, standardization, commonality, inter operability, cost-effective maintenance/support and training. Rationalization should be on lines of specialization, combat effectiveness and cost effectiveness with the underlying philosophy that services retain core areas of competence while integrating core competence of other services in their plans. Air Defence must remain the preserve of the air force. In a nuclear environment, this can not be over emphasized.

Affordable Security

While there was much relief at the incremental increase in defence budget in the Finance Bill for 2000-2001, this still amounted to less than 3% of the GDP. High technology weapon systems have increased in costs by up to twenty times in the last two decades, far surpassing normal inflation or foreign exchange variations. Corresponding maintenance and manpower costs have also increased disproportionately. Some 20 % of modernization and maintenance costs of the services are incurred in foreign exchange. Continuing erosion in the rupee value puts further pressure on the service financial planners. Analysts have opined that if the current ad hoc and somewhat disjointed approach to security, force and equipment planning continues then even a 5% GDP defence budget may be inadequate, clearly not an affordable option for developing India.

- Criteria of affordability must now guide the very basis of national security planning. A top to bottom integrated approach rather than a distributive "do with what you get" approach. This calls for a major change in both mindset and procedures. The alternative is fragmented investments leading to poor defence returns on investments.
- A National Security Policy determined at the cabinet level should guide the MOD's defence strategy. This strategy will need to be translated by an integrated military mechanism into force development objectives for each service and specific military mission jointly and singly.
- Blind pursuit of high technology/high cost weapon systems is wasteful. Recent conflicts with extensive use of air power have revealed the limitations of such an approach.
- Notwithstanding the perpetual demand for more resources, the IAF surrendered upwards of Rs 1500 crores in FY 1999-2000, due to procedural delays, clearly highlighting the urgent need for restructuring and decentralizing the defence financial management system.

SUMMARY

- A National Security Policy determined at the cabinet level should guide the MOD's defence Strategy. This strategy will need to be translated by an integrated military mechanism into force development objectives for each service and specific military missions jointly and singly.
- Decision-making delays are costing the nation dear in security terms and in lives of military personnel. There is urgent need for restructuring and decentralizing the defence financial management system.
- Service HQ need to be integrated with the Ministry of Defence (MOD) and a Combined Defence Staff concept responsible for integrated operational planning and execution constituted.
- Service roles and missions need to be rationalized such that duplication and wastage is avoided.
- There is need for rationalization of air assets so as to benefit from economies of scale and specialization with the air force (with the exception of fleet-borne operations).
- Recognition that the army and navy also need airborne missions and therefore decentralizing operational command and control towards operational efficacy is needed.
- Formation of a Technology Commission towards rationalization of Defence Research & Development and Production is required. and control.

Reference & Further Readings

1. *Securing India's Future in the New Millennium*—Countering Missile Threats by K. Subrahmanyam.
2. *India's Nuclear Bomb* by George Perkovich.
3. *Securing India's Future In The New Millennium*—Nuclear Deterrent Posture by Brahma Chellaney.
4. *Impact of Emerging Technologies on Air Power*—USI Paper 1/98 by Air Marshal Bharat Kumar (Retd).
5. RAND-1996. Strategic Information Warfare—A New Face Of War by Roger C. Molander, Andrew S. Riddile, Pete A. Wilson.
6. *Weapons Of Mass Protection—Non-Lethality, Information Warfare And Air Power in the Age of Chaos* by Chris Morris, Janet Morris, Thomas Baines.
7. *Securing India's Future In The New Millennium*—The Role of Science and Technology by P.V. Indiresan.
8. *Engineering Excellence: Cultural and Organizational Factors* by D. Christiansen. IEEE Press, New York 987.
9. *The Defence Industry* by Jacques Gansler. MIT Press 1980.

10. Indian Defence Review. 'Challenges facing Indian Aerospace Industry'—Air Marshal B.D. Jayal (Retd).

11. *The Economist.* Survey Of The World Economy. 28 September 1996.

12. Global Trends 2015—A Dialogue About the Future With Non-government Experts NIC 2000-02, December 2000.

13. *Securing India's Future In The New Millennium*—Challenges To India's Security In The New Millennium by Brahma Chellaney.

14. *The Principles of War in the 21st Century: Strategic Considerations* by William T. Johnsen, Douglas V. Johnson II, James O. Kievit, Douglas C. Lovelace, Jr and Steven Metz.

15. Operation Desert Storm: Operation Desert Storm Air War (Letter Report, 07/02/96, GAO/PEMD-96-10).

16. The US Military's Soft Ribs and Strategic Weaknesses-PLA-October 2000.

17. *A Strategy For Long Peace* by Stevens Kosiak, Andrew Krepinevich & Michael Vickers CSBA Report.

18. Reforming the National Security System—Recommendations of the Group of Ministers—February 2001.

19. Indian Nuclear Doctrine-National Security Advisory Board.

20. Strategic Survey 1998/99 Strategic Policy Issues.

21. MOD Annual Report 1997-98.

22. *Securing India's Future In The Millennium*—Energy Security For India-Frederik Grare.

23. Indian Defence Review. Indian Nuclear Doctrine-A Discussion-Air Marshal B.D. Jayal.

24. Strategy, *Microsoft ® Encarta ® 98 Encyclopedia © 1993-1997.*

25. *Shape and Size of the Indian Navy in early 21st Century* by Vice Admiral R.B. Suri.

26. FIZA'YA Psyche of The Pakistan Air Force by Pushpindar Singh, Ravi Rikhye, Peter Steinemann.

27. Securing India—Strategic Thoughts and Practice: Essays by George Tanham Manohar-1996.

28. *Defending India* by Jaswant Singh.

29. *India's Emerging Nuclear Posture* by Tellis.

30. *Future Imperiled—India Security in the 1990's & Beyond Edited* by Bharat Karnad, Viking Penguin-1994.

31. Doctrine of the IAF War Strategic Cell. Air HQ.

32. *Indian Air Force-Trends and Prospects* by George Tanham & Marcy Magnon (RAND-1994).

33. *Air Supremacy: The Enduring Principle*—Air Commodore P.L. Gover.

34. *War in the Third Dimension: Essays in Contemporary Air Power* (London: Brasseys, 1986).

35. *War in the Third Dimension: Continuity, Innovation and Convergence* by Air Vice Marshal R.A. Mason.

36. *India's Defence Spending: Assessing Future Needs* by Air Commodore Jasjit Singh.

37. *Air Power: A Centennial Appraisal* by Air Vice Marshal Tony Mason (UK: Brassey's, 1994).

38. *Weapons of Peace* by Raj Chengappa.

39. *Firepower in Limited War* by Robert H. Scales JR.

40. *The Indian Air Force-A balanced Strategic and Tactical Application* by Air Vice Marshal V. Kapila.

41. *The Impact of Emerging Technologies on Air Power* by Air Marshal Bharat Kumar-USI Paper 1/98.

42. *The Armageddon Factor* by Dr Sanjay Badri-Maharaj.

43. *The Changing Face of Nuclear Warfare* by Lawrence Martin. Harper & Row publishers, New York.

44. *The Future of Land Warfare* Chris Bellamy, Croom Helm Ltd., Bakenham, UK.

45. *Stability in South Asia* by Ashely Tellis, Natraj Publishers, New Delhi.

46. *Low Intensity Conflicts in India* by Lt. Gen. V.K. Nayar, PVSM, SM (retd) USI publications.

47. *China's Changing National Security Doctrines* by Swaran Singh, Delhi Papers No. 9, IDSA, New Delhi.

48. Nature of Future Wars—Military Research Project, DSSC, Wellington.

49. Proceedings of a Seminar on command and Staff Challenges in the 21st Century, DSSC, Wellington.
50. Jawaharlal Nehru—India's Foreign Policy; Selected Speeches September 1946-April 1961 Publication Division Government of India.
51. Military Balance 2000-01.
52. SIPRI Year book 2000-Stockholm International Peace Research Institute. Stockholm, Sweden.
53. Strategic Survey 1999-2000, Institute for Strategic Studies, London.
54. Asian Strategic Review 1998-1999, IDSA, New Delhi.
55. Asian Defence Year Book 2000-01.

Index